Pushing the Boundaries of Latin American Testimony

Pushing the Boundaries of Latin American Testimony
Meta-morphoses and Migrations

Edited by
Louise Detwiler and Janis Breckenridge

palgrave
macmillan

PUSHING THE BOUNDARIES OF LATIN AMERICAN TESTIMONY
Copyright © Louise Detwiler and Janis Breckenridge, 2012.

All rights reserved.

First published in 2012 by
PALGRAVE MACMILLAN®
in the United States—a division of St. Martin's Press LLC,
175 Fifth Avenue, New York, NY 10010.

Where this book is distributed in the UK, Europe and the rest of the World, this is by Palgrave Macmillan, a division of Macmillan Publishers Limited, registered in England, company number 785998, of Houndmills, Basingstoke, Hampshire RG21 6XS.

Palgrave Macmillan is the global academic imprint of the above companies and has companies and representatives throughout the world.

Palgrave® and Macmillan® are registered trademarks in the United States, the United Kingdom, Europe and other countries.

ISBN: 978–0–230–33847–0

Library of Congress Cataloging-in-Publication Data

Pushing the boundaries of Latin American testimony : meta-morphoses and migrations / edited by Louise Detwiler and Janis Breckenridge.
   p. cm.
   ISBN 978–0–230–33847–0 (alk. paper)
   1. Latin American literature—20th century—History and criticism.
   2. Reportage literature, Latin American—History and criticism.
   3. Literature and society—Latin America.   4. Mass media and culture—Latin America.   I. Detwiler, Louise, 1965–
   II. Breckenridge, Janis, 1970–
   PQ7082.R46P68 2012
   980.03—dc23   2011031571

A catalogue record of the book is available from the British Library.

Design by Integra Software Services

First edition: January 2012

10 9 8 7 6 5 4 3 2 1

Printed in the United States of America.

Louise Detwiler: In memory of my family in the immaterial world, to the celebration of my husband and daughter in the material one, and on behalf of the love that connects us all.

Janis Breckenridge: To my parents for "raising me right" and always believing that I could do and be absolutely anything I wanted. It is your unwavering support that has made that true. And to my G-ma for always taking an interest. I miss you more than I can say.

Contents

Acknowledgments ... ix

Introduction: Points of Departure ... 1
Louise Detwiler and Janis Breckenridge

Part I Moving Theories: Neoliberalism and Coalitions

1. Writing Fabio Argueta: Testimonio, Ethnography, and Human Rights in the Neoliberal Age ... 11
Leigh Binford

2. Testimonio and Its Travelers: Feminist Deployments of a Genre at Work ... 37
Patricia Connolly

Part II Positioning Oppositional Performances: Clandestine, Reluctant, and False Witnesses

3. Hiding the Camera in Miguel Littin's *Acta general de Chile* ... 57
David William Foster

4. Guerrilla Narratives through the Kaleidoscope of Time: Rereading Resistance in Nicaragua ... 71
Julia M. Medina

5. Bearing False Witness? The Politics of Identity in Elsa Osorio's *My Name Is Light (A veinte años, Luz)* ... 87
Nancy J. Gates-Madsen

Part III Connected Communities: Emerging Contexts and Merging Mediums

6 Testimony in Truth Commissions and Social Movements in Latin America 109
Lynn Stephen

7 Rumors as Testimonios of Insile in *La mujer en cuestión* (The Woman in Question) by María Teresa Andruetto 131
Corinne Pubill

8 Accomplishing "Tellable-Tellings": Managing Displays of Faith on Live Radio 147
Melissa Guzman

9 Embroidered Discourse/s Break the Silence: The CPR-Sierra of Guatemala (Re)vive Testimonio 165
T. M. Linda Scholz

Part IV Novel Landscapes: Counter-Geographies, Graphics, and Terra-Trauma

10 Ciudad Juárez as a Palimpsest: Searching for Ecotestimonios 181
Alice Driver

11 Drawing the Line between Memory, History, and Artistic Re/creation: Miguel Gallardo and Carlos Giménez's Graphic Testimonies 201
Janis Breckenridge

12 Witnessing the Earth through Gaspar Pedro González's *El 13 B'aktun: la nueva era 2012*: (*13 B'aktun: Mayan Visions of 2012 and Beyond*) 221
Louise Detwiler

Conclusion: "Something That Might Resemble a Call": Testimonial Theory and Practice in the Twenty-First Century 239
Kimberly A. Nance

Notes on Contributors 249

Index 253

Acknowledgments

It is thanks to testimonio that we began to follow and admire each other's work, became conference colleagues, and then great friends. "We should work on a book together sometime soon!" we would say to each other over the years. And it is thanks to at last having simultaneous sabbaticals that we managed to turn our vision into a reality with this edited collection. We'd like to thank our respective institutions, Salisbury University (Fulton School of Liberal Arts) and Whitman College, for the gift of time devoted to research and writing. Working nearly daily as a team (JaMA/DeLO) on opposite coasts over the past year has been a remarkable journey of collaboration, patience, and encouragement. We are grateful as well to our talented contributors and editorial assistant, Sarah Nathan, whose prompt and thorough attention to our many requests made this process a truly positive experience. We appreciate that all of you believed in us enough to see our collective project through to its fruition. Deserving special recognition is the very talented Darius Detwiler, whose tailor-made cover art captures the heart and soul of this collection. Above all, we are indebted to the courage of so many witnesses across the globe who have shared, and who continue to share, their life stories in the name of peace and justice.

Introduction

Points of Departure

Louise Detwiler and Janis Breckenridge

The essays in *Pushing the Boundaries of Latin American Testimony* showcase a new generation of scholarship on a hybrid, and sometimes maddening yet always fascinating, subgenre of Latin American literature: testimonio. The contributors included here often make only a sideways glance to the saturated debates of previous decades. A core group of pro- and anti-testimonio critics were at the top of their theory game in the 1980s and 1990s—a time when Rigoberta Menchú became *the* icon for those multilayered debates. Thereafter, the new millennium brought with it an air of (r)evolutionary movement for the exchange of information across the globe and, within the academy, across the disciplines. Yet, scholars were still clinging to Rigoberta Menchú and other classic testimonios, such as *Biografía de un cimarrón (Biography of a Runaway Slave)* by Cuban writer Miguel Barnet, in their efforts to theorize outward and upward regarding complex issues of representation in peace and social justice work. Indeed, Arturo Arias's collection of essays, *The Rigoberta Menchú Controversy* (2001), ushered in the first decade of the new millennium.

However, to many of us following these debates, it appeared as though these issues were again being batted back and forth in a never-ending, pendulum-like cycle between "the subaltern can speak" and "the subaltern cannot speak." While we in no way discount the profound substance of these scholarly discussions and owe much to them, we also note that it is time for testimonio de jure of scholarship to move forward because testimonio de facto on the ground has undergone a profound metamorphosis and many migrations: from discipline to discipline and border to border; from text to textiles, radio, and graphic art; from transcribed and written to spoken, public, and performative; from fixed contexts to interactional ones; and from nonfiction to fiction and film. Included in these movements is the key figure of the *testigo*, or eyewitness. In the informant role, the eyewitness described in these pages may be invented, false, hidden, or disengaged while living in insile (internal exile), or even nonhuman.

Within a few years following Arias's collection, three particularly noteworthy projects surfaced within Testimonio Studies. In 2004, Linda S. Maier and Isabel Dulfano published *Woman as Witness: Essays on Testimonial Literature by Latin American Women*. This volume of essays responds in part to the fact that, with very few exceptions such as Rigoberta Menchú, testimonio criticism has long focused on male-authored narratives and has been carried out by male scholars; yet, most testimonios have come from female witnesses. This long-standing neglectful approach within a very rich field of study goes hand-in-hand with the need for more theorizing about the ways in which women and testimonio, or gender and genre, fit exceedingly well together for a whole host of reasons explained in the collection. Also permeating many of these essays is the sense that testimonio cannot, has not, and should not fade away in spite of scholarly statements to the contrary. We wholeheartedly agree with Isabel Dulfano's statement that "[w]hat humankind does merit is the continued examination of the personal histories of all people and discourses" (95).

Another significant contribution appeared in 2005, with Joanna R. Bartow's *Subject to Change: The Lessons of Latin American Women's Testimonio for Truth, Fiction, and Theory*. In her study, Bartow adeptly makes a solid case for a testimonial informant who, it must be recognized, will evolve over time. She focuses closely on the degrees of agency the informant possesses to represent herself within the dynamics of the mediation process with the transcriber, who also must evolve. She examines relationships such as these not only within the testimonio project, but also within the shared conceptual spaces of testimonio and feminist theories and testimonio and fiction. As the title suggests, Bartow's study ultimately contributes as well to the fact that the reception of testimonio has changed from transparent and innocent to more critical and complex (29). She pays particular attention—through masterful close readings of works by Clarice Lispector and Diamela Eltit—to the paradoxes inherent in the testimonial project and subject, to discursive violence, to shifting silences and acts of appropriation, and to translating identity.

Kimberly Nance's *Can Literature Promote Justice? Trauma Narrative and Social Action in Latin American Testimonio* (2006) represents a third major contribution to Testimonial Studies within this time period. In this brilliantly researched study, Nance approaches testimonio with the tools of classical rhetoric and with a focused target on the reader. Put simply, she queries whether testimonio truly prompts readers to act upon the injustices they encounter while reading. She warns that some narratives not only "let the general reader off the hook, but also may even dissuade a reader from taking any sort of action at all" (92). Among her conclusions is the notion that perhaps testimonio criticism needs to avoid the love it/hate it extremes that have tended to characterize the corpus for so long. She writes in her conclusion, "From Poetics to Prosaics," that what is needed is "a shift from fantasy relationships with testimonio—to a harder, less glamorous, and less ideologically pure alternative" (158).

The essays in this volume are very much "impure" and therein lies their strength. They break free from the classic boundaries established by foundational critics such as John Beverley, George Yúdice, Marc Zimmerman, and many other distinguished scholars. Indeed, as new-to-the scene scholar Hans M. Fernández Benítez posits so convincingly in his recent essay " 'The moment of testimonio is over': problemas teóricos y perspectivas de los estudios testimoniales" (" 'The moment of testimonio is over': Theoretical Problems and Perspectives of Testimonial Studies"):

> no estaría mal considerar la existencia de nuevos estudios testimoniales basados en una *episteme* testimonial renovada que siga promoviendo una conciencia y solidaridad internacional a favor de los derechos humanos en el "Tercer Mundo," pero que no se agote en categorías y conceptos monolíticos de análisis y que, además, . . . precise una ética de trabajo intelectual para el latinoamericanismo de hoy (it would not be a bad idea to consider the existence of a new kind of Testimonial Studies based on a renovated testimonial *episteme* which continues to promote international solidarity and consciousness of human rights in the "Third Word," but which does not wear itself out with monolithic categories and concepts, and which also requires an intellectual work ethic for today's Latin Americanism).
>
> (67)

We believe that with the new decade upon us, *Pushing the Boundaries of Latin American Testimony* fulfills this notion of a renovated testimonial *episteme*. Linda S. Maier wisely notes in her introductory essay, "The Case for and Case History of Women's Testimonial Literature in Latin America," that although scholars are quick to mention Beverley's statements regarding the passé status of testimonio, "he also points out its inherently shifting nature" (4). Testimonio in these pages indeed shifts, moving well beyond the familiar scenario of the professional writer/journalist/sociologist who, in solidarity, records the urgent and contestatory life stories of oppressed voices living at the margins of their societies.

Instead, what we find here are ecotestimonios, novel witnesses, anti-testimonios, meta-testimonios, and graphic testimonios. In some cases the urgency is palpable, such as in Lynn Stephen's study of oral testimonio's role in embodied public testimony in Oaxaca, Mexico, or in Alice Driver's quest to geographically locate memories of feminicide victims in Ciudad Juárez. In other cases, the tone is irreverent, as in Julia Medina's study of the revolutionary witness who never wanted to be a revolutionary in the first place. In parallel fashion, Corinne Pubill examines how the power of rumor serves an anti-testimonial function by misrepresenting and ultimately isolating the witness. Similarly, Nancy Gates-Madsen identifies a dynamic wherein the testimonial task of writing/righting wrongs can, ironically, serve to perpetuate those wrongs. Leigh Binford's essay is sweeping and metadiscursive as he reflects on a testimonio that was shared, but never formally written down. He provides an impressive range of interdisciplinary connections as he follows testimonio's trek across time and across the disciplines.

Along these lines, our inclusion of disciplines usually not represented in testimonio scholarship has been deliberate. Melissa Guzman's conversational analysis approach to religious testimonios and T.M. Linda Scholz's incorporation of communication studies into her essay about the CPR-Sierra of Guatemala represent fields that have been absent from previous scholarly conversations. Similarly, Patricia Connolly and Janis Breckenridge take testimonio to new lands, via the Sangtin Writers in India and visual narrations about the Spanish civil war and its aftermath. Louise Detwiler's essay pushes testimonio even farther: into the realm of the spirit world, also known as the fifth dimension.

The subtitle, *Meta-morphoses and Migrations*, is meant to prompt readers to acknowledge that voice and the interdiscourses of history/story are everywhere and always, and that there is no one way to "do testimonio." If this is the case, however, then how do we know that it's testimonio and not something else? This question has been thoroughly addressed by both first- and second-wave testimonio scholars based on a fairly strict formula that in many cases these essays simply do not follow. While all tend to recognize testimonio as a composite narrative, here we resist endlessly picking apart that exceptional quality such that we move into yet another round of cognitive paralysis and demise. Instead, we have chosen to appreciate how testimonio does, in fact, represent the complexities and injustices of a rapidly changing world, rather than lament how it does not. Call it third wave, or post postmodern, or what you will, but we take a more intuitive approach to testimonio, akin to Debra Castillo's notion of women's texts and their "subjunctive mood" (63). When it's there, we know it. A "testimonio mood" of sorts, to borrow her term.

We envision, in fact, that testimonio scholarship of the future will scrutinize and embrace entirely different realms of subjectivity, such as that of the cyborg, the nonhuman, or some other cognitive, referential, or linguistic arena not yet articulated as of this writing. Taking the pulse of autobiography in their new edition of *Reading Autobiography: A Guide for Interpreting Life Narratives*, Sidonie Smith and Julia Watson refer to the expansion of their field—more broadly referred to there as life writing—into the realm of the human genome and cognitive science as examples of contemporary contexts (225). They note as well that "as the corpus of texts and media expands, the debates shift" (234). In sum, by not pinning testimonio down too strictly, we may better follow its sojourns into the future.

The essays that follow are grouped around broad themes. Part I, "Moving Theories: Neoliberalism and Coalitions," shows how testimonio has migrated across disciplines and across borders. Part II, "Positioning Oppositional Performances: Clandestine, Reluctant, and False Witnesses," examines testimonio through the lens of anomalous witnesses who at times deliver their stories in opposition to transparency and institutional definitions of truth, regardless of the political persuasions behind that truth. Part III, "Connected Communities: Emerging Contexts and Merging Mediums," focuses on locating testimonio beyond the text and within the usually spontaneous, but at times authoritatively managed, realm of social interaction. In Part IV, "Novel Landscapes: Counter-Geographies, Graphics, and Terra-Trauma," the essays trace lives and life systems through both literal and figurative landscapes of memory.

Readers will appreciate the many noteworthy subthemes that materialize across these four sections. Often, the authors point out that a layered approach to testimonio production creates room for the emergence of more than one voice and more than one story. This might mean text next to or within embroidery, words accompanying body, multiple speakers in conversation, or a contrapuntal engagement of ideology. Decoded together, these layers produce their own testimonios in a kind of *mise en abyme* framework. Other contributors share their disappointment that institutions and organizations have appropriated testimonio for their own agendas, often at the grave expense of silencing the next cohort of pressing narratives. Still others find that testimonio itself can serve to silence; yet, that silence might in some way conjure up representation in need of inquiry. While these subthemes may not be entirely new, their mediums and/or terms of production and reception often are.

Smith and Watson write that "as practices of narrative identity multiply and shift in the decades to come, scholars of life narrative will continue to contribute to rich dialogues about their significance in understanding the intersections of self, community, and geopolitical transits" (234). Our vision for this volume aligns with this forward-looking notion of dialogues in motion. We would add that narrative motion in these times often outpaces the rate and degree of change of times past. Therefore, while some might contend that there is no more room for testimonio talk, this collection suggests that perhaps the conversation has just begun.

Works Cited

Arias, Arturo, ed. *The Rigoberta Menchú Controversy*. Minneapolis: U Minnesota P, 2001. Print.

Barnet, Miguel. *Biografía de un cimarrón*. La Habana: Instituto de Etnología y Folklore, 1966. Print.

Bartow, Joanna. *Subject to Change: The Lessons of Latin American Women's Testimonio for Truth, Fiction, and Theory*. Chapel Hill: U of North Carolina P, 2005. Print.

Castillo, Debra A. *Talking Back: Toward a Latin American Feminist Literary Criticism*. Ithaca: Cornell UP, 1992. Print.

Fernández, Benítez Hans M. " 'The moment of testimonio is over': problemas teóricos y perspectivas de los estudios testimoniales." *Ikala: revista de lenguaje y cultura* 15.24 (2010): 47–71. Print.

Maier, Linda S. "Introduction: The Case for and Case History of Women's Testimonial Literature in Latin America." *Woman as Witness: Essays on Testimonial Literature by Latin American Women*. Ed. Maier, Linda S. and Isabel Dulfano. New York: Peter Lang, 2004. 1–17. Print.

Maier, Linda S., and Isabel Dulfano, eds. *Woman as Witness: Essays on Testimonial Literature by Latin American Women*. New York: Peter Lang, 2004. Print.

Menchú, Rigoberta, and Elisabeth Burgos. *Me llamo Rigoberta Menchú y así me nació la conciencia.* Barcelona: Editorial Argos Vergara, 1983. Print.

Nance, Kimberly A. *Can Literature Promote Justice? Trauma Narrative and Social Action in Latin American Testimonio.* Nashville: Vanderbilt UP, 2006. Print.

Smith, Sidonie, and Julia Watson. *Reading Autobiography: A Guide for Interpreting Life Narratives.* 2nd ed. Minneapolis: U of Minnesota P, 2010. Print.

PART I

MOVING THEORIES: NEOLIBERALISM AND COALITIONS

CHAPTER 1

WRITING FABIO ARGUETA: TESTIMONIO, ETHNOGRAPHY, AND HUMAN RIGHTS IN THE NEOLIBERAL AGE

Leigh Binford

For some time I have been working on a project, still incomplete, that involves my brokering of the testimonio of one Fabio Argueta, a Salvadoran citizen in his early sixties, relatively short of stature and plump, and saddled with a host of physical problems, most of which resulted from his participation in that country's revolutionary war.[1] Since the war ended in 1992, Fabio has led a rather quiet life as a small storekeeper and as the head of a family that includes a half dozen children of various ages. But in talking to Fabio about his life, and in particular his participation in the Christian Base Communities of the progressive church in the early 1970s, and then his incorporation into the Peoples Revolutionary Army (ERP) faction of the Farabundo Martí National Liberation Front (FMLN), you begin to develop an appreciation for the courage, resourcefulness, analytical skill, and strategic calculation that he displayed from an early age, and that he especially put to the service of progressive, even utopian, change.

I decided that his story should be told; he accepted the idea, and between 1992 and 1994, we met on a dozen occasions and taped Fabio's story more or less chronologically, beginning with his birth in El Mozote in 1943 and ending with the ethnographic present in Cuscatancingo, a working class neighborhood of San Salvador, the nation's capital. I supposed at the time that even though the war had ended, I would coauthor or edit Fabio's *testimonio* much in the way that other anthropologists had done for and with other testimonial subjects. Perhaps I was even naive enough at the time to believe that *Fabio's Story*, as the manuscript came (rather uncreatively) to be called, might represent a real piece of People's History, the, or rather a, subaltern perspective on the Salvadoran revolution (see Randall).

But I failed to factor in how changes then taking place in the world might inflect on the reception of *testimonio*, which even if it has a lengthy ancestry, gained particular fame during the seventies and eighties period of Latin American rebellion and revolution. The very definition of *testimonio* drew upon social upheaval, as John Beverley wrote in a 1989 essay: "The situation of narration in *testimonio* has to involve an urgency to communicate, a problem of repression, poverty, subalternity, imprisonment, struggle for survival, and so on, implicated in the act of narration itself" ("Margin" 26).

In an age of Latin American rebellion and revolution, *testimonio* seemed an appropriate medium for expression of the voice of those without voice: workers and peasants, men and women, Indian and ladino struggling to bring down repressive military dictatorships. Dozens of *testimonios* were constructed with the assistance of sympathetic Western intellectuals, some of them anthropologists, and a few *testimonios*, such as *I, Rigoberta Menchú*, even won large audiences and international acclaim. But what happens to *testimonio* when the revolutionary "state of emergency" that popularized it as a literary form of protest is terminated and when the armed leftist organizations that provided so many testimonial subjects are defeated or transform themselves into legal political parties? What happens to *testimonio* when the brutal military dictatorships of the seventies and eighties give way to electoral democracies characterized by political competition and less overt forms of repression, and when the newly hegemonic neoliberal economic model offers an appearance of choice and opportunity for all—*even if* most studies of income distribution indicate that such models, put into practice, are more exclusionist than the client-centered import substitution models that they replaced (see Portes and Hoffman)? And finally, what happens to *testimonio* when many of the same literary critics who championed it in the eighties make an about-face and decree its declining relevance, arguing that subaltern subjects must find new forms of representation more in tune with postmodern culture and identity politics—which have ostensibly substituted for modernist culture and class politics?

Following theorists Pierre Bourdieu and William Roseberry in terms of reconfigurations in fields of power, these events problematize my project, as a brief recapitulation of Fabio's life should make clear. Fabio was born in 1943 in El Mozote, a small, dispersed village in the northern highlands of Morazán. As is well known, El Mozote lent its name to what may be the largest single massacre in modern Latin American history, committed by the U.S.-trained Salvadoran special forces Atlacatl battalion in December of 1981 (Binford, *El Mozote*; Danner).[2] But Fabio spent only nine years in his birthplace. A violent conflict with an alcoholic uncle drove his parents to move five miles south near Meanguera township, where he spent most of his childhood, adolescence, and young adulthood. Fabio inherited a few plots of agricultural land when his father died, and for some years, he combined farming with small-scale commerce. In 1970, at age twenty-seven, his life took an unexpected turn when he was selected by northern Morazán's priest to attend a lay catechist training center run mostly by U.S. and Spanish Jesuits in the adjacent department of San Miguel.

In the Centro Reino de la Paz training school, better known as El Castaño, Fabio was exposed for the first time to the progressive theology of the Second Vatican Council. He learned about God's and the church's "preferential option for the poor" and its advocacy for the development of the whole person, that is, development in material as well as spiritual aspects. Of equal importance, Fabio and the other students in El Castaño acquired a series of practical skills that the Jesuit fathers judged necessary if they were to become promoters of social and economic, as well as religious, development in their home communities. Here, I'm talking about skills related to community organization, public speaking, cooperative development, agricultural technology, and in some cases, basic health care. The most important lesson communicated by the center staff was dignity: that the students were deserving, that they merited a better life, that they were capable of attaining it through working with others (Binford, "Peasants").

Fabio and other catechists returned to the Morazán highlands eager to put their newfound knowledge into practice, and though they were impeded for a time by Father Andrés Argueta, the conservative priest who had sent them, and who was clearly shocked and disturbed by the result, many of them soon developed a relationship with a young, radical priest appointed in 1973 to lead a newly created parish centered in the town of Torola. Thus began the Christian Base Community movement in the Morazán highlands.

Fabio was among the most active, resourceful, and successful of catechists, traveling widely in the region preaching the Word, organizing base communities, working on house construction and other projects to aid the poorest of the poor, and in coordination with the young priest, interpreting the Bible in the context of local history and social problems. Even if not representative of a clearly defined social class (see Roseberry 109–16), he and others like him were, in my view, legitimate organic intellectuals in the Gramscian sense of a strata of persons who "coming into existence on the original terrain of an essential function in the world of economic production... give [their social group]... homogeneity and an awareness of its own function not only in the economic but also in the social and political fields" (Gramsci 6).[3]

However, the experiment was doomed by a political structure under assault that was unable to tolerate even rather benign self-help projects, particularly when those projects alerted a poor, exploited, and oppressed peasantry and rural proletariat to the social and political causes of subordination. Harassed by soldiers, spies, and paramilitary agents, in 1974 Fabio and other catechists began to collaborate with regional representatives of the ERP. Even as they continued with religious and community development work, they also played key roles in recruiting area workers and peasants to clandestine Military Committees, which trained secretly in remote areas, preparing themselves for the coming civil war. In 1977, Fabio was arrested by the National Guard and brutally tortured for almost three weeks, until public pressure forced his release. He then went completely underground, and following the outbreak of civil war in 1980, became one of the region's most renowned political organizers, working in the guerrilla rear guard of northern Morazán with civilians and combatants alike.

Finally, in 1988, chronic health problems related mainly to his torture eleven years earlier forced his retirement from the zone. Guerrilla commanders smuggled Fabio out of the country, and he spent the last four years of the war in Managua, Nicaragua, organizing Salvadoran refugees; he returned to El Salvador following the signing of the Peace Accords in 1992. With a loan related to his ex-combatant status, Fabio established a small store in the front room of his rented house in the working class neighborhood of Cuscatencingo in San Salvador—where I first met him—but recurring asthma attacks, a hernia, and a weak heart limited both his political and economic activities.

In outline, this is the story that Fabio tells. But with the war over and six elections—four presidential, six legislative and municipal—celebrated since 1994, it would seem to be of limited contemporary relevance. In the postwar context, Fabio's life story becomes just another life history as opposed to a testimonio. Joana O'Connell alluded to this terrain shift in a 1998 paper titled "Rereading Salvadoran *Testimonio* after the Cease-Fire":

[N]ow that the war is over—or at least the "hot war" of active military engagement and not the quieter one of economic and social violence—how do our readings [of wartime *testimonio*] have to change? In other words, since, to my mind, *testimonio* is best understood as a kind of textual production that foregrounds the "doing" of the text—its forms of moral or ethical intentionality and how those constitute readers as doers in their respective social and political contexts—then what happens to the urgent call to action when the armed struggle has been suspended, some of the exiles have returned home, and political engagement in El Salvador and in the U.S. must find other channels to effect change?

(3–4)

It is particularly difficult for testimonial texts to "constitute readers as doers" when the FMLN, which won the March 2009 national elections following many years as the second power in El Salvador to the conservative National Republican Alliance (ARENA) Party, split into *los Ortodoxos* (orthodox) and *los Renovadores* (renewal) wings, with the latter advocating for many classic neoliberal social and economic formulas—electoral politics, fiscal responsibility, open markets, foreign investment—rejecting any pretense that these might be mere transitory measures on the "road" to socialism.[4] Indeed, in early March of 2002, the *Renovadores* broke definitively with the FMLN and took the first steps toward the formation of a new social democratic party, which they tentatively called the *Movimiento Renovador* (Renewal Movement). If class is on the decline and if vanguard movements seeking to "lead the revolution" really have been replaced in El Salvador and elsewhere by nonclass or cross-class new social movements—feminists, environmentalists, urban popular movements, gays and the like—characteristic of a fragmented, postmodern culture, then subaltern agents would be advised to abandon class-based politics in order to seek new forms of cultural and political expression that better accord with their own complex social positionalities (see Beverley, *Subalternity*).

I comment more on this problem later in the chapter. But for the moment I want to discuss two additional objections that potential testimonial brokers such as myself must confront. One has to do with a turn away from testimonio on the part of many of the very literary critics who previously wrote favorably about it. The other involves anthropologists and their appropriation of testimonial forms to the writing of ethnography.

Literary Criticism

To begin, the turn away from testimonio on the part of literary critics has been partly a product of their increasing skepticism about the possibility of representing subaltern voices, whether via testimonio or some other literary or nonliterary form. From the beginning, literary critics interrogated the limits as well as the possibilities of testimonio, and elaborated on a series of obstacles that blocked access to the true voice of the other. These obstacles included everything from the unequal power relations entailed in the staging of the interviews, to the editorial functions exercised by the intellectual broker or interlocutor (in the case of Fabio's testimonio, I am that interlocutor), the resistances put up by the testimonial subject to telling all to an audience of mostly middle class cosmopolitan readers, and the interpretative strategies through which those readers unconsciously domesticate difference (turn difference into sameness) or essentialize it (e.g., racialize or ethnicize it) (Sommer, "No Secrets" and "Rigoberta's Secrets"; Achugar; Sklodowska). Majority opinion seems to have been that the popularity of testimonio could be attributed to the fact that it produced a "truth effect"—the reader's perceived access to the truth of the other, which is obviously not the same as referential truth itself. Insofar as the production of a testimonio involves maneuver by various agents within different social fields of power, and an end product that is necessarily shaped by these maneuvers, I think that their work exerted a salutary effect on cosmopolitan readers' desires to know others' lives and their belief that through a work of literature they might be able to do so with considerable precision.

From the beginning, testimonio has had an ambivalent relationship with the literary establishment. It is, after all, a hybrid form, representing the conversion of oral testimony into writing. By equating history and literature with writing (and modern culture) and folktales and testimonies with orality (and traditional culture) (Levi-Strauss), Western intellectuals have vigorously defended their disciplines in order to prevent their contamination by an indigestible Other. But testimonio, written like literature and occasionally endowed with recognizable artistic merit, generated a provocative debate over the definition of Literature itself, the potential for subaltern subjects to communicate through it, and their historic exclusion from it. Moreover, testimonio served as a medium through which literary theorists could seriously rethink the refusal of their own discipline to make room for subaltern others, and to acknowledge that historically the discourse of Literature has been a discourse of exclusion.

Hence John Beverley opined that *I, Rigoberta Menchú* is "the most interesting work of literature produced in Latin America in the last fifteen years," but went on to argue that general acceptance of that fact neutralizes the work's subversive potential. The work loses its sense of "a provocation in the academy, a radical otherness," and becomes another sign of multinational citizenship: a must read for the well-educated future banker, steward of industry, or stock market trader. Beverley stated that he would like his students to understand "that almost by definition the subaltern, which will in some cases intersect with aspects of their own class or group identity, is not, and cannot be, adequately represented in literature or in the university, that literature and the university are among the institutional practices that *create* and sustain subalternity" ("Margin" 271, emphasis in the original).

Note that Beverley has moved the discussion away from the epistemological status of testimonio or even its political relevance to so-called Third World political struggles by focusing on its relevance to the politics of academia. Obviously, struggle over the presence or exclusion of the dominated groups within academia *does* have implications for struggles within the Third World, insofar as education plays an important role in the reproduction of the political and cultural hegemony of dominant groups. But this analytical displacement—I can't think of another way to describe the situation in which *we* appropriate *their products* in order to promote *our interests*, even when those interests are progressive in a general sense—makes it quite easy to lose sight of the original goals of these books. I doubt that Rigoberta Menchú pondered over the definition of Literature at the moment she consented to tell her story to Elisabeth Burgos-Debray, though statements in her testimonio indicate that she understood quite well the role of Literature in the reproduction of the system of domination against which she was struggling.

The insights of Beverley and others are useful, albeit too pessimistic, particularly when they conclude that testimonio is elicited, formed, and disseminated through power/knowledge systems that invariably neutralize the subversive potential that testimonio might have in other contexts, as, for instance, when oral histories or testimonies circulate within dominated groups themselves.[5] Abstract analyses of this sort, which owe much to the Michel Foucault of *Discipline and Punish*, overlook the way that readers bring their own lives and the contradictions active in them to their reading experience (see Binford and Harding). Which is to say that the context that shapes their reading experience reaches *beyond* academia or literary institutions to encompass a much wider field of thought and action—a point made over fifteen years ago by Janice Radway in *Reading the Romance*. In a sense, the meta-theoretical critique affirming the impossibility of representing the voices of others in testimonio is in part a product of frustrations related to the fact that the revolutions with which some literary critics identified failed to materialize. They were then led to examine more closely their own discipline and its complicity with the defeat of progressive forces, a necessary step to be sure, but one that can also result in a reduction of the opportunities for the poor and oppressed to have their (mediated) voices disseminated among a wider reading public (see Eagleton 25).[6]

Let me provide one example of this dynamic. Gareth Williams (244) comments on a case cited by John Beverley in his book *Against Literature*. Alan Carey-Webb of the University of Oregon discussed how students in an undergraduate course used *I, Rigoberta Menchú* to question their own position in the world as well as the purposes and methods of education, and found in Guatemalan society "many attractive features that they found lacking in their own lives" (qtd. in Beverley, *Against Literature* 91; see Carey-Webb). Williams comments critically that "Rigoberta Menchú and the Maya-Quiché are [here] viewed as an expression of value: that of carrying the load of a single social, global function; becoming the means by which the First World can reflect upon itself and define its own areas of struggle and political engagement. The Latin American subaltern becomes everything the United States lacks and craves in order for it to think itself" (244). While theoretically correct, Williams overlooks how even inward-turning readings can contribute to an eventual subversion of the dialectic of domination *if*, articulating with real, *nonliterary* contradictions in people's lives, they stimulate readers to rethink the world and their place in it, and to make the decision to participate in collective efforts to change social relations in ways that favor the global majority. Using *I, Rigoberta Menchú* to question the social order in one's immediate surroundings may be a first step to the development of a critical social consciousness capable of linking the here with the there and the now with the then. Finally, the recent history of U.S. intervention in Central America suggests that structural changes in those (and other) underdeveloped countries are dialectically related to internal political changes in the United States, making the local appropriation of *I, Rigoberta Menchú* relevant to extra-local and extra-national social change. Poststructuralism is of limited utility when it comes to thinking the operation of power in its nondiscursive mode, or of approaching discourses, even internal disciplinary discourses, as multiple and conflicting—variously "residual," "dominant," and "emergent," to adapt Raymond Williams's (121–27) terminology—rather than manifesting a relatively seamless operational form.

I return now to John Beverley's statement that testimonio was part and parcel of a particular class-based, revolutionary politics that was displaced by neoliberal capitalism and its accompanying postmodern identity politics—movements turning around ethnicity, gender, ecology and so on—as the principal means of resistance. The salience of identity politics in Latin America, as in the United States, is palpable, but that does not mean either that class politics is absent or that the identity-based New Social Movements (NSMs) are "as 'classless' or as loath to confront state power and address material concerns as some theorists suggest" (Edelman 20). James Petras and Timothy Harding recently discussed a "third wave" of leftist politics in Latin America that "emerges as a response to the negative consequences of neoliberalism and frustration with the ineffectiveness and unresponsiveness of the existing center-left electoral parties and coalitions" (5).[7] They note that movements like Mexico's EZLN (Zapatista Army of National Liberation), Brazil's MST (Landless Workers Movement), Columbia's FARC (Revolutionary Armed Forces of Colombia), and Bolivia's *cocalero* unions are "developing a broad agenda that goes beyond sectoral reforms to a national transformation ... moving from local to national struggle" (6) and conclude that "[t]he movement from protest to politics, from local to national action, from sectoral transformation to national-popular revolution has begun" (7). Even if overly optimistic—as the Mexican government's "containment" of Zapatista protest indicates—this reading of the current conjuncture does, at least, suggest that the political cartography of contemporary Latin America is too complicated to be represented in terms of a simple transition from interventionist states/class politics/modernist cultures to neoliberal states/identity politics/postmodernist cultures. Class remains an important axis of struggle in Latin America, for which reason it is too soon to dismiss testimonio as a medium for the current and future projection of subaltern voices (see Guttman, *Romance* 117–20).

Ethnography

Just as some literary critics have reevaluated testimonio and moved into the terrain of autocritique and meta-critique, some anthropologists have embraced testimonio and argued, at least implicitly, for a rather direct access to the real. I want to be clear that anthropologists don't produce testimonio so much as exercise what I call the "testimonial function." I think of the testimonial function as the self-inscription of the anthropologist as witness to poverty, oppression, and struggle. It cannot be testimonio because anthropologists are not and cannot be true testimonial subjects with an organic connection to and an ontological experience of that which they narrate. However committed they may imagine themselves to be to others, anthropologists eventually go home—home being some other place—or else they quit being anthropologists.

The testimonial function is not new to anthropology, but it used to be relegated to field memoirs published after the author's scientific bonafides had been established via the production of "serious" ethnography. However, during the last fifteen years, it has become much more popular and widespread, partly because of a poststructuralist-inspired suspicion of the generalization and analysis that characterized those ethnographies, and a desire to offer accounts that better reflect the complex, messy, heterogeneous first-order experience of fieldwork.[8]

For instance, Lila Abu-Lughod (*Writing Women's Worlds* and *Writing Against*), Michael Jackson (*Minima Ethnographica*), and Ruth Behar (*Vulnerable*) sustain that all *abstractions*—which theories and generalizations certainly are—produce *essentialisms*, which Jackson pejoratively defines as involving "a facile ironing out of difference in the search for administrative order" (200). They believe that when represented in this manner, other cultures come to be contrasted with our own in ways that help to perpetuate if not increase the distance between self and Other, when the job of ethnography should be to reduce that distance, or what is practically the same thing, to represent others as being as multidimensional and complex as ourselves: other human beings suspended, like us, in " 'webs of significance' [and, I might add, networks of material and nonmaterial relationships] that he [*sic*] himself has spun" (Geertz 4). Anthropology does not generally accomplish that humanistic task. As a professional discourse that elaborates on the meaning of culture in order to account for, explain, and understand cultural difference, anthropology ends up constructing, producing, and maintaining difference. Anthropological discourse helps give cultural difference (and the separation between groups of people that it implies) the air of the self-evident (Abu-Lughod, *Writing Women's Worlds* 12). Extreme conceptions of cultural difference can even lead to "neoracism," defined by Etienne Balibar as "a racism whose dominant theme is not biological heredity but the insurmountablility of cultural differences" (qtd. in Moreiras 47). The turn to testimonial-style ethnographic work seems aimed at restoring that "trace of the real" characteristic of testimonio that disappears when the mess of daily life in the field, which Renato Rosaldo likens to a "garage sale," is transformed through careful sorting and analysis into ethnographic texts as formal and contrived as a museum exhibition (58).[9]

Without belaboring the point, I find myself troubled by the relatively uncritical acceptance of personal narrative as superior to the more traditional discursive strategies used to stage ethnographies. Radical proponents of the testimonial function in anthropology seem unconscious of, and if conscious of then untroubled by, the possible effects of their editorial decisions. They seem unconcerned with ways these texts might be read or misread by readers unfamiliar with the social and cultural situations the authors elicit. Consider, for instance, the abstract of a recent article by Ruth Behar, one of the most committed practitioners of the testimonial function in anthropology:

> This article is a meditation on the way ethnography, as a method and form of expression, has informed a range of reflexive anthropological journeys in Spain, Mexico, and Cuba. It uses a poetic sense of reflexivity to explore the embedded nature of personal experience within the ethnographic process. Borrowing the metaphor of "the lost book" from a fictional story by Agnon, the article explores the contradictory dynamic that emerges in witnessing loss and simultaneously wanting to preserve culture. Ultimately, the article urges ethnographers to pay attention to intuition, serendipity, and unexpected moments of epiphany in the quest for ethnographic ways of knowing, while encouraging ethnographers to present their findings in a wider variety of literary and artistic genres.
>
> ("Ethnography" 15)

It is precisely in this vein, I believe, that Michel-Rolph Trouillot opined that the postmodern disintegration of the divide between self and other has left anthropologists in the contemporary human sciences without a clear object of study. Anthropology was historically founded on the premise of a "savage other" that played an important role in the construction of the "civilized self." But the global spread of culture and commodities has muddled the difference, leaving anthropologists shaken and confused. Quoting Truillot:

> His favorite model has disappeared or, when found, refuses to pose as expected. The fieldworker examines his tools and finds his camera inadequate. Most importantly, his field of vision now seems blurred. Yet he needs to come back home with a picture. It's pouring rain out there, and the mosquitoes are starting to bite. In desperation, the baffled anthropologist burns his notes to create a moment of light, moves his face against the flame, closes his eyes, and, hands grasping the camera, takes a picture of himself.
>
> (35–36)

A wonderful send-up of contemporary ethnography faithful to Trouillot's comment appeared in *Krippendorf's Tribe* (in Spanish, *Una Familia de Indios*), a film starring Richard Dreyfuss and Gina Elkins. Dreyfuss plays a bumbling anthropologist who leaves New Guinea and returns to his university empty handed after having failed to locate an uncontacted, likely mythical, New Guinea "tribe." Desperate, he invents the "Shelmikamu" (a compendium of the names of his three children) to satisfy funders, university officials, and an expectant public, and films his children and himself disguised in fictive native garb acting out fantasy rituals in his backyard. A few skeptics in the department go to New Guinea in order to invalidate the claims, but a quick cell phone call to a friendly (and modernized) group of natives has them, too, acting out the savage script in order to preserve the anthropologist's reputation.

My point is not that anthropologists should forsake the testimonial function. Creatively employed, it permits readers to grasp how others, like themselves, strategically maneuver on local power fields, even if the fields and the strategies are different. It may thereby contribute to the "strategic humanism" that Lila Abu-Lughod believes necessary in a world experiencing a recrudescence of essentialisms: ethnic, cultural, gender, racial. But anthropologists are not and cannot be testimonial subjects. They will always see and record the world through particular lenses; the colors and shapes of which are not usually detailed in testimonial-style ethnographic writing. Let me note that this trend, too, can have negative consequences for the production of testimonio, for if the voices of anthropologists, through the testimonial function, come to substitute for the voices of those whom they study, well, then, testimonio would seem to have been stripped of its raison d'être. In a more critical vein, the testimonial function also points us toward the limits of anthropological work in general, for if we acknowledge—which I am not ready to do at the moment—that the best anthropology is that based exclusively on personal narrative, then the next logical step would be to eliminate the anthropologist and restore the voice of the informant, or better yet, have the informant write the ethnography—and do away with the ethnographer.[10]

BETWEEN DON TASO AND ESPERANZA: "BEARING WITNESS IN HARD TIMES"

Two ethnographic-style testimonials (or testimonial-style ethnographies) mark the extremes, if not the limits, of ethnography's appropriation of testimonial discourse. In the historical distance lies Sidney Mintz's *Worker in the Cane: A Puerto Rican Life History*—analyzed with considerable sensitivity by Florencia Mallon—which tells the story of don Taso, an honest and admirable Puerto Rican sugarcane worker. Closer to the present, we find Ruth Behar's flamboyant *Translated Woman: Crossing the Border with Esperanza's Story*, which recounts the life of Esperanza, an itinerant market woman from a rural town in central Mexico. Mintz was a key figure—along with Eric Wolf, June Nash, and others—in the development of a historically sensitive, political economic approach in anthropology. *Worker in the Cane* manifested Mintz's early interest in the social relations and political orientations of Puerto Rico's rural, sugarcane proletariat. Thirty years later, "identity" had largely eclipsed "class" for a generation of younger anthropologists trained during the Reagan years, a point reflected in Behar's choice of Esperanza as informant, the features she emphasized, and the discursive strategy she employed in presenting them.

I am interested in these two works insofar as they might be employed to inform—even if by way of negative example—Fabio's testimonio cum life history. After all, the works fall on either side of the period of "high" revolutionary insurgency in Latin America. This was so *even though* Mintz wrote on the eve of the Cuban Revolution (and almost a decade after the truncated Bolivian one), and *even though* Guatemalan revolutionary groups were several years away from laying down their arms when Behar penned *Translated Woman*. In short, these books represent two possibilities by means of which testimonial subjects, through their anthropological or non-anthropological interlocutors, might "bear witness in hard times" (Mallon 311). A brief examination of the poverty, want, high levels of criminality and gang warfare, broken promises, and growing international migration in El Salvador could be easily mustered to show that, indeed, hard times are here particularly for the rural, and all but a fraction of the urban Salvadoran population (see Lauria-Santiago and Binford; Moodie). Of course, hard times are not specific to the periods following "negotiated revolutions" or defeated insurgencies; a majority of people experience hard times during nonrevolutionary periods and in spite of efforts to avoid them, as a function of the forces that impinge upon them and which they strive to negotiate, not the least as a consequence of the normalized operation of capitalism.[11]

Translated Woman

In *Translated Woman: Crossing the Border with Esperanza's Story,* Behar juxtaposed the taped, transcribed, and edited life story of Esperanza, a poor, widowed peasant woman from the rural town of Mexquitec (near San Luis Potosí, Mexico) with discussion of their changing relationship and commentary on her own history as a Cuban-born Jew raised by immigrant parents in New York City, to which the family migrated in 1962 when Behar was five years old. Esperanza narrates a life of maltreatment and betrayal on the part of men—father, husband, and son—as well as women who cover up for them that left her with a *cólera* (rage), a potentially dangerous internal state in Mexican rural, folk medicine that could have lethal consequences for the protagonist or for those close to her.[12] Esperanza had sworn off entangling liaisons with males—although she continued to entertain lovers—and experienced temporary cathartic release from her "martyrdom" by joining a cult devoted to Pancho Villa, the legendary Mexican revolutionary, whose spirit frequently spoke to her through Chencha, a mysterious and sexually ambivalent necromancer.

For her part, Behar discusses an unresolved, conflictive relationship with her father. In one dramatic incident, Behar recounts how when she was in her early twenties, her father, angered by her distance and apparent self-indulgence while a scholarship student at a prestigious private eastern college, tore up before her eyes a packet of loving, albeit questionably sincere, letters that she had mailed to her parents from school (326–27). This was merely one among a number of other experiences that Behar narrates as a denationalized Latina border crosser attempting to find both her way and her identity in the United States—like Esperanza, a translated woman. Behar discusses her struggles at school, the Latino/a "slot" into which she was to be inserted when she obtained a multiyear (but not tenure-track) contract at the University of Michigan, and the tenacity with which she negotiated immediate tenure from that university when, having been awarded the prestigious five-year "Big Mac" or MacArthur Genius Fellowship, she suddenly became a hot academic commodity.

Without attempting to measure one form of suffering against another, it is difficult to know how, precisely, to relate Behar's history to that of her informant, Esperanza, who was physically knocked about and mentally abused as a child, and later, wife; saw four (of her nine) children expire at early ages; and remained a member of the Mexican rural, working poor in 1993, 63 years after her birth and the year that *Translated Woman* was published. Behar is, like Esperanza, a "halfie" embodying elements of the subaltern, but I do not believe that this status in itself extends Behar a "special pass" for doing ethnography in just any area of rural (or urban) Latin America. The difference in privilege is enormous, as even Behar is drawn to point out (236–43, 337), and it grows larger toward the end of her work in Mexquitec, as the author's academic career takes off.

Behar says that she discovered her own voice through that of Esperanza, renouncing earlier efforts to be, as she says, a "second-rate gringa," and embracing an identity as a feminist Latina:

> Because of my father's shame [of her peddler grandfather in Cuba], it didn't occur to me at first that my work with Esperanza, the Mexican street peddler, was also a bridge to my own past and the journey my family has made to shift their class identity. How many cultural and class borders I, too, have crossed to end up in the position of being able to turn away the peddler that came to my door [once in Mexquitec], while in all good conscience devoting years to writing up hundreds of pages of another peddler's life story.
>
> (337)

This and other statements sketch the outlines (and many of the details) of the classic immigrant rags-to-riches story, albeit one marked by continuing familial tensions and personal doubts—which Behar would continue to explore in later writings ("Introduction," "Writing," *Vulnerable Anthropologist*)—around her relationship with her father and her own insecurities. Despite the occasional commentary on class, it is ethnic and gender identity that ties this book (as well as Behar and Esperanza) together: Esperanza as a dark-skinned *mestiza* peasant and widow occupying a subordinate position in the rural Mexican class/gender hierarchy, yet one who makes her living selling to the privileged Mexican urban middle class; Bejar as a Latina and Jewish immigrant from a working class family attempting to find a comfortable place in the Anglo-dominated academic world. Neither exhibits an interest in class politics.

Worker in the Cane

Worker in the Cane chronicles the life of don Taso, a poor, rural, Puerto Rican sugarcane proletarian, from 1908 (his year of birth) to 1949. In the abstract, Taso was no different from thousands of other rural proletarians relegated to a variety of taxing, dirty jobs in and around the cane plantations for most of their working lives. But Taso attracted Mintz's attention—much as Fabio attracted mine—for his energy, intelligence, and inquiring mind. Taso pondered his surroundings, even as he remained, inescapably so, a product of them. Much of Taso's account of his life is given over to his struggle to find employment and feed and clothe a growing family, his search for stable housing outside the control of the sugarcane industrialists, and his political support of first the Socialist, and later, the Popular Party. In Mintz's rendering, Taso recounts his life—including traumatic periods of blacklisting and economic desperation, grave illnesses, intrafamily conflicts, and the deaths of three children—in a controlled, often reflective voice culturally appropriate to an adult, rural, Puerto Rican, South Coast male. However, the reader does learn that Taso's perspective on his difficult past has been constructed from a more psychologically placid and more economically and socially stable present. By the time Mintz conducted these life history cum testimonial interviews, Taso had resolved his housing problems, obtained year-round and relatively well-paid employment, experienced the miraculous cure of a debilitating, lifelong hernia, and was no longer the object of accusations of marital infidelity on the part of Elí, his spouse. Taso and Elí attributed some of these improvements to their conversion to the Pentecostal church. Indeed, the ecstatic religious experiences of a lifelong skeptic and rational thinker piqued Mintz's interest in don Taso's story (5) and weigh heavily in Florencia Mallon's commentary on the resulting product (see Mallon).

While the religious angle is undoubtedly important—and says as much about Mintz as it does about his informant—I am interested in gleaning *Worker in the Cane* for insights into the potential of testimonio and anthropology to "bear[ing] witness in hard times." In a broad political sense, times were just as hard, *if not more so,* during Latin America's "prerevolutionary" period of the forties and early fifties as during the "postrevolutionary" period of the nineties and the first decade of the new millennium.[13] Mintz, of course, was writing in the first period, when progressive U.S. academics were venturing out from under the dark shadow cast by Macarthyism, and in opposition to the evolutionist triumphalism Walt Rostow &

company (for whom all societies were on track to become, sooner or later, like the United States), who were beginning to detail the contradictions and human costs of rapid capitalist development. Thus, a key feature of *Worker in the Cane* is the back and forth movement between Taso's detailed personal chronicle of his strategic maneuvering, and Mintz's more condensed efforts to contextualize that account by explaining in broad strokes how a paternalistic, hacienda-based sugar society was giving way to far more individualized relationships promoted by the modernizing, U.S.-owned sugar companies. They are two approaches—one a life history/testimonio, the other a historical sociology—of representing a deepening process of rural proletarianization:

All jobs in the cane were now standardized, with stipulated minimum wages, and piecework survived only in particular jobs—such as cane cutting—where the decision to work by wage or by incentive was up to the workers themselves. Nearly all perquisites provided to workers in place of cash had been eliminated. Child labor laws were in force. Mechanical devices were by this time essential in the fields, and the value of all manual skills had declined.

(207)

Mintz concludes that by the end of the forties, "[t]he maturation of a rural proletariat—landless, wage-earning, store-buying, and economically homogeneous—was complete" (207). The upsets, disjuncture, confusions, displacements, and multiple sufferings that accompanied this process played key roles in Mintz's explanation of Taso's evangelical conversion (255–58), a conversion that, in conjunction with a series of betrayals and disappointments (151–53, 196–98, 204, 209), effectively removed him from active politics.[14] It is here that we encounter one of the key dilemmas posed by *Worker in the Cane,* namely, the deepening rural proletarianization entailed a double process of homogenization and differentiation that involved on the one hand "the maturation of a rural proletariat" that "began to think of themselves as members of a national class" and on the other, increasing awareness "of their separateness and individuality" (207).[15] Mintz registers these contradictions, and he situates Taso squarely at the center of them, but he never arrives at a fully satisfactory assessment of the protagonist. Taso is the subject of Mintz's prerevolutionary lament for the human costs of capitalist "progress":

As Taso revealed what he could of his life and how he tried to make sense of it, I became newly aware that most people in the world today still live and die without fulfillment. At the same time they are so muted by inexorable circumstance that the more fortunate of us are rarely compelled even for one moment to reflect upon the toll. And yet these human beings are not so thwarted as it might seem. They make do with what they have, and at times they can manifest a nobility and courage that I am awed by.

(11)[16]

But Mintz refuses to pity—itself a form of "victimization"—his friend and informant because to do so would degrade "the meaning of Taso's life to himself and to those who know and love him" (277). While preferable to Behar's dehistoricized and decontextualized testimonio of Esperanza, Mintz fails to adequately explain the role that Taso played in producing and reproducing the conditions that subjected and bound him. Certainly, *some* choice was involved in Taso's decision to abandon the Socialist Party, and later, to retire from efforts to create an alternative, more democratic rural agricultural workers union. Like Mallon, Mintz offers testimonio as a form of "reality check" through which we might get a glimpse behind the veil of the triumphalism cast by hegemonic discourse—developmentalist in the fifties, neoliberal in the nineties—in order to contemplate the human costs of uncontrolled market capitalism. But having done so, what then?[17]

Neoliberalism, Testimonio, and Emergent Discourses and Practices

Another way to read prerevolutionary testimonios like *Worker in the Cane* and to think about "postrevolutionary" or neoliberal testimonio as something more than "bearing witness in hard times" requires that we interrogate "emergent," albeit unrealized, discourses and practices embedded in the narratives of testimonial subjects. Even when dealing with past events, testimonio often highlights personal and social transformation, those moments when social structures and relationships that were hidden and obscure are cast into the light and sharpen in focus, to be struggled over and (ideally) superseded as opposed to lived within. Taso's active role as treasurer of the newly formed local branch of the General Workers Confederation (CGT) reflected a growing consciousness on his (and others') part that the old paternalistic relationships were breaking down and that most rural workers were becoming substitutable cogs in the sugar machine. Although introduced from without, the idea of a union would not have gathered force locally had it not responded to the felt needs of a critical mass of rural workers. When the authoritarian management style of the union president alienated workers who "had bad things happen to them" (198), Taso worked to help establish a more democratic, independent union. That union, too, failed, in part because of a rural *habitus* shaped by decades if not centuries of promises and betrayals, perpetrated as frequently by members of subaltern classes as by the local bourgeoisie and petty bourgeoisie. As Taso noted, "They start one union over here and another over there, and that's the way it always goes" (200).

Mintz aids the reader in understanding Taso's story by providing the necessary background and context. Yet Taso's narration outruns his efforts—not because *language* as an abstract system of significations contains a "surplus," which is to say that meaning multiplies and proliferates through every effort to tie it down, but because discourses and practices invariably say more than the actors speaking and struggling from within; hegemony can make consciousness. This brings me to two main points: testimonio is not only about "bearing witness in hard times" because it offers us the image of emergent discourses and practices, recounted after the fact by those closest to testimonial subjects. In some cases, the discourses/practices blossom and assume the forms of a counter hegemony or an alternative hegemony; in others, they fizzle away, are co-opted, or are suppressed. Even more important is the *fact* of emergence itself, the possibilities these discourses and practices represented, and the way the experiences of testimonial subjects prod *us* to historicize the present in order to "seize hold of a memory as it flashes up at a moment of danger" (Benjamin). However, given that testimonial readers also think and act from within hegemony, testimonio's progressive relevance—as opposed to its mere documentation of the cost of neoliberal capitalism—cannot be left up to the reader, unaided by the interlocutor, to decide.

All that I have said does not eliminate the problem of communicating Fabio's story and interrogating the lessons it might hold. Even if testimonio is a literary form theoretically relevant to the current conditions of struggle and resistance under neoliberal capitalism, there remains the practical problem of convincing readers of that fact. The ideas herein represent my understanding of some of the features of the changing academic field of power upon which I operate. I am convinced that to offer *Fabio's Story* in a "typical" testimonial format in which the interlocutor, following a short introduction, gives over the bulk of the work to the (mediated) voice of the testimonial subject would be to condemn it to oblivion. Few publishers would be capable of assessing this manuscript as anything other than another life history of the Salvadoran war with little or no relevance to the current situation in El Salvador or any other country in Latin America (or elsewhere). I've always found it interesting, and I suppose that this is a measure of the problem we face, that the "public" seems to have an insatiable curiosity about the lives of the so-called rich and famous and a veritable lack of curiosity about the lives of the poor and downtrodden. Those who have attained wealth and fame attract as objects of class fantasies, the poor and destitute are repudiated as objectifications of what downward mobility might look like. Readers and viewers tend to individualize the former—every renowned athlete or actor or financier is different—and essentialize the latter (see Binford, *El Mozote*: chapter 1).

In this war of movement, I too must move and adjust, and hope that Fabio, with whom I have not spoken in a dozen years, will understand. As it evolves, the book is becoming a combination of Fabio's testimonio and a commentary on both the genre and its critics. Furthermore, in each chapter I analyze Fabio's life experience as it relates to the relevant social science literature. In other words, I seek to accord the ideas of Fabio, whom I have characterized here and elsewhere as an organic intellectual (Binford, "Peasants"), the respect that I would grant to those of any university trained academic. Finally, I suggest how this testimonio—as a story of ideas and actions, of suffering and struggle—might be brought into the present, a living memory that, creatively interpreted, can indeed inform our understanding of a social process that is, in a truly dialectical sense, both the same and very different from the one Fabio recounts. *Fabio's Story*, of which this essay, appropriately modified, is intended to be a part, is destined to be a hybrid one: a testimonio that will, if successful, offer a "trace of the real" in the Lacanian sense; a conversation among intellectuals of various sorts, mediated by myself; and a critical and reflexive inquiry into the economic, social, and political conditions that led Gayatri Spivak to sustain—and many others to agree with her—that "the subaltern cannot speak."

Notes

1. Earlier (and different) versions of this essay were presented at the University of California, Davis, in November of 2001, Hartwick College in April of 2002, the Colegio de Michoacán (Mexico) in 2005, and a seminar organized by Francisco Gómez in Puebla (Mexico) in 2008. Modifications followed suggestions made by Francisco Gómez, Sergio Zendejas, Judith Adler Hellman, Ricardo Macip, Gavin Smith, Susana Narotzky, and Lesley Gill, none of whom bear responsibility for the final result.

2. On the role of the United States in training generations of repressive Latin American military officers, see Lesley Gill, *The School of the Americas: Military Training and Political Violence in the Americas.*
3. Roseberry sought to supersede the strict division between "peasant" and "proletarian" by analyzing proletarianization as a world historical process with different consequences in particular times and places. He noted that "Our concepts of peasants were always idealized statements that had to be mediated by an understanding of the history of particular social formations in which peasants have played a role. The best of the definitions were simply ways of talking about social relationships rather than attempts to construct elaborate typologies in which peasantries became reified as a type in an evolutionary sweep or a group in a complex whole" (194). Viewed in this way, there is no singular, categorical peasantry and thus no specific form of peasant politics distinct from proletarian politics.
4. In early March of 2002 the *Renovadores* separated definitively from the FMLN, defining themselves as social democrats in contraposition to the "communists" of the FMLN.
5. For poststructuralist literary critics, as for the French philosopher/historian, power is *not* an attribute of individuals but a simultaneous principle/effect of relations internal to discourse and action.
6. While extreme, Terry Eagleton's position on poststructuralism merits consideration: "Post-structuralism, which emerged in oblique ways from the political ferment of the late 1960s and early 1970s, and which like some repentant militant became gradually depoliticized after being deported abroad, has been among other things a way of keeping warm at the level of discourse a political culture which had been flushed off the streets. It has also succeeded in hijacking much of that political energy, sublimating it into the signifier in an era when precious little subversion of any other sort seemed easily available. The language of subjectivity has at once ousted and augmented questions of political action and organization" (25).
7. The first wave of left politics in the mid-sixties to mid-seventies, which included the Chilean Socialists, the Bolivian MIR, and others, has been "largely decimated and/or co-opted." The second wave, located in Central America and Brazil (FSLN in Nicaragua, FMLN in El Salvador, PT in Brazil, URNG in Guatemala, and PRD in Mexico), were the revolutionaries of the eighties and became the electoral reformers of the nineties. According to Petras and Harding, "The basic weakness of the second wave of the left is its tendency to compromise with the center, shedding demands for radical changes in land tenure, property ownership, and control over banks and foreign trade. It functions largely as an ineffectual congressional opposition, confined to criticism and denunciations. Apart from election campaigns, it is unable or unwilling to engage in mass struggles, displaying

increasing immobilism and disconnection from its original mass base" (4, see also Petras and Veltmeyer).
8. Philippe Bourgois (*Search* and "Continuum") is one ethnographer strongly committed to the testimonial function (or personal narrative) who is vehemently *not* poststructuralist. Nonetheless, I have criticized his use of the testimonial function, and he has responded to that critique (Binford, "Violence"; Bourgois, "The Violence"). For somewhat different reasons, I have serious reservations about the work of Matthew Guttman (*Romance* and *Meanings of Macho*), another political economy oriented ethnographer.
9. Carolyn Nordstrum, known for her work in the areas of war, violence, corruption, and (il)legality, is another advocate of the testimonial function. She eschews theorizing contemporary economic relations in part because "Our theories are constructed to fit the narrow confines of our discipline. We may even begin to think in neat units of analysis. These categories make perfect sense unless we try to apply them to the way people actually live their lives" (20–21). Michael Taussig's *Law in a Lawless Land* attempts to reproduce in writing the emotional experience of living in a Colombian town controlled by paramilitaries. Yet his critique of ex post facto explanation mirrors that of many other advocates of the testimonial function: "And this of course is what people like me are meant to do, too: find the underlying logic that will make sense of the chaos. Your disorder; my order. Find the paths through the forest and over the mountains. Talk their language. Determine their self-interest. Square it out into real estate called 'territory.' Then dip it all into a fixing solution like developing a photograph. But what if it's not a system but a 'nervous system' in which order becomes disorder the moment it is perceived?" (17–18).
10. In a world without significant differences in wealth and power, such might be the result, for all people would enjoy the "right of refusal" to be made anthropological subjects, a right that today is enjoyed by a small minority.
11. For a U.S. example see Ehrenreich.
12. Esperanza blames herself for the loss of one of her infant children, who suckled her milk during one of her fits of *cólera* (Behar, *Translated* 66–68).
13. "Hard times" may be more striking subjectively when they follow times when major structural change has been—or at least seems to be—on the plate, but this is not a prerequisite. Hard times are "hard" precisely because of the "easier" (or less hard) times that preceded them, regardless of an external observer's evaluation of that earlier period.
14. For instance, Mintz states that "The revivalist churches are the churches of the detribalized, the deculturated, and the disinherited. They fill many needs for lower-class people who, one way or another, have lost their stake in 'the old ways.' The revivalist churches provide

15. Speaking of modernism and postmodernism in particular—but I think referring to capitalism in general—David Harvey notes the complex and contradictory aspects of capitalist accumulation: "Within this matrix of internal relations, there is never one fixed configuration, but a swaying back and forth between centralization and decentralization, between authority and deconstruction, between hierarchy and anarchy, between permanence and flexibility, between the detail and the social division of labour.... The sharp categorical distinction between modernism and postmodernism disappears, to be replaced by an examination of the flux of internal relations within capitalism as a whole" (*Condition* 339, 342). These "internal relations of capitalism as a whole" have implications for the analysis of groups and individuals (also see Harvey, *Enigma*).
16. In a statement to the same effect, Mintz notes, "It was my hope that the remarkable intelligence and articulateness of the protagonist—a man who had very little formal education and had lived a very hard life—would reveal itself successfully to the interested reader, and thus illuminate the immense human potential, often unrealized, that lies outside our reach because our social and economic system often destroys individual capacities before they can blossom" (xii).
17. Much depends on the author's political stance, the choice of testimonial subject, and the way the testimony is mediated and contextualized. Mallon selected Isolde Reuque, an honorable social activist who has dedicated her life to promote Mapuche culture and politics, but who has for many years worked within the state and allied, even if only tactically, with the Christian Democratic Party. Taken as the representation of the Mapuche struggle for Western readers, her life idealizes democracy and gradualism—a step-by-step advance within the confines and constraints of peripheral, neoliberal capitalism. Moreover, Mallon's extreme effort at "horizontality," through which she strived to minimize rather than exploit her power to shape the context within which Isolde's voice is projected, resulted in a book that, at least for readers with little experience of post-1978 Chilean history, presents severe difficulties in comprehension. Is there nothing more left than to work from within the state, seeking gradual *paso-a-paso* (step-by-step) gains (see Reuque)?

Works Cited

Abu-Lughod, Lila. "Writing Against Culture." *Recapturing Anthropology.* Ed. Richard Fox. Santa Fe: School of American Research, 1991. 137–62. Print.

———. *Writing Women's Worlds: Bedouin Stories*. Berkeley: U of California P, 1993. Print.
Achugar, Hugo. "Historias paralelas/Historias ejemplares: La historia y la voz del otro." *Revista de crítica literaria latinoamericana* 36 (1992): 49–71. Print.
Behar, Ruth. "Ethnography and the Book that was Lost." *Ethnography* 4.1 (2003): 15–39. Print.
———. "Introduction: Out of Exile." *Women Writing Culture*. Ed. Ruth Behar and Deborah Gordon. Durham: Duke UP, 1995. 1–29. Print.
———. *Translated Woman: Crossing the Border with Esperanza's Story*. Boston: Beacon, 1993. Print.
———. *The Vulnerable Anthropologist: Anthropology that Breaks the Heart*. Boston: Beacon, 1996. Print.
———. "Writing in My Father's Name." *Women Writing Culture*. Ed. Ruth Behar and Deborah Gordon. Durham: Duke UP, 1995. 65–82. Print.
Benjamin, Walter. "Theses on the Philosophy of History." *Illuminations*. New York: Harcourt Brace Jovanovich, 1968. 253–64. Print.
Beverley, John. *Against Literature*. Minneapolis: U of Minnesota P, 1993. Print.
———. "The Margin at the Center." *The Real Thing: Testimonial Discourse and Latin America*. Ed. Georg M. Gugelberger. Durham: Duke UP, 1996. 23–41. Print.
———. *Subalternity and Cultural Representation: Arguments in Cultural Theory*. Durham: Duke UP, 1999. Print.
Binford, Leigh. *The El Mozote Massacre: Anthropology and Human Rights*. Tucson: U of Arizona P, 1996. Print.
———. "Peasants, Catechists, Revolutionaries: Organic Intellectuals in the Salvadoran Revolution, 1980–1992." *Landscapes of Struggle: Politics, Society, and Community in El Salvador*. Ed. Aldo Lauria-Santiago and Leigh Binford. Pittsburgh: U of Pittsburgh P, 2004. 105–25. Print.
———. "Violence in El Salvador: A Rejoinder to Philippe Bourgois's 'The Continuum of Violence in War and Peace: Post Cold War Lessons from El Salvador.'" *Ethnography* 3.2 (2002): 179–97. Print.
Binford, Leigh, and Wendy Harding. "How First World Students Read Third World Literature." *Translation Perspectives VI: Translating Latin America*. Ed. William Luis and Julio Rodríguez-Luis. Binghamton: SUNY Center for Research in Translation, 1991. 145–52. Print.
Bourgois, Philippe. "The Continuum of Violence in War and Peace: Post Cold War Lessons from El Salvador." *Ethnography* 2.1 (2001): 5–34. Print.
———. *In Search of Respect*. 1996. Cambridge: Cambridge UP, 2002. Print.
———. "The Violence of Moral Binaries: Response to Leigh Binford." *Ethnography* 3.2 (2002): 221–31. Print.
Bourdieu, Pierre. "Social Space and Symbolic Power." *In Other Words: Essays Toward a Reflexive Sociology*. Palo Alto: Stanford UP, 1990. 123–39. Print.

Carey-Webb, Allen. "Teaching, Testimony, and Truth: Rigoberta Menchú's Credibility in the North American Classroom." *The Rigoberta Menchú Controversy*. Ed. Arturo Arias. Minneapolis: U of Minnesota P, 2001. 309–31. Print.

Danner, Mark. *The Massacre at El Mozote*. New York: Vintage, 1994. Print.

Eagleton, Terry. *The Illusions of Postmodernism*. London: Blackwell, 1996. Print.

Edelman, Marc. *Peasants against Globalization: Rural Social Movements in Costa Rica*. Palo Alto: Stanford UP, 1999. Print.

Ehrenreich, Barbara. *Nickel and Dimed: On (Not) Getting By in America*. New York: Owl, 2001. Print.

Geertz, Clifford. "Thick Description: Toward an Interpretative Theory of Culture." *The Interpretation of Cultures*. New York: Basic, 1973. 3–30. Print.

Gill, Lesley. *The School of the Americas: Military Training and Political Violence in the Americas*. Durham: Duke UP, 2004. Print.

Gramsci, Antonio. *The Prison Notebooks*. Oxford: Oxford UP, 1971. Print.

Guttman, Matthew C. *The Meanings of Macho: Being a Man in Mexico City*. Berkeley: U of California P, 1996. Print.

———. *The Romance of Democracy: Compliant Defiance in Contemporary Mexico*. Berkeley: U of California P, 2002. Print.

Harvey, David. *The Condition of Postmodernity*. London: Blackwell, 1989. Print.

———. *The Enigma of Capital and the Crises of Capitalism*. Oxford: Oxford UP, 2010. Print.

Jackson, Michael. *Minima Ethnographica: Intersubjectivity and the Anthropological Project*. Chicago: U of Chicago P, 1998. Print.

Lauria-Santiago, Aldo, and Leigh Binford, eds. *Landscapes of Struggle: Politics, Society, and Community in El Salvador*. Pittsburgh: U of Pittsburgh P, 2004. Print.

Levi-Strauss, Claude. *The Savage Mind*. Chicago: Chicago UP, 1966. Print.

Mallon, Florencia E. "Bearing Witness in Hard Times: Ethnography and Testimonio in a Postrevolutionary Age." *Reclaiming the Political in Latin American History: Essays from the North*. Ed. Gilbert M. Joseph. Durham: Duke UP, 2001. 311–54. Print.

Mintz, Sidney. *Worker in the Cane: A Puerto Rican Life History*. 1960. New York: Norton, 1974. Print.

Moodie, Ellen. *El Salvador in the Aftermath of Peace: Crime, Uncertainty and the Transition to Democracy*. Philadelphia: U of Pennsylvania P, 2010. Print.

Moreiras, Alberto. *The Exhaustion of Difference*. Durham: Duke UP, 2001. Print.

Nordstrum, Carolyn. *Global Outlaws: Crime, Money, and Power in the Contemporary World*. Berkeley: U of California P, 2007. Print.

O'Connell, Joana. "Rereading Salvadoran *Testimonio* after the Cease-Fire." Latin American Studies Association. Palmer House Hilton Hotel, Chicago. Sept. 24–26, 1998. Presentation.

Petras, James, and Timothy Harding. "Introduction: Radical Left Response to Global Impoverishment." *Latin American Perspectives* 27.5 (2000): 3–10. Print.

Petras, James, and Henry Veltmeyer. *Globalization Unmasked: Imperialism in the 21st Century*. London: Zed, 2001. Print.

Portes, Alejandro, and Kelly Hoffman. "Latin American Class Structures: Their Composition and Change during the Neoliberal Era." *Latin American Research Review* 38.1 (2003): 41–82. Print.

Randall, Margaret. "¿Qué es y cómo se hace un testimonio?" *Revista de crítica literaria latinoamericana* 36 (1992): 21–45. Print.

Reuque Paillalef, Rosa Isolde. *When a Flower is Reborn: The Life and Times of a Mapuche Feminist*. Ed. and trans. Florencia E. Mallon. Durham: Duke UP, 2002. Print.

Rosaldo, Renato. *Culture and Truth: The Remaking of Social Analysis*. Boston: Beacon, 1989. Print.

Roseberry, William. *Coffee and Capitalism in Venezuela*. Austin: U of Texas P, 1983. Print.

Sklodowska, Elzbieta. "Spanish-American Testimonial Novel—Some Afterthoughts." *The Real Thing: Testimonial Discourse and Latin America*. Ed. Georg M. Gugelberger. Durham: Duke UP, 1996. 84–100. Print.

Sommer, Doris. "Rigoberta's Secrets." *Latin American Perspectives* 18.3 (1992): 32–50. Print.

———. "No Secrets." *The Real Thing: Testimonial Discourse and Latin America*. Ed. Georg M. Gugelberger. Durham: Duke UP, 1996. 130–57. Print.

Spivak, Gayatri. "Can the Subaltern Speak?" *In Other Worlds: Essays in Cultural Politics*. London: Routledge, 1987. 66–111. Print.

Taussig, Michael. *Law in a Lawless Land: Diary of a Limpieza*. New York: New, 2003. Print.

Trouillot, Michel-Rolph. "Anthropology and the Savage Slot." *Recapturing Anthropology*. Ed. Richard Fox. Santa Fe: School of American Research P, 1991. 17–44. Print.

Williams, Gareth. "The Fantasy of Cultural Exchange in Latin America." *The Real Thing: Testimonial Discourse and Latin America*. Ed. Georg M. Gugelberger. Durham: Duke UP, 1996. 225–53. Print.

Williams, Raymond. *Marxism and Literature*. Oxford: Oxford UP, 1977. Print.

CHAPTER 2

TESTIMONIO AND ITS TRAVELERS: FEMINIST DEPLOYMENTS OF A GENRE AT WORK

Patricia Connolly

> *Seven women, seven lives, countless aspirations, worlds, dreams, and struggles. Sometimes, the threads of our lives get entangled with one another, and at others, they isolate themselves and scatter.*
>
> (Sangtin Writers 3)

So mark the opening lines of the Sangtin Writers' *Playing with Fire: Feminist Thought and Activism through Seven Lives in India.* This collaboratively written narrative interweaves nine testimonial voices—seven of which belong to village-level NGO activists in Uttar Pradesh—in its exploration of a collective feminist methodology through which to realize more egalitarian organizing efforts. The *sangtins*'[1] penetrating words strongly resonate with a poetics of solidarity articulated by many polyvocal feminist testimonios that actively foreground the material and ideological conditions that wedge themselves between the felt realities and the hopes and dreams of the women located at the center of their narratives. The multi-layered tensions articulated in this passage—between the individual and the collective, between oppressive realities and the promise of liberated futures—remain a staple in such works as they illustrate the effects of macrosocial power structures in women's daily lives while documenting how women actively struggle against processes of marginalization. Published in 2006, *Playing with Fire* is a fiercely committed and energized piece of testimonial literature that challenges John Beverley's absolutist claim that "the moment of testimonio is over" ("The Real Thing" 280). Rather, this essay argues that contemporary feminist polyvocal testimonios importantly re-envision and re-energize the testimonial genre by utilizing it as a methodological tool to realize the creative and political visions of activist women's groups in their socially situated contexts.

This essay engages with a selection of testimonios compiled by activist women's groups from distinct geopolitical locations: Sangtin Writers, *Playing with Fire: Feminist Thought and Activism through Seven Lives in India* (2006); Latina Feminist Group, *Telling to Live: Latina Feminist Testimonios* (2001); Beverly Bell, *Walking on Fire: Haitian Women's Stories of Survival and Resistance* (2001); and Sistren Theatre Collective, *Lionheart Gal: Life Stories of Jamaican Women* (1986). A brief overview of each text's trajectory and stated goals attests to testimonio's ability to traverse increasingly diverse (cultural, political) terrain.

Sangtin Writers' *Playing with Fire (PF)* is set in Sitapur District of Uttar Pradesh, India, an area thick with donor-funded development initiatives. The collective formed out of concern for how the non-governmental organization (NGO) that (at one time) employed eight of the nine *sangtins*[2] reinforces social hierarchies along the lines of class, caste, and religion through bureaucratic practices that undermine the organization's stated efforts to "empower" underclass women, including undervaluing the knowledge and labor of the village-level activists who consist *of* and work directly *with* the women the organization purports to serve.[3] *PF* confronts the limitations and possibilities of NGOs' abilities to enact foundational social change.

Going back 20 years to a text that documents the collective dialogic processes that inform the story-based form of consciousness raising that the Sistren Theatre Collective (founded in 1977) uses as the seeds of creation for its theater productions, *Lionheart Gal (LG)* charts a complex picture of pressing social concerns faced by (mainly) black working-class Jamaican women. The editor and then theatre director Honor Ford-Smith suggests that the stories reveal the impact of development on women and "illustrate ways in which women can move from the apparent powerlessness of exploitation to the creative power of rebel consciousness" (xiii). The book's topics range from early motherhood to intimate partner violence, working and living conditions, education, and political participation and rebellion, thoroughly dispelling the idea that "women's issues" remain in the terrain of the private sphere.

Beverly Bell's *Walking on Fire (WF)* is aimed at complicating static, monolithic representations of Haitian women by focusing on the creative means of resistance Haitian women use to *bat tenèb*, "beat back the darkness" (xiiv). Similar to *LG*, this collection focuses on a number of social issues that testify to the ways in which domestic and international policies destabilize women's struggles to maintain economic stability and cultivate dignified lives, while simultaneously attesting to the "rebel consciousness" that keeps these women's hopes and dreams alive. *WF* differs from the other texts in that Bell does not write as an immediate member of a women's collective. Rather, Bell conducts interviews with women from several organizations, providing a broader picture of the diverse ways Haitian women engage in resistance efforts.

The Latina Feminist Group's *Telling to Live (TL)* stretches the idea of testimonio by bringing it into the realm of the U.S. academy. The collective was configured by a group of Latina academics with the goal of working with the sociohistorical differences that cut through the pan-ethnic configuration of "Latinas" in a way that becomes glossed over in solidarity efforts. The book testifies to the ways in which testimonio became a central methodology in conveying themselves to each other and in theorizing *Latinidades*.

Out of these four feminist polyvocal testimonios, all but *PF* position the various women's narratives side by side within the narrative frame; *PF* further complicates this polyvocal form by "braiding" together individual voices and interweaving the stories with a collaboratively generated comparative analysis within the body of a thematically framed chapter. With the exception of *WF*, these texts emerge as part of established collectives serving as by-products that seek to document brief moments of much longer political journeys. Each work acknowledges the politics of language and differently employs a decolonizing use of standard English by "bending" it to serve its immediate needs. These texts also employ metaphors that firmly anchor them to the cultural spaces from which their narratives emerge. Additionally, *PF* and *WF* directly insert themselves in ongoing debates on the politics of knowledge production.[4]

The term "feminist" is employed by the four primary texts discussed in this essay to refer to a self-conscious political posturing that embodies an awareness of the interconnectedness of social inequalities while granting particular attention to the ways that gendered cultural oppressions and material poverty attach themselves to women's bodies in different geopolitical locales. Additionally, this qualifier signals an egalitarian and politically motivated mode of inquiry that is evidenced in feminist testimonio's use of nuanced collaborative methodologies attentive to the possibilities and foreclosures of differently positioned women coming together to work around collectively defined sets of social issues.

While traditional testimonios have employed an "I" that is "we"[5] to provide a sustained situational analysis of how larger power structures are felt and experienced at the level of marginalized social actors, contemporary feminist testimonios often incorporate multiple voices and subject positions. This polyvocal structure mitigates the genre's reliance on metonymy by allowing speakers to be explicitly named and differentiated within the body of the text.[6] This collective resonance positions culture as a contested terrain while highlighting how the similarities and divergences between individual accounts enable a three-dimensional understanding of sociohistoric conditions in a situated context. Through the heterogeneity of experience and perception, fragmented truth claims subtly emerge; these then need to be pieced together and worked through in order for epistemic wholeness to more thoroughly materialize. The effect is a dynamic, multi-voiced framework that necessarily interrupts homogenous, monolithic representational practices.

While literary criticism on testimonio has overemphasized the power differentials between (first world) reader and (third world) text, often foreclosing possibilities of testimonio's successful navigation of these tenuous relations through stated function and embodied form, multi-voiced feminist testimonios fiercely insist on a bidirectionality of power that refuses to fully yield interpretive power to the reader. In each of these texts the traditional dynamic of the testifier/witness is challenged, complicating and reclaiming the genre from a simplistic politics of recognition. Specifically, these feminist renderings of testimonio recreate and revitalize the genre through a poetics of polyvocality and a process versus product-based approach that deliberately blurs the lines between witness and testifier. Such conceptual reframing undermines the masculinist notion of testimonio as a means to a political end. Rather, the processes of writing and telling become critical moments of praxis in the face of diffuse power structures. The increasing geopolitical diversity and structural complexities espoused by feminist testimonios extend the epistemological and political reach of this hybrid writing form.

Travels and Translations: Reconsidering the Theoretical Terrain of "The Real Thing"

Polyvocal feminist testimonios are not without precedent. As Linda Maier addresses in *Woman as Witness: Essays on Testimonial Literature by Latin American Women,* testimonio has been saturated with women's voices since its inception as a contemporary genre (2). Two paradigmatic examples—*I, Rigoberta Menchú* and *Let Me Speak! Testimony of Domitila*—feature women's testimonies, and are in turn edited and translated by women, not to discount the innovative contributions of feminist oral historian Margaret Randall. Nevertheless, the gendered dimensions of these critiques—the truth claims they put forth about women's lived experiences—have rarely been the focus of extended scholarly inquiry (Maier 2). Ironically, as more activist women's groups utilize the genre for their explicitly feminist creative and political work, their efforts have coincided with its declared metaphoric death.

In "The Real Thing," John Beverley states that "the moment of testimonio is over... the originality and urgency... that drove our fascination and critical engagement with it, has undoubtedly passed" (280–81). Both earlier and later in this essay, Beverley calls attention to how the "status of the testimonial narrator is a subject in her own right, rather than as someone who exists *for us* [the critics]" (268), and that "the way in which subaltern groups themselves appropriate and *use* testimonio... has not been addressed adequately" (280). Yet, in the above passage, Beverley undermines these alternate claims by framing testimonio as a passing academic fad that within the logic of capitalism could only briefly engage the "fascination" of Latin American literary critics.

As a literary academic, the point for Beverley is that "new forms of political imagination and organization are needed; that, as in everything else in life, we have to move on" (282). But if the testimonial moment is "over," how does Beverley account for the ways in which testimonios are emerging in new geopolitical sites and structural forms? Why should these formulations be categorized outside of testimonio? While not discounting the important work his definition allowed for in identifying testimonio as a distinctive genre worthy of literary attention, Beverley's canonical categorization serves a much less radical function in our current social landscape in its inability to account for the ways in which the genre continues to transform itself—or rather—has been transformed by those who seek to use its pedagogical force for their own political and creative needs.

Beverley's dismissal maintains echoes of the theoretical tensions between "original" and "copy" explored by Edward Said in "Traveling Theory" and "Traveling Theory Reconsidered":

> [T]heories sometimes "travel" to other times and situations, in the process of which they lose some of their original power and rebelliousness... the first time a human experience is recorded and then given a theoretical formulation, its force comes from being directly connected to and organically provoked by real historical circumstances. Later versions of this theory cannot replicate its original power; because the situation has quieted down and changed, the theory is degraded and subdued, *made into a relatively tame academic substitute for the real thing.*
> ("Traveling Theory Reconsidered" 436, emphasis added)

In "The Real Thing," we hear an almost identical sentiment when Beverley claims that while testimonio was once "intimately linked to international solidarity networks in support of revolutionary movements or struggles around human rights, apartheid, democratization... [d]etached from these contexts, it loses its special aesthetic and ideological power" (281). In both Said's and Beverley's musings, there is legitimate concern over how far radical ideas can stretch before losing their integrity and oppositional consciousness. But as Said concedes in a radical re-envisioning of his original essay, this perspective forecloses the possibility of theories igniting passion in readerships removed from their immediate "originary" context but who perhaps reside in situations with parallel sociopolitical circumstances, allowing the theory to grow fertile roots on seemingly foreign soil.

In revisiting the "inevitable" domestication of a theory as it travels further from its originary site, Said fathoms the possibility of "an alternative mode of traveling theory, one that actually develop[s] away from its original formulation... [and] flames out, so to speak, restates and reaffirms its own inherent tensions by moving to another site" (438). By the end of "Traveling Theory Reconsidered" Said completely retracts his earlier argument, claiming instead that the "point of theory... is to travel, always to move beyond its confinements, to emigrate, to remain in a sense in exile... This movement suggests the possibility of actively different locales, sites, situations for theory" (451–52).

Said's revised understanding of traveling theory is useful for contesting Beverley's argument on several levels. In a literal sense, testimonio is taking root in new geopolitical spaces. This migration is in turn engendering new possibilities for the formulaic construction of the genre as it becomes utilized by differently located groups for their sanctioned social issues. As academics, our analytical frameworks and tools for understanding testimonio must therefore also "travel" in order to do justice to this expanding body of work. But where and how can testimonio travel without losing the ember of its existence? How to make it "flame out"?

It is not insignificant that the genre of testimonio, as we currently understand it, came to be in a dynamic Latin American social landscape marked by cultural revolutions, dictatorships and *los desaparecidos* (the disappeared ones), struggles for land rights, and legal recognition. Yet, it need not be *contained* by this context; to do so would be to neglect to recognize the broader political possibilities it engenders. Recent books such as Sharmila Rege's *Writing Caste/Writing Gender: Narrating Dalit Women's Testimonios* necessarily complicate understandings of testimonio as mere cultural imports—troubling any easy understanding of "original" and "copy"—by illustrating how Indian women have been "doing" testimonio without calling it as such, or in fact ever hearing the term. By limiting our understanding of testimonio to a specific geopolitical site, or in terms of a list of imposed genre conventions, such texts highlight the risk of ignoring the underlying *ethos* and political and cultural immaterialities that define this flexible, grounded writing form. To return to Said's articulated tension between "original" and "copy," I argue that we need to question the productivity of a teleological, lineage model of origins in the first place if, in fact, the point of theory *is* to travel, and is *always already* traveling.

In the remainder of this essay attention turns to the representational practices utilized by a particular strand of contemporary co-travelers: feminist polyvocal testimonios. These texts enable an expansive understanding of the genre's formulaic and political possibilities by entering into dialogue with the intentions of the producers of testimonio and how these goals become embodied by the works themselves. The collaborative ethos that underpins these collections serves as a catalyst for the innovative collective methodologies undertaken throughout the body of these texts and positions feminist polyvocal testimonios as pieces of a larger transnational critique of power in its gendered dimensions.

Rendering an Absent Polyphony Present: Feminist Polyvocal Testimonios, Variations on a Theme

It is commonplace to identify testimonio by its use of a representative "I" set in metonymic relation to the experiences of the "we" whereby "individual testimony evokes an *absent polyphony of other voices*" (Zimmerman 112, emphasis added). Yet, as early as Margaret Randall's foundational *Cuban Women Now* (1974) and *Sandino's Daughters: Testimonies of Nicaraguan Women in Struggle* (1985), there were already testimonios in the process of rendering an otherwise "absent polyphony" *present*. Many of Randall's innovative feminist oral history methods have "traveled" into contemporary feminist polyvocal testimonios. Rather than subsuming disparate sets of experiences under one voice meant to represent the many, Randall conducted multiple oral histories with the women involved in these cultural revolutions and positioned their interview responses *side by side* each other within the narrative frame. Randall's formatting complicates the reader's relation to her work by extending the dialogic function of testimonio from one of text to reader to the participants themselves. A careful reader does not encounter a series of individual interviews but is rather able to hear a conversation emerging between interviewees, a result of placing differing accounts of specific events in close proximity. By letting the contradictions remain, Randall makes room for the epistemological possibility of coexisting truths. Her narratives resist stasis by representing the fluidity of truth and insisting upon the dynamicity of cultures in flux.

In considering the number of contemporary polyvocal feminist texts that emerge as by-products of women's collectives, it is clear that Randall's emphasis on dialogic processes between participants—the importance of witnessing themselves and each other—has been heard. *PF, WF, TL,* and *LG* all attest to this. But while each employs a polyvocal framework, their utilizations of this underlying structure vary in purpose and form. Whereas *WF, TL,* and *LG* position individual women's stories as stand-alone narratives within the body of the text, *PF* opts instead for a "braiding" of the collective's voices to further represent their bond as *sangtins* without glossing over the disparate positionalities and power differentials that exist within the group. While blended in the sense of interlocking narratives, this "chorus" does not remain constant; rather, we are told, "[a]s one of us speaks, the voice of the second or third suddenly blends in to give an entirely new and unique flavor to our music. Our notes blend, disperse in ones or twos or sevens, and regroup" (Sangtin Writers xxxiv). Beyond the musicality of this metaphor, it highlights the fluid, deliberate shifting of voice(s)—at one moment featuring the particular experience of one woman, augmented by a differing experience of another, then rejoining to produce a collective reading of what these dissonances mean: "While Radha was subjected to scornful meddling for not producing a child after three years of marriage, here was Sandhya, feeling a different kind of pressure: *not* to have one" (59).

These "variations" on similar cultural experiences remind us how social structures enact themselves differently on the bodies of disparately positioned social actors while referring back to the "same economy" (Scott 779). But *PF*'s deployment of polyvocality is not only for poetic effect. As members of a collective organized to confront the ways NGOs define "poor rural women's issues" without the input of women who occupy these social positions, the *sangtins* are committed to representing themselves as knowledge producers who do not need to rely on outside interpreters: "We want to interrupt the popular practice of representation in the media, NGO reports, and academic analysis, in which the writing voice of the one who is analyzing or reporting as the 'expert' is separated from the voice of the persons who are recounting their lives and opinions" (Sangtin Writers xxxiv).

Of the other texts, *TL* stands out in its production of a collaboratively generated chapter. The collection's multilayered introduction, "*Papelitos Guardados (Guarded Writings)*: Theorizing *Latinidades* Through *Testimonio*," is the result of group writing and reflection. While the book is collaborative in the sense of collective workshopping, the narratives themselves remain authored by single *testimoniadoras*: "Many of us, in one way or another, are professional *testimoniadoras* (producers of *testimonios*) . . . [yet many of us] had not yet experienced being on both sides of the process, sharing and generating our own *testimonios* with each other as Latina scholars" (2). Sharing their testimonios with each other became a vital part of their collective process. As stated by Luz Acevedo, "*nudos de poder* (nodes of power) could be loosened and united through a process of collaboration and polyphonic negotiation of difference" (261). Rather than resolve these representational struggles by submerging differences beneath an I-slot, members of the collective have final say on the framing of their particular stories. This choice is particularly poignant, considering that the collection emerged from U.S. Latina academics wanting to work through the sociohistorical complexities that are erased in pan-ethnic solidarity efforts.

WF is concerned with countering the "bare life" representations of Haitian women perpetuated through international circuits. Bell frames the polyphonic functionality of her text by suggesting: "The women's diverse responses to their realities call for expansive analyses, challenging monolithic assumptions often made about people in poor and black countries. Through their *istwa* (stories) the *griyo* (storytellers) defy cultural and gender essentialism and implicitly rebuff any attempt to create a paradigm or symbol of 'Haitian woman'" (xvi).[7] The women's stories are positioned side by side, and Bell thematically organizes the narratives around different forms of resistance ("Resistance in Survival" and "Resistance as Expression"), providing brief introductions to each section by drawing upon the women's stories as the basis for the analyses.

Similar to how Bell frames the collection's narratives within the oral Haitian tradition of *istwas* and *griyos*, in *LG* Ford-Smith suggests that the collection "draws on a legacy of tale-telling which has always preserved the history of Caribbean women...[since the] tale-telling tradition contains what is most poetically true about our struggles" (xv). In "Rock Stone a River Bottom No Know Sun Hot," the narrative voice illustrates this by recounting a saying her mother used to repeat: "'Member seh man a green lizard,' she used to say. 'Man is a ting weh change. Di instant when dem see one next woman, dem no waan bodder deal wid yuh, especially when dem see yuh tight pon yuh money.' Yuh see, she was disappointed by a man and dat cause her fi go tru a whole heap" (45). Meant to teach her daughter to be wary of relationships with men, her mother's encoding of men as "green lizards" illustrates the pedagogical creativity of the folk tradition, while the daughter's decoding (marked by, "Yuh see") highlights how the faculties of the imagination are also used to interpret social truths.

Ford-Smith's decision to convey these tales in Jamaican Creole furthers how the collection's polyphonic framework resonates with culturally specific storytelling practices. She also speaks directly to the epistemological importance of reading across individual accounts: "The stories can be read individually as accounts of ways in which women come to terms with the difficulties in their personal lives. However, within each story there are different emphases such as work, housing, relations with men and children; so that taken together, they are a composite woman's story, within which there are many layers of experience" (xiii). Ford-Smith's authorial directive to read across individual narratives, to engage with the "many layers of experience," reinforces the overarching political and intellectual benefits of rendering the "absent polyphony" *present*.

Rather than subsuming disparate experiences under a collective "I" that represses difference in an effort to maintain a united front, polyphonic testimonios illustrate how social truths speak louder and fuller when contradictions are encouraged to resound. In this way, feminist testimonios push beyond considering testimonio as a predefined genre. Rather, they employ this hybrid writing form as a tool—or *methodology*—capable of nurturing political projects that maintain a commitment to working through difference. It is this idea of testimonio as methodology that explains feminist testimonios' decidedly process rather than product-based approach.

Testimonio as Methodology: Process, Pedagogy, and Praxis in Activist Women's Writings

Through the processes of telling, testimonio prompts its testifiers to gain insight into how their personal experiences are informed by sociohistorical conditions, in turn increasing their level of critical consciousness. Feminist polyvocal testimonios' commitment to a process-based approach is evident on several textual levels, but is most apparent through their development of extensive methodology sections (the introduction usually serves this function) and by discursively framing the texts in terms of labor. If the text is the result of a women's collective it also documents how the group's collaborative processes of writing and reflection become translated into book form and how the book connects to their larger commitments. As *WF* and the work of Margaret Randall illustrate, even when a feminist testimonio is not the result of a collective process, the methodology sections intricately document the extent to which feminist collaborative methodologies have been employed, in turn challenging the dichotomization of theory and method. By insisting on this process-based approach, feminist testimonios offer nuanced engagements with questions of privilege and power in collaborative projects and remind us that the organization and production of knowledge are of equal importance as the final product.

These extended methodology sections are marked by a painstaking focus on documenting the level of thought, consideration, and labor involved in the processes of memory and dream work that produce the final written document. Out of the four texts engaged in this essay, *PF* and *TL* house the most extensive methodology sections; they are also the most explicit in framing their books in terms of labor and work. In the introduction to *TL*, the Latina Feminist Group informs the reader that the production of the text "involved an elaborate collaboration and division of labor among eighteen women of diverse Latina backgrounds... [w]hen we think about the work we have accomplished, we envision not only the product but the human connection between us, the *cariño* (affection), *respeto* (respect), and commitment to each other" (xi). Similarly, a subsection of *PF*'s introduction is devoted to "The Labor Process" (xxix). In this way, feminist testimonios mark how the work of writing and reflection holds meaning for the participants/writers/tellers themselves by making these accumulated (political, intellectual, emotional) labors visible to their readership. This is especially true of testimonios that are authored as part of a collective where significant effort goes into documenting such details as how and when the collective first emerged; the issues around which the group organizes; the conditions under which the members met; critical dates, events, and stages that shaped the process and form of book writing; internal and external challenges and how they have been addressed; and how the book fits into the collective's larger goals and political platform.

In addition to introductions doubling as methodology sections, feminist testimonios actively frame how they want the book to be understood by addressing what they hope to accomplish through this discursive representation of their labors. These framings are as diverse as their social situations. While *WF* places importance on diversifying representations of "poor Haitian women," the *sangtins* downplay their concern with representational "accuracy," arguing instead that the "usefulness or effectiveness of *PF*, then, can be assessed...on the basis of whether and how it can become a part of the authors' individual and collective agency and serve activism" (154). In *LG*, Ford-Smith focuses on the importance of creative expression in women's processes of self-actualization by suggesting that the stories "attest to the fact that when women select their own creative organisational forms, they begin to build a base from which they do transform their lives" (xx). Ford-Smith places particular emphasis on Sistren's *collective* creative process; for Sistren, a central function of *LG* moves beyond gaining recognition for the lives of working class Jamaican women by illustrating the type of knowledge that can be produced when linking the creative and political through artistic collaboration.

Still, testimonios purposely engage a transnational audience to bring attention to their struggles, and the methodology sections serve an important pedagogical function by emphasizing the particularities and cultural situatedness of their place-based critiques for a readership unversed in these specificities. *PF*, *WF*, and *LG* each incorporate brief histories and statistics meant to raise the consciousness of their readership by introducing critical aspects of the cultural landscapes with which they engage. As a text set in the political landscape of the U.S. academy, *TL* differently situates its place in genealogical relation to Chicana feminist thought. These place-based framings occur on other textual levels as well. As stated, Bell and Ford-Smith locate the women's stories within Haitian and Jamaican cultural folkloric traditions. *PF* locates the place-based ethos of the *sangtins'* analyses by documenting how this text, a translation of the Hindi book *Sangtin Yatra*, is meant to bring attention to the disciplinary action brought against them for writing critically of NSY (xiii). The "place" that *PF* occupies is therefore as situational and ideological as it is geopolitical; by cultivating a transnational network of solidarity, it places itself in a larger struggle over knowledge production.

This process-based approach is central to creatively redirecting the power differentials involved in third world women's voices being marketed to a first world audience, especially when traditional renderings of testimonio have positioned the genre as a means to a political end. In form and function, feminist testimonios critique this assumption by emphasizing how the labors of writing and reading, remembering and dreaming constitute political *work*. An anticapitalist sentiment in itself, these pieces insist that it is through processes of writing and reading, of listening and telling where the real work—on the part of the participants—lies, and not in the finished document itself. As such the "work" of feminist testimonio begins long before individual texts reach a reading audience.

The blurring of witness and testifier is perhaps most notably attained by how the narrators are discursively framed as "*sangtins*," "Sistren," "*testimoniadoras*," and "*griyos*," culturally resonant terms that denote a commitment to reciprocity, accountability, and solidarity. The methodology sections are also foundational for redirecting the relationship between reader and text. Beyond this, the blurring of witness and testifier occurs on two main registers: at the level of collective process, and at the level of the written text.

PF provides the clearest example of this textual blurring. The chapter "From the Streets of Babul to the Wetness of *Aanchal*" is concerned with themes of adolescence, marriage, and motherhood and consists of interlocking snippets of each autobiographer's narrative. Once all of the seven voices have spoken, a comparative analysis highlights the extent to which these stories have already been witnessed through the *sangtins'* dialogic processes: "The families of Garima, Sandhya, Shikha, and Pallavi were economically more secure and resourceful than were Radha's and Chaandni's parents. For this reason, the sorrows that fell into the laps of these four women involved fewer pains of livelihood and hunger and more aches of middle-class respectability and caste-based social status" (48). Through these interpretive codas the *sangtins* take control of how their stories will be received, interrupting the reader's consumption of their stories with evidence of how the collective has already thoroughly processed these accounts.

Other narrative tactics employed by the *sangtins* include a use of direct address and the rhetorical deployment of questions: "What are we trying to tell you, our readers, by engaging in this exercise of writing? Are these stories important simply because they were articulated as a result of a collective process?" (61). As highlighted by Kimberly Nance in *Can Literature Promote Justice? Trauma Narrative and Social Action in Latin American Testimonio,* the use of ambivalence within the narrative frame is an established trope of "deliberative" testimonio (35). These might be central questions with which the collective has grappled, but their inclusion in the text marks them as a meta-rhetorical device that forces the reader to confront these same questions. The other collections similarly employ direct address in the form of questions posed to the reader. In *LG*'s "Veteran by Veteran," the narrative voice concludes an analysis of the Jamaican working class landscape with: "Yuh see how it go? After yuh get nice lickle house and a live up and plenty people all plant up dem garden, dem start up dem war. Is like politicians no waan working class people fi live good for when dem have dem political differences is always inna di working class area dem fight it out" (170).

In *WF,* Bell actively anticipates and redirects the voyeuristic gaze of the book's readership through careful introductory framings of each section. Her insistence on referring to her interviewees as *griyos*/storytellers rather than as "participants" is a discursive choice that necessarily confers the women with more agency and creativity. "The Women of Millet Mountain" specifically attests to how productions of storytelling are always already happening between Haitian women; the book becomes framed as an extension of the storytelling processes that Haitian women employ in their daily lives. If the telling of *istwas* is familiar territory for the women whose narratives collectively comprise *WF,* for others, testimonio becomes a learned technique. In *TL,* the Latina Feminist Group suggests that "[t]hrough *testimonio* we learned to translate ourselves for each other" (11).

In *LG,* Ford-Smith emphasizes the necessity of collective dialogic interpretations of written testimony: "Each finished testimony still remains to be discussed as fully as it deserves within the group. In a sense until this is done, the work process will not be complete" (5). While a wider readership is invited to engage with the knowledge produced by Sistren, the group's internal discussions are most salient to the forwarding of their goals. In this way, feminist polyvocal testimonios redefine the dialogic function of traditional testimonio by insisting that their primary relationship is with the women who have braved and bared their stories through extensive processes of telling, writing, and reflecting, often in a collaborative setting, not the normatively defined "primary" relationship between reader and text.

COLLECTIVE JOURNEYS OF CREATION: TESTIMONIO AS A POETICS OF SOLIDARITY

[T]his collective journey of creation has united us in a closed fist. We hope that this fist will continue to become stronger and that we will gain the support and strength of many, many fists like ours.

(Sangtin Writers 131)

At its core, testimonio insists that cultural resistance matters. It recognizes that writing and reading perform social functions, and that through an intentional crafting of these tools, the lives, experiences, and critical insights of ordinary people living on the (material, cultural) margins of society can be drawn upon to expose oppressive power structures and incite radical social change. Outside of the narrow academic parameters that require it to fit preexisting genre expectations, the ember of testimonio insists that narrative can be used to communicate an urgent social problem. Testimonio can serve as a vital political tool in the crafting of alliances and in conceptualizing the sociopolitical responsibility of those who enter into alliances.

Feminist polyvocal testimonio therefore offers one particular way, or *methodology*, of telling a story about how the social landscape actively shapes and affects the gendered existence of the women at the center of the narrative account. By documenting not only the stories of the women involved, but also the underlying methods and labors that inform the texts, feminist polyvocal testimonial literature extends the epistemological and political reach of the testimonio genre. This is primarily accomplished through a poetics of polyvocality, a process versus product-based approach, and a blurring of witness and testifier. Although I have artificially separated these three methods for the purposes of analysis, they are mutually reinforcing in *practice*.

Despite the diverse forms and functions of these polyvocal feminist texts, Ford-Smith aptly states the shared testimonial ethos that connects these works: "The women who speak in these stories are not unique... Their lives here show that women are actively creating solutions, that they are not passively awaiting outside agitators to 'stir them up' into action" (xxx). By claiming memory and dream work as important modes of critical praxis, these texts employ testimonio as a methodology for organizing and present themselves as partial blueprints for social action. Each text offers itself up in the spirit of coalitional alliance that is attuned to a complex politics of difference with the hope that their contributions will spark in others the desire to dream, fight, and translate those struggles into a conceptual and story-based mapping of existing social conditions in all of their gendered dimensions.[8]

Notes

1. "Sangtin" refers to an Awadhi (an oral, local language of Uttar Pradesh) word meaning "of solidarity, of reciprocity, of enduring friendship among women" (Sangtin Writers xxiii). The original Hindi edition of *PF* is titled *Sangtin Yatra,* translating as "a journey of sangtins" (xxiii).
2. Nari Samata Yojana (NSY) is a pseudonym employed by the *sangtins* to refer to this NGO that operates under the banner of women's empowerment. Eight of the nine *sangtins* were at one time employed by NSY and their experiences with the organization prompted the formation of the collective. One of the *sangtins'* main critiques is that while NSY seeks to "empower" *dalit* women (lower caste affiliation), most of its village-level employees are *sawarn* (higher caste affiliation).
3. *PF* weaves together the voices of nine *sangtins,* seven of whom become the "autobiographers." This narrative choice was made to mitigate the effects of significant power differentials existing between the seven village-level activists and the regional NGO coordinator and U.S. academic also a part of the collective.
4. *TL* straddles English and Spanish. *LG* echoes the phrasings of oral Jamaican Creole. *PF* and *WF* serve as translations from Hindi and Haitian Creole, with key phrases expressed in the original languages. *PF* uses the metaphor of "monsoon clouds" to address the weight of the tears the women experienced when sharing their stories (9). In *WF,* Bell describes the conditions of poor Haitian women: "Popular snacks in Haiti are *peze souse,* squeeze and suck, frozen pops... The *istwas* in this chapter are told by women being consumed like a *peze souse*" (24). *PF* and *WF* also explicitly name the women at the center of their texts as "knowledge producers," contesting current trends in development initiatives that frame participant testimonies as "raw material" in need of further "expert" analysis.
5. For discussions of metonymy in testimonio, see Sommer and Zimmerman.
6. In each collection, the women were provided with a choice of address. In *LG,* the women remain anonymous. In *PF,* pseudonyms are used

within the narrative frame, but the work is published under the authors' real names. In *WF,* all women chose to use their real names except for two, who also employ pseudonyms in their daily life. *TL* names the women who participated in the project, but some individual narratives are authored anonymously.
7. Bell explains her use of *istwa/griyo*: "Borrowing on the tradition of the venerated storyteller, which stretches back to Africa and extends across Haiti, those who give their *istwas* here are termed *griyo*... The women in *Walking on Fire* are far younger than traditional *griyo* elders, and to my knowledge none holds this honor in her own family or village. Yet in this book, they are the keepers and recounters of history, truth, and wisdom" (xv).
8. Thank you to Amy Kaminsky and Richa Nagar for their continued support and insightful feedback. Thank you also to Edén Torres whose visual of the "ember" of testimonio helped to inspire the trajectory of this essay.

Works Cited

Barrios de Chungara, Domitila. *Let me speak! Testimony of Domitila, a Woman of the Bolivian Mines.* Ed. Moema Viezzer. Trans. Victoria Ortiz. New York: Monthly Review, 1978. Print.
Bell, Beverly. *Walking on Fire: Haitian Women's Stories of Survival and Resistance.* Ithaca: Cornell UP, 2001. Print.
Beverley, John. "The Real Thing." *The Real Thing: Testimonial Discourse and Latin America.* Ed. Georg Gugelburger. Durham: Duke UP, 1996. Print.
Latina Feminist Group. *Telling to Live: Latina Feminist Testimonios.* Durham: Duke UP, 2001. Print.
Maier, Linda S. "Introduction: The Case for and Case History of Women's Testimonial Literature in Latin America." *Woman as Witness: Essays on Testimonial Literature by Latin American Women.* Ed. Linda S. Maier and Isabel Dulfano. New York: Peter Lang, 2004. Print.
Menchú, Rigoberta. *I, Rigoberta Menchú: An Indian Woman in Guatemala.* Ed. Elisabeth Burgos-Debray. Trans. Ann Wright. London: Verso, 1984. Print.
Nance, Kimberly A. *Can Literature Promote Justice? Trauma Narrative and Social Action in Latin American Testimonio.* Nashville: Vanderbilt UP, 2006. Print.
Randall, Margaret. *Cuban Women Now: Interviews with Cuban Women.* Toronto: Women's, 1974. Print.
———. *Sandino's Daughters: Testimonies of Nicaraguan Women in Struggle.* Ed. Lynda Yanz. Vancouver: New Star, 1981. Print.
Rege, Sharmila. *Writing Caste/Writing Gender: Narrating Dalit Women's Testimonios.* New Delhi: Zubaan, 2006. Print.

Said, Edward. "Traveling Theory." *The World, The Text, and The Critic.* Cambridge: Harvard UP, 1983. Print.

——. "Traveling Theory Reconsidered." *Reflections on Exile.* Cambridge: Harvard UP, 2003. Print.

Sangtin Writers, and Richa Nagar. *Playing with Fire: Feminist Thought and Activism through Seven Lives in India.* Minneapolis: U of Minnesota P, 2006. Print.

Scott, Joan W. "The Evidence of Experience." *Critical Inquiry* 17.4 (1991): 773–97. Print.

Sistren with Honor Ford-Smith. *Lionheart Gal: Life Stories of Jamaican Women.* Ed. Honor Ford-Smith. London: Women's, 1986. Print.

Sommer, Doris. "Not Just a Personal Story: Women's *Testimonios* and the Plural Self." *Life/Lines: Theorizing Women's Autobiography.* Ed. Bella Bordzki and Celeste Schenck. Ithaca: Cornell UP, 1988. Print.

Zimmerman, Marc. "*Testimonio* in Guatemala: Payeras, Rigoberta, and Beyond." *The Real Thing: Testimonial Discourse and Latin America.* Ed. Georg M. Gugelburger. Durham: Duke UP, 1996. Print.

Part II

Positioning Oppositional Performances: Clandestine, Reluctant, and False Witnesses

Chapter 3

Hiding the Camera in Miguel Littin's *Acta general de Chile*

David William Foster

> *Somos el último ejército prusiano que queda en el mundo. (We are the last Prussian army remaining in the world.) (Chilean general, qtd. by narrator in chapter two of* Acta general de Chile*)*
>
> *En realidad había motivos de sobra para temer que la policía tuviera noticia de mi presencia en Chile, y de la clase de trabajo que estábamos haciendo. Llevábamos casi un mes en Santiago, los equipos habían sido vistos en público más de lo que convenía, habíamos hecho contacto con gentes muy diversas, y muchas personas sabían que era yo quien dirigía la película, [...] y en la vida real ya no comportaba como un clandestino demasiado riguroso. (In reality, there were more than enough motives to fear that the police had news of my presence in Chile and the type of work we were doing. We spent almost a month in Santiago, the equipment had been seen in public more than was suitable, we had made contact with a great diversity of people, and many knew that it was I who directed the film, [...] and that in real life I was not behaving as a very rigorous clandestine person.)*
>
> (García Márquez 119)

One of the two abiding themes of documentary film theory, in its characterization as sociohistorical testimony in form and in function, centers on the question of the intrusive camera.[1] Although the experience of social subjects with the presence of a camera in their lives varies widely, it is customarily assumed that one will perform one's life differently in conformance with the degree to which a camera is there to record it. That is, the presence of the camera, not to mention the support personnel and other technical apparatuses accompanying the camera, will serve to make individuals conscious enough of themselves, their bodies, their interactions such that their being in the world, which is what the camera may have wanted to capture in the first place, is purportedly denaturalized and rendered unauthentic. To whatever degree there is a belief that so-called real people behave in so-called real ways as they move through life and to whatever degree a documentary may wish to capture such supposed real behavior, the production of a documentary grounded in this belief will want to proceed on to capture the individuals in such a way that they are not conscious of being recorded: this is often called the "fly on the wall" approach to documentary production. To be sure, much newsreel footage is produced in this fashion, and narrative filmmaking is almost universally grounded in the convention that the universe it portrays is not aware of the fact that it exists for the camera's viewing, and through the camera, for our viewing.

An ethics of representation is not operant in the case of narrative filmmaking, not at least for the universe and its characters being represented, although there are very real ethical considerations vis-à-vis the audience, in terms of reliability and honesty of conception, verisimilitude and coherence, and trust with respect to the fictional contract. By contrast, the documentary as a mode of the testimonial contract, with rare exceptions, includes proscriptions on the abuse of confidence of historical individuals by recording them without their knowledge and consent, and this often includes caveats as regards how, even though they are aware of being filmed, the record of their lives is subsequently utilized and edited.

In the case of documentaries that are more similar to journalistic footage, in the sense that the immediacy of the event and/or the intent is to capture a large swath of human experience rather than individual stories, the ethics of representation takes into account the impossibility of obtaining individual permission for purposes of interpreting general and large-scale occurrences, although there is a measure of caution as regards what may slip over into the invasion of individual privacy. Existing in the world and its collective social circumstances is, today, an implied consent to the possibility of one's presence in that world being recorded for any number of subsequent reportorial uses.[2]

Miguel Littin's[3] *Acta general de Chile* (1986) presents a rather unique twist on the ethics of representation. A filmmaker in Chile before the 1973 neofascist military coup that drove him into exile and that, essentially, destroyed serious filmmaking in Chile along with professional photojournalism, Littin, a decade after the military coup (1985, to be exact), decided to return to Chile clandestinely to film the report on the society that had been created by the Pinochet dictatorship. In this sense, *Acta* is a sequel to Patricio Guzmán's *Batalla de Chile*, which describes the sociopolitical climate in Chile in the approximately two years preceding the destruction of the Salvador Allende government by the September 11, 1973, military revolt.

Narratively, Guzmán's *Batalla* ends with the bombing of the Moneda Presidential Palace, its takeover by military troops, and the death/suicide of the constitutional president. Chronologically, Guzmán's final image is that of General August Pinochet along with his junta comrades addressing the Chilean nation as to the details of the significant institutional change the military has brought about. Guzmán's filming crew had been able to move with freedom around Santiago and the rest of Chile recording the footage that would be assembled. However, in exile in Cuba, into *Batalla,* after the coup, Guzmán no longer had access to the nation, so to speak. This is a circumstance signaled by his detention in the Estadio Nacional and the circumstances whereby his raw footage ran the risk of being confiscated and destroyed by the junta government. The fact that it was saved by the intervention of the Swedish government has given us what is unquestionably the most famous documentary produced to date in Latin America. From that point forward, at least forward to a then incalculable moment when democratic culture could return to Chile, news reporting and other forms of testimonial documentary were controlled by the ruling junta in order to maintain a univocal public discourse that systematically excluded alternative interpretations. The official system was predicated on the assumptions that no dissident reporting could take place, and concomitantly, nor could any broadcasting of dissident voices. The circuit of reportorial/documentary commentary was hermetically sealed.

However, Littin's clandestine return to Chile in 1985 broke such a seal—at least in part. While he could not aspire to any broadcast in Chile of what he was about to film, his presence in that society became a significant reinterpretation of the dissembling fly on the wall of documentary filmmaking. If Guzmán often pretended to be interviewing for a conservative television channel to garner the unrestrained opposition to Allende of a segment of the Chilean citizenry,

Littin would also engage in a charade, mount a disguise, and dissemble with regard to what he was doing in order to obtain the raw material subsequently assembled into the four capítulos (chapters) of the 240 minute-long *Acta*. The actual story has a dimension of an adventure novel, and therefore it is no surprise that it has been told as such by the Colombian novelist Gabriel García Márquez. In this sense, Littin's *Acta* effects a change on the ethical question of clandestine photography.

The ethics of documentary customarily preclude any intervening in the privacy of individuals, who have a reasonable expectation that their intimate lives will not be recorded unbeknownst to them, such that we have access to intimate lives only because that access has been duly authorized. In the case of *Acta,* the life of a society is at issue, and it is a society access to which is proscribed by unconstitutional circumstances. *Acta* circumvents a proscription, but it does so in order, precisely, to underscore the illegitimacy of that proscription. The audience will be told that the camera has deliberately intruded upon, not an individual life, but a social life without authorization and that the circumstance of that intrusion seeks to be rhetorically effective in direct proportion to the illegitimacy of the proscription.

As has been pointed out, Littin's goal is not to denounce the details of life under dictatorship: Littin and other Chilean exiles did that with highly effective eloquence on, as one says, the stage of world opinion on the basis of evidence of Pinochet tyranny that was readily available from sources that did not require travel to and filming in Chile. Many news sources had, in fact, accomplished that, and narrative fiction, in the way in which fiction can be so compelling in its representation of lived human experience, had also made its own effective contribution.[4]

Rather, Littin's main goal was to accomplish a particular *effect*—that of the infiltration (in reality, five different camera crews from several countries were involved,[5] in different points of Chile) of the camera into spaces in which the uncensored camera was expressly forbidden to go. The fact that much of Littin's footage involves interviews with people who knew they were being interviewed does not lessen the importance of that effect, since what is significant is the use to which that footage is put in a text that cannot be publicly exhibited in Chile. That *effect,* even today, 20 years after the return by Chile to constitutional democracy, is still operant when one views *Acta* and grasps the historical conditions of its production: the fact that it is a documentary based on a camera not hidden from individuals, but from a society whose government had sought to ban the camera of critical commentary.

Acta is not the story of those conditions of production, although a separate documentary could well be made about them. Rather, it is a series of testimonies about Chile from within during the height of the Pinochet dictatorship whose overall effect is to underscore the false legitimacy of that dictatorship and the unconstitutional provisions that sustained it. Implicitly, *Acta* is more the story of the intrusive camera than anything else, even when the camera is not, reflexively or autoreferentially, the subject of its own gaze.

As in the case of the monumental projects like Guzmán's *Batalla de Chile* or Solanas's *La hora de los hornos,* the four hours are not one seamless document, but rather a series of fragments that coalesce under the general title. The first part of the documentary interviews individuals who, alternatively, support and are opposed to Pinochet; as a consequence, what we have is a journal of testimonies that are of interest because of their diversity and the strength of their conviction, one way or another, with regard to the dictatorship. In a sense, the opinions of those who support Pinochet are grimly more fascinating, since they are the fundamental motivation for the existence of the documentary. If it were not for the dictatorship, Littin would not have been in Chile filming the interviews for *Acta*. And since the audience of *Acta* and what they presume to know about Littin echo the opinions of the opposition, the audience does not have quite the implicit metastructural dimensions that those of the opposition do. The first part also includes interviews with individuals whose lives have been disastrously affected by the regime.

The second part of the film is devoted to northern Chile and its history of neglect and poverty, exacerbated by policies of the regime.[6] The third part focuses on the Chilean exiles[7] in Argentina and various examples of resistance to the dictatorship within Chile, especially university student movements, ending with an interview with an armed revolutionary group.[8] Finally, *Acta* closes with a chapter devoted to the death of Allende based on filmed sources and interviews, including affirmations as to the continued importance of Allende for the resistance and as a symbol for the return to democracy in Chile.

Because of its metastructural nature, the following will mostly be concerned with the first part of the documentary. As intrinsically interesting as parts two and three are, they only minimally expand on the circumstance of the clandestine camera. And while part four is dramatically very effective, it is documentary in the way in which all fiction is documentary, but is not a strictly documentary filmmaking project as such.

Acta does, in fact, open with a preliminary metacritical dimension, as the camera records Littin's arrival at the central train station in 1985. There is a voice-over in Littin's own words that transcribes his highly evocative reaction to see the city, shrouded in morning mist, for the first time in a dozen years. In this evocation, the crucial phrase is that of "la ciudad oculta" (the hidden city): Santiago as a city in which many of the most important events of its inhabitants are, one might say, hidden from view. While the camera records the particular material quality of the early morning streets of Santiago's center—the city that is explicitly on view—the voice-over begins the process of reporting on those facets of national life, such as resistance to the dictatorship, that are not materially or explicitly on view.

As the camera watches Littin watching the city, we see a landscape free of oppositional discourse: there are no campaign posters, no protest manifestations, no graffiti, nothing to disrupt the bland texture of apparent urban conformity. This rhetorically charged introit, "lleno de interrogantes" (full of questions), quickly moves, however, away from the transcription of Littin's clandestine arrival and his personal undertaking to the series of interviews that make up the bulk of the first of the four segments of the film. The rhetorical question—"¿Qué significa vivir bajo la dictadura de Pinochet?" (What does living under the Pinochet dictatorship mean?)—posed by the voice-over, which represents Littin's interior monologue as he travels through the streets of the city, is answered by the first interviewee in an appropriate discursive transition, as she begins "Significa vivir..." (It means to live...).

The predicated *significa* (means) is thus a controlling textual device throughout this segment. The voice of the interior monologue poses the question, and the interviewees undertake to answer it, with that predicate being the bridge between the two, between the director behind the camera and the real Chilean citizens who testify to (or before) that camera. As one might expect, the individuals interviewed do not neatly divide themselves into those who support the government and those who are opposed to it. And as one might suspect, the latter far outweigh the former, and the confirmation lies not only in the expected fact that the director might find more of them,[9] but in the particular litany of grievances that they have to articulate. These grievances divide themselves into three groups, and while they are all subtended by the repudiation of the military dictatorship, each group has its particular emphasis. Littin does not present them in a rigorously expository manner, but alternates them, increasing rhetorical effect and diminishing the sense of a systematic political denunciation.

The first group consists of talking heads;[10] a minute or so into each person's statement, an imaginary typewriter writes out their name and organizational or institutional identification. Some are, evidently, more interesting or eloquent than others, such as Pinochet's ex-Minister of Justice, who underscores the legitimacy of her office and her particular administration of it. By contrast, a former military interrogator describes his activities in detaining and torturing suspected opponents, an activity that he alleges to have provoked his revulsion. The camera allows these individuals to testify, although the narrator may subsequently comment on or refute the statements of those who support/have supported the regime.

The second group consists of poetic interludes that may also be built around interviews. This is the case with a brief excursus regarding the particular poverty of the port city of Valparaíso, once one of the most important of all the Pacific Coast ports, but now, at least as the camera shows us, a vast shanty town, its port installations abandoned or underutilized.[11] Various individuals speak to the impoverishment of life for Chileans such as those who live in Valparaíso, who, as a consequence, seem to stand in for all Chileans (at least until the second segment of *Acta*, set in the regionally impoverished North). I use the term "poetic interlude" because music and poetic texts are included as a backdrop to a survey of images of impoverishment, which are only commented on indirectly.

Finally, the third group of images are the testimonies (apparently read off of a prompter, because of the totally formal nature of their articulation and the unmoving pose of the body speaking them)[12] regarding disappeared family members. As one might expect, these declarations are the most moving, since, although the actual facts are missing in most cases, the concept of "disappeared person" has behind it the narrative trajectory of detention, incarceration, torture, further detention, possible assassination, and burial in a mass grave; customarily, no official trace of a person's movement along this trajectory is kept and it is virtually impossible for either the relative or organized human rights organizations to trace any whereabouts. The pained expression of those reporting on such disappearances, the understanding of that narrative trajectory, the fact of a disappearance without any available trace, and the accumulated posted images in the room where most of the testimonies are given are all details that contribute to the particular impact of these interviews.

It is not really that *Acta* provides in and of itself a counterweight to the silence of the regime and the silence that it, transitively, imposes on the survivors of the disappeared, as well as the other victims of the particulars of the regime (such as impoverishment, which seems to have been a deliberate part of the dictatorship's policies). The very existence of human rights organizations, some connected to the Chilean Church and some connected to international agencies, means that there was a place for the discussion of the disappeared and related abuses. This discussion might not have taken place in the public arena (either extemporaneously or through established media), but it did take place across a broad spectrum of the Chilean citizenry.

In this sense, *Acta* does not serve to lift an absolute silence, but, echoing the key word of its title, it does serve as a testimonial documentary act of the sort that still could not be made openly in Chile at the time. If the articulation of human rights abuses is not totally consigned to clandestinity, Littin's project is not either, since, as the accumulation of Chileans who speak for the record increases as the film progresses, the more the lonely figure of Littin emerging from the central train station in the opening sequence of *Acta* is replaced by the number of individuals and the groups of individuals who cluster around his camera. Indeed, accumulation is a principal rhetorical feature of *Acta*, especially in this first part, and it not only is part of the recording of increasing numbers of individuals who have suffered at the hands of the regime, it is also an index of the growing resistance taking place at that time, barely five years before the regime change in favor of a return to constitutional democracy. Indeed, Littin makes room to show the large public protests that had become a part of national life by 1985. (It is unclear if the brief images of the government's response to these protests in the form of water cannons turned on the protestors were something one of Littin's crews filmed or if they were news footage from another source.)

The first chapter of *Acta* ends with the camera once again focusing on Littin as he moves through the city. In the transition from the foggy lassitude of the opening scenes to the dynamic conclusion of a society ready for a change, Littin now moves through densely populated spaces: the streets, a public market, one of the heavily traveled bridges over the Mapocho River that runs through central Santiago. It is fall, and the waters are still flowing rapidly, reinforcing Littin's interior monologue about an awakening Chilean society. Immediately prior to these closing images of Littin, the soundtrack captures voices singing about "las buenas nuevas... a mi pueblo que comienza a despertar" (the good news... for my people about their awakening).

Littin's last set of interviews before this strongly voiced envoi focuses exclusively on women. Taking up the much vaunted topic of women's public assertiveness in Chile, *Acta* sees in women's ad hoc societies an alternative to stagnated dictatorial structures. Women have organized themselves into groups to complement, supplement, and overcome the practices of the dictatorship. Women's initiatives involve human rights watches, food distribution centers (which continue a practice instituted, as Guzmán shows in *Batalla*, by food shortages provoked by opposition tactics to Allende back before the coup), and dining rooms (the so-called *ollas populares*, people's kettles) to feed those who cannot adequately feed themselves. This particular focus on women, the source and staple of the Chilean family, as the narrator states in words that are more often articulated by the Catholic right, rounds off the accumulative process that is the backbone of the first chapter of *Acta* and what comes off as a mosaic of collective resistance that intersects the personal tragedies of the disappeared. This interplay between lament and resistant promise, between oppressed individuals and the awakening collective may be viewed as promoting a particular ideological agenda with regard to Chile. One could hardly have expected it to be otherwise, given Littín's history and the circumstance of the filming of *Acta*. But aside from that, the interplay of these diverse elements and the fluidity of movement from one segment to another keeps *Acta* from being a collection of just so many talking heads.

Littín himself ties together not only the first chapter, which is the most important segment of *Acta* because of the way in which it provides a survey of the sociopolitical circumstances of Chile in 1985, but the four parts as a whole. Not only is his the principal narrative voice, but throughout, we see him at strategic moments as the various expository segments unfold, reminding us that he is the witness in the first instance of the Chile he is surveying and that it is his camera that is transmitting his particular vision. In this way, *Acta* is not an objective newsreel, but a very personal interpretation, as principled as that interpretation may be in terms of the accumulated weight of evidence it marshals as part of its testimony. It is important to recall that the word *acta*, while it refers to an official or a quasi-official document, derives from the Latin verb *agere*, whose basic meaning for this context is "to set in motion," in the sense of conducting the business of state. Littín's choice of term to describe his documentary, first of all, plays off the fact that it is a supplement to the documents of state that cannot exist because of repression and censorship. Because the de facto military government is illegitimate, it is necessary for the ad hoc document of the filmmaker to undertake to testify in a clandestine and resistant fashion that tyranny cannot allow. In this sense, Littín's film prefigures the acts of a truth commission that has not yet, unlike Argentina's Comisión Nacional sobre la Desaparición de Personas (CONADEP, see published document, *Nunca más [1984]*), come into being.

But there is another resonance for the word *acta* in Littin's film, and that is in juxtaposition to the official founding document of the Chilean people, the *Acta de independencia de Chile* (1818). One of the witnesses of Allende's last hours in the Moneda describes how she receives from Allende for safekeeping the presidential copy of the *Acta de independencia*, which she carries with her as she leaves the Moneda during the final bombardment. She goes on to relate how the document is brutally taken from her by a military man who detains her as she exits the building; without consulting the document, he rips it up, presumably assuming that it is some final statement for posterity of Allende or some important document she has chosen, or been chosen, to safeguard. Whatever the degree of accuracy of this testimony might be, Littin would be offering it, at a strategic moment in his narrative of the death of Allende and the overthrow of his constitutional presidency, as an inevitably symbolic gesture of the destruction by the military of Chilean historical integrity as constituted by the *Acta de independencia*. In turn, in the wake of the destruction of that *Acta*, Littin's *Acta*, making as it does its own contribution to the restoration of constitutional democracy in Chile,[13] becomes an effective supplement to the original historical document.

Notes

1. The other is the invisible narrator as the so-called voice of God.
2. For example, street scenes in a frequent movie set like New York City take place in an area that has been demarcated by signs announcing that filming is taking place and that an individual's entrance into that space is an implied consent to being filmed, and subsequently, to appear in passing in the final product.
3. His name appears also as Littín, as in García Márquez's book; however, Littin seems to be the more common form. See the early French interview with Littin on his work (Chanan 53–65).
4. See the Skármeta anthology of writing about the coup and both internal and external exile.
5. *Acta* was, however, produced by TV Española.
6. This segment of Littin's documentary is constructed around how the city of Antofagasta, where Chileans from all over the country went to work in, first, the saltpeter (nitrate) fields, and then, the copper mines in the nineteenth century, is a symbol of the Chilean proletariat, the city where Luis Emilio Recabarren founded the Chilean Communist

Party in 1922 (earlier dates are given, but they are usually taken to refer to precursors of the Communist Party, strictly speaking). Littin deals with this history in his narrative film *Actas de Marusia* (1985). Yet Antofagasta is also the symbol of the exploitation of Chile and the Chilean worker by foreign interests that control the mineral extraction of the area. It is this fundamental contradiction—quintessential Chile versus foreign exploitation—that structures this segment of *Acta*. The story of this exploitation included the violent death of over 7,000 workers during the first quarter of the twentieth century. The Chilean Army has a long and bloody history as agents of this violence, and Littin's narrator underscores the continued presence of the military in the Chilean north, the manner in which it is a vast *cuartel* (barracks), and how it is the most visible face of a country under fascist rule. It is in this way that this chapter of *Acta* forms an integral part of the story of Chile under dictatorship that is central to the first chapter.

7. On the cinema of Chilean exile, see Schumann (200–05). Littin is mentioned, but not *Acta*.
8. The group is the Frente Patriótico Manolo Rodríguez, and the motif of clandestinity in *Acta* is of special importance here. Access to the group involved considerable negotiation and travel to an unknown (or, at least, unannounced) destination, and the spokespersons do not allow themselves to be filmed directly. This is the only moment in the four chapters of *Acta* that we actually see one of Littin's camera crew. Although we see them setting up their equipment, ironically, it is only to film the spokespersons for the FPMR in dark shadows: that is, the recorded filming is of a nonfilming, which testifies to the deep clandestinity of this armed resistance group.
9. This is irrespective of what the actual scientific demographic of the moment might have been, although it is important that 1985 corresponds with the time in which the tide of support is beginning to turn against Pinochet and will result in the vote that is the beginning of the regime change that will come in 1990.
10. Mouesca, in her excellent overview of Littin's film work, states categorically: "Littin no es documentalista, de modo que lo mejor de [*Acta*] son aquellas secuencias que apoyan una narración en que la intención subjetiva—subrayar la emoción que vive un exiliado en el encuentro con lo propio después de muy largos años de ausencia— obtener un verdadero e intenso lirismo" (105) (Littin is not a documentalist, and the best part of [*Acta*] involves those sequences that support a narration in which the subjective intention—the underscoring of the feelings experienced by an exile in the encounter with his own roots after long years of absence—is successful in achieving a true and intense lyricism). By contrast, there is a certain degree of documentariness in many of Littin's films, such as his inaugural narrative film, *El chacal de Nahueltoro* (1969), on an infamous murderer who,

through a process of self-redemption, becomes a folk hero before he is executed by the state. *Alsino y el cóndor* has the Nicaraguan civil war in the 1970s as a prominent backdrop. As Greenfield says with regard to *Chacal*, "Littin's style is documentary and journalistic" (122). Chávez discusses *Alsino* as an eminently political film.

11. One sequence includes images of the famous Valparaíso outdoor elevators that climb the steep hills around the port. The comment is made that the English built 40 of them (the first began operation in 1883), but only 15 are in operation today.
12. In one case, at least, a woman reads from a text held in front of her.
13. One of the final images of the documentary is a sign carried high in a demonstration that reads "Chile quiere democracia" (Chile wants democracy).

Works Cited

Acta general de Chile. Dir. Miguel Littin. Chile/Cuba. Dur. 240 min. RTVE, 1986. Film.

Actas de Marusia. Dir. Miguel Littin. Mexico. Dur. 110 min. CONACINE, 1976. Film.

Alsino y el cóndor. Dir. Miguel Littin. Nicaragua/Cuba/Mexico/Costa Rica. Dur. 89 min. Nicaraguan Film Institute, Cuban Institute of Cinematographic Art and Industry, Latin American Production of Mexico, Costa Rican Cinematographic Co-Operative, 1982. Film.

El chacal de Nahueltoro. Dir. Miguel Littin. Chile/Mexico. Dur. 95 min. Centro de Cine Experimental de Universidad de Chile, 1969. Film.

Chanan, Michael, ed. *Chilean Cinema*. London: British Film Institute, 1976. Print.

Chávez, Daniel. "*Alsino y el cóndor*, hacia una crítica del espectador latinoamericano y nicaragüense." *Chasqui: revista de literatura latinoamericana* 37.2 (2008): 27–47. Print.

García Márquez, Gabriel. *La aventura de Miguel Littín clandestino en Chile*. Buenos Aires: Editorial Sudamericana, 1986. Print. Published in English as *Clandestine in Chile: The Adventures of Miguel Littín*. Trans. Aza Zatz. New York: Henry Holt, 1987. Print.

Greenfield, Conetta Carestia. "The New South American Cinema: From Neo-Realism to Expressive Realism." *Latin American Literary Review* 1.2 (1973): 111–23. Print.

La hora de los hornos: Notas y testimonios sobre el neocolonialismo, la violencia y la liberación. Dir. Octavio Getino and Fernando E. Solanas. Argentina. Dur. 260 min. Grupo Cine Liberación, 1973. Film.

Mouesca, Jacqueline. *Plano secuencia de la memoria de Chile; veinticinco años de cine chileno (1960–1985)*. Madrid: Ediciones del Litoral, 1988. Print.

Nunca Más: Informe de la Comisión Nacional sobre la Desaparición de Personas. Buenos Aires: Editorial Universitaria de Buenos Aires, 1984. Print.

Schumann, Walter, and Peter B. Schumann. *Historia del cine latinoamericano*. Trans. Oscar Zambrano. Buenos Aires: Editorial Legasa, 1987. Print. Trans. of *Handbuch des lateinamerikanischen films*. Frankfurt: Vervuert, 1982.

Skármeta, Antonio, ed. and prologue. *Joven narrativa chilena después del golpe*. Clear Creek: American Hispanist, 1976. Print.

Chapter 4

Guerrilla Narratives through the Kaleidoscope of Time: Rereading Resistance in Nicaragua

Julia M. Medina

In Latin America, guerrilla warfare, used for gaining political and representational agency, declined as a mode of resistance and struggle at the end of the cold war. The peace treaties of El Salvador in 1992 and Guatemala in 1996 put an end to the era of *el guerrillero* (the guerrilla fighter). Since then, traces of this Janus-like figure have shaped a lingering nostalgia for a kind of revolutionary mysticism, as well as an ideological disenchantment associated with post–cold war politics that gave rise to neoliberal hegemony across the continent.[1]

In the context of the "posts" (postrevolutionary, post–cold war, post–armed resistance, postmodern, postnational, and postmemory), what is the role of testimonial guerrilla narratives in the current cultural landscape? Are they a moot historical artifact? How do guerrilla narratives figure into the political and cultural imaginary? Is there an ethical content inscribed in the narrative form of guerrilla accounts? Is that ethical and ideological content grounded in the time of its production? How do such narratives read after their referential urgency has passed?[2] How and can they be written from the distance of time?

To begin addressing these questions, this essay will retrospectively consider the case of Omar Cabezas' *La montaña es algo más que una inmensa estepa verde* (1982) *(Fire from the Mountain: The Making of a Sandinista)*. This text, published during the height of revolutionary fervor in Nicaragua, gained much international circulation through many editions and translations during the 1980s. Written and published 20 years after the armed struggle, Juan Sobalvarro's *Perra vida: memorias de un recluta del servicio militar* (2005) (Life's a bitch: memoirs of a military service conscript)[3] recounts his experience as a draftee during the civil war that followed the revolution, and unlike Cabezas' account, chronicles his unwilling participation in the anti-imperialist struggle of the Sandinista Revolution. The point of reading these texts and their respective titles side by side, or contrapuntally, is not to negate or privilege a specific version of that history, but rather to discuss the trajectory of both the role of testimonial narratives and the role of its readers through the lens of the guerrilla experience.[4] These narratives provide valuable registers of historical and critical contexts in which they were produced and discussed. Whereas Sobalvarro faces the challenge of being a conscript, Cabezas reaffirms the Civilization versus Barbarism paradigm in the form of the lettered city versus the rural world, or *ciudad/campo* (city/country). Because armed struggle is understood to have been one of the preconditions for the development—or perhaps for the reception, as Sklodowska has suggested ("Spanish American")—of testimonial narrative, it is a pertinent point of entry.[5]

By limiting the scope of this analysis to accounts of guerrilla warfare in Nicaragua, I seek to address the testimonial narrative in light of the postrevolutionary context as analogous to "post-testimonio" inquietudes. Guerrilla narratives allow us to delve into the fissures of critical approaches that have dominated the discussion of testimonial narratives, given that written testaments of armed participation appealed to an imaginary of solidarity, or as Moreiras has eloquently argued, to a "poetics of solidarity" (203). The way testimonios have been read has kept them contained to their historical milieu, and therefore, many have deemed them as (im) passé. However, despite the fact that the guerrilla narratives discussed here were written within different political contexts, they articulate concrete and localized objectives.

As testimonios, these texts were not written to fulfill a desire for third-world literature or to act as a gateway to the transnational public sphere of identity politics (Gugelberger 1–2). Texts such as these have been written to serve a specific, localized historical purpose. Critical reception of these narratives has overlooked the fact that they are also read in the context in which they are produced. It is not only a matter of North American academics co-opting the subjectivity/experience of the narrator. It is a question, rather, of erasing the existence of a local constituency capable of reading, understanding, and appreciating these works, that is, overlooking the reception of those who are the implied referents and whose lives have been directly affected by the (hi)story they convey. The time of testimonio is not over, but the way in which testimonio texts are read remains to be redefined as a transnational experience. As such, guerrilla narratives serve as tools that present/produce a kaleidoscopic effect of history that distorts, mirrors, and transforms our understanding of the context they depict.

During the height of discussions surrounding the genre, John Beverley defined testimonio as "a new form of narrative literature in which we can at the same time witness and be a part of the emerging culture of an international proletarian/popular-democratic subject in its period of ascendancy" (43).[6] If the narrative form is a witnessing portal of a certain subject in a specific period, then how does it read in hindsight? How does the form retain its specificity, and therefore, what can it tell us once ascendancy has been obtained? Is testimonial narrative constrained to the time and the conditions that define its enunciation? Sklodowska's initial skepticism best anticipated the problem. She questioned, for example, if testimony presented a subaltern voice or a mediated narrative, that is, whether a textual construct is staged for the reader *(Testimonio)*.

As many critics have noted, Leonel Delgado Aburto among them, Cabezas is not a subaltern subject nor was he one at the time of his writing ("Proceso cultural").[7] He is better categorized under the tradition of Bernal Díaz del Castillo and other such conqueror-warriors, with the twist of orality and the national vernacular added to the mix, as Coronel Urtecho might have seen him.[8] Given that he did not write his account during his time as a militant for the revolution but rather three years later as a statesman for the Sandinista government, I see him more as a continuation of nineteenth-century writers turned statesmen and vice versa.[9]

On the other hand, Juan Sobalvarro's text was written decades after his participation in the war and was published locally by a small press in Nicaragua. As a journalist and a poet, Sobalvarro was a cultural figure within the Central American context at that time. Both of these guerrilla narratives problematize the already slippery category of testimonio due to their positionality within subaltern subjectivity, as well as their historical moment.

Irrespective of their place in the testimonial trajectory, these narratives provide an ideal space for examining ideological content as they negotiate the commodification of the historical processes that esteem testimonio as a genre. In framing these readings, I am reminded of one of Walter Benjamin's theses on the philosophy of history: "History is the subject of a structure whose site is not homogeneous, empty time, but time filled by the presence of the now" (261). Given that the historical content of these nonfiction texts is understood from an autobiographical experience, how do we read guerrilla narratives synchronically?

The Sandinista Revolution provides a fascinating case study of the *guerrillero,* for, unlike El Salvador, the Funes presidency represents the rise to power of the FMLN (Farabundo Martí National Liberation Front) within the context of the democratic process subsequent to the armed struggle.[10] The rise, fall, and resurgence of the FSLN (Sandinista National Liberation Front) presents a case in which guerrilla warfare not only succeeded in 1979 with the triumph of the Sandinista Revolution, but also then had to defend that project in a sustained armed struggle lasting almost a decade in light of the counterinsurgency movement orchestrated and financed by the United States.[11] Fifteen years after its electoral defeat in 1990, the FSLN regained political control through the democratic process in 2006, thanks in large part to the failures of neoliberal economic and social policies. The texts discussed here speak to the guerrilla experience at different stages in these struggles.

A 23-year gap separates the publications of Cabezas' testimonio and Sobalvarro's memoir. Cabezas' text, published in 1982, recounts the initial stages of resistance formation in the late 1960s, as well as the armed struggle that triumphed in 1979. His text undertakes what Delgado Aburto calls "a romantic foundational-nationalism" (*Márgenes* 116).[12] The importance of disseminating, establishing, and forging a romantic foundational-nationalism is linked to the pressure that U.S. aggression imposed on civil society, much of which took the form of an economic and military assault. The date of Cabezas' publication marks the onset of the counterinsurgency war launched in part by the United States with the Contras.[13] At this crucial time for the consolidation of the Sandinista political project, his narrative links the Nicaraguan Revolution to the Cuban model, following Ché Guevara's revolutionary subjectivity of the *guerrillero* and of the New Man.[14] By linking both revolutionary movements, Cabezas' account mythologizes the struggle while emphasizing its historical inevitability. As Mantero correctly reminds us, Cabezas' text responds to a systematic national project that sought to legitimize the Sandinista Revolution in light of its geopolitical context (48). The production of his text further emphasizes the Cuba-Nicaragua connection, since it was first published in Havana as winner of the 1982 Casa de las Américas prize.

In terms of production, it is important to comment on the performative male/macho posturing within the text. In an interview with Edward Waters Hood, Cabezas explained: "Entonces pasa que, grabábamos, hacíamos el amor, a veces apagábamos la grabadora, a veces no apagábamos la grabadora, seguíamos haciendo el amor, y así" (Cabezas, "Testimonio" 114). [Then we recorded, made love, sometimes we turned off the recorder, sometimes we didn't turn off the recorder, we continued making love and so on.] He continued, "Y entonces, para mí, grabar se convirtió en una forma de comunicar, y hacer el amor es comunicar, y hablar es comunicar" (115). [And so for me, recording became a way to communicate, and making love is a way to communicate, and talking is communicating.] Recording a testimonio is a common procedure, particularly when an intermediary transcribes the interview as recorded from a "non-lettered" subject. The context of sexual intercourse in the telling of the story indicates a desire to make love to the experience/historical juncture being conveyed, while at the same time, it inadvertently trivializes the conditions under which the transcription took place. And, because Cabezas' text is a narrative that accounts for *guerrillero* subjectivity, the sexually charged, meta-testimonial characterization of its production emphasizes the performative character of hypermasculinity.

In contrast, Sobalvarro's memoir was published in Nicaragua in 2005, 15 years after the Sandinistas' electoral defeat and one year before Daniel Ortega won the presidential elections in his fourth attempt for the presidency since 1990. Although Sobalvarro had wanted to write about his experience for years, he chose to do so at that time in order to "contribuir a la memoria histórica que se puede transmitir a las nuevas generaciones" ("Memorias"), that is, contribute to the historical memory that can be handed down to new generations. With the imminent triumph of Daniel Ortega's presidency a year later, the timing of this publication can be understood as a cautionary tale to a generation of people of voting age without direct memory of the 1980s. Furthermore, Sobalvarro's account does not narrate the struggle of defeating Somoza and establishing the revolution, but rather portrays his experience as a conscript in the civil war against the U.S. backed counterinsurgency. In terms of the production of the text, Sobalvarro explains in his epilogue:

Hace seis o siete años empecé a escribir este testimonio con mucha rabia, pensaba en un principio descargar en este relato toda mi frustración por los recuerdos de la guerra y la revolución. Sin embargo, el testimonio se fue dando casi como un juicio hacia mí mismo y creo que no podría ser de otra manera, porque no soy como ciertos tontos que ven héroes en la guerra o creen que la guerra por sí misma es heroica. Si alguna virtud proveyera la guerra, en todo caso esta no podría ser más que la de exhibir las peores canalladas de los seres humanos. (261) [Six or seven years ago, I began writing this testimony with a lot of anger, thinking that in this narrative I would discharge all of my frustrations over the memories of the war and the revolution. However, the testimony was almost turning into a judgment of myself and I think that it could not be otherwise because I am not like some fools who see heroes in war or believe that war in and of itself is heroic. The only virtue war may have is that it displays the most despicable traits of human beings.]

Consistent with the guerrilla context therein represented, Sobalvarro's meta-testimonial account eschews male posturing and romantic protagonism. Reading Cabezas' testimonio from hindsight, as well as Sobalvarro's memories, creates a complexly layered effect on the reception of various stages of guerrilla warfare and politics in Nicaragua.

This kaleidoscopic effect can be anticipated from the respective titles of the accounts. The Spanish title of Cabezas' narrative, *La montaña es algo más que una inmesa estepa verde* (literally translated as The mountain is something more than an immense green steppe), presents the geography of the struggle as something more than what it is, or as Saldaña-Portillo describes, "the guerrilla's theater of operation... a tabula rasa on which a new revolutionary subjectivity and a new revolutionary culture will be inscribed" (73–74). Rodríguez describes the mountain as "the symbiosis of the feminine-masculine," and continues by noting that "over the feminine body of the mountain men engender the fatherland" (46). Delgado Aburto categorizes the mountain—along with other peripheral spaces—as a margin to be probed by the cultural hero (*Márgenes* 109). The elliptic translation of the Spanish title to *Fire from the Mountain: The Making of a Sandinista* resonates with Cabezas' personal transformation from *guerrillero* to politician and with the political transformations of Nicaragua itself. This mistranslation, or marketing ploy, speaks to the fetishization of the historical processes that esteem testimonio (and the guerrilla account) as a genre, while further exemplifying the commercialization and romantic circulation of such narratives within the North American academy. In reference to testimonial narrative in Central America, Arturo Arias explains: "[u]ndoubtedly, Central American literary discourse has been disempowered politically while, paradoxically, being empowered as a commodity by globalizing trends" (25).

On the other hand, Sobalvarro's title, *Perra vida: memorias de un recluta del servicio militar* (roughly translated as Life's a bitch: memoirs of a military service conscript), emphasizes the involuntary nature of his participation in the civil war with the word "conscript" and the exclamatory phrase, "life's a bitch," a morning slogan that was repeated every day by one of the narrator's co-combatants. In addition, the noun *perra* (bitch) alludes to the fact that the young conscripts were known as "los cachorros de Sandino" (Sandino's pups)—hence, offspring of history, and in turn, of the conscript life. In the titles of these narratives, then, mysticism and resentment become mirrors that distort, yet capture, the historical representation of guerrilla warfare.

The first line of each account also conveys the distorted conditions of the authors' enlistments. Cabezas recalls: "Recuerdo que ingresé al Frente después de unas vacaciones, después que me bachilleré" (11). [I remember that I joined el Frente after vacation, upon completing high school.][15] The petit bourgeois tone of this phrase suggests that joining the struggle was an alternative to vocational training. In this lies the strategy of the testimonio, since the narrator does not claim to be committed to the cause, but rather enticed by the lore of a fraternal network. What Cabezas seeks to highlight with this beginning and throughout his narrative is the transformation of the petit bourgeois into a group with a revolutionary consciousness and thereby the creation of the New Man, a conversion that takes place upon living on the mountain. Yet, as Yúdice has stated: "Cabezas' 'new man' repeats patriarchal privilege in the guise of a Sandinista uniform" (17).

In the case of Sobalvarro, his story begins in 1983 when he was a junior in high school. At that time, the Sandinista government began collecting signatures to support a law of military service.[16] His enlistment a year later takes place at Sobalvarro's high school, where Sobalvarro and his classmates are called to duty during one of the weekly rallies, with no possibility of avoiding it; hence the title of the first chapter, "Voluntarios a güevo" (Volunteered by the balls).

Consistent with historical counterpoint framed by these accounts, each text represents a different stage of the struggle. For Cabezas, it was the organizational period at the end of the 1960s, as well as the insurrection in the late 1970s. For Sobalvarro, it was the fight for sovereignty in the 1980s. Guerrilla warfare is depicted in ways that correspond to their relationship to the struggle and to the struggle's relationship to history. Both men refer to the fear, hunger, and discomfort of being on the mountain. Yet, oddly, Cabezas' account maintains an elliptical void of actual fighting. He alludes to the omnipresent fighting but avoids direct description.

While Sobalvarro's story also avoids the details of the fighting, his narrative does not omit combat nor his own participation in it, including his own injuries acquired in battle. In retelling his experience with warfare, Sobalvarro admits to his own tactical mistakes as well as to his fears and/or his desire to kill a superior. There is no pretense of stoic heroism in his representation of the armed struggle. As such, one of the few intertextual references to Cabezas' account is precisely during battle, where Sobalvarro exclaims:

> Entonces recordé los testimonios de los guerrilleros y ahora me parecían novelitas amorosas comerciales, ellos describían sus cruzadas como campañas de hombres llenos de amor, como que destilaban amor ¿y a la hora de matar a dónde se iba el hijueputa amor? ¿y a la hora de las jerarquías, dónde paraba el compañerismo? (202) [Then I recalled the *guerrilleros*' testimonios and now they seemed like commercial love stories, they described their crusades like advertisements for men full of love, like they were oozing love? Where did fuckin' love go at the time of killing? And at the time of hierarchies, what happened to camaraderie, where did it end up?]

From the vantage point of time, the realities of the fighting come to the forefront of the narrative, whereas the details of ideological transformation are cast as romantic and unrealistic historical posturing.

The ideological content thus marks the form of the texts, as well as their historical content. Critics have already discussed the ideological discrepancies found in Cabezas' testimonio.[17] The most compelling case, made by Saldaña-Portillo (who does not directly reference Cabezas' text but revolutionary movements in general), states that these movements "subscribe to a developmentalist model of revolutionary subjectivity, consciousness, and agency" (6). In other words, "the discourse of development captures the imagination of these revolutionary movements, often to the detriment of the constituents the movement sought to liberate though their anti-imperialist struggle" (4–5). In so doing, these revolutionaries cast the subaltern, that is, the peasants, as isolated premodern communities that need to enter into modern rationality under the guidance, of course, of the *guerrilleros*. Like Ché Guevara and Mario Payeras, Omar Cabezas falls into this trap of revolutionary rhetoric.

Returning to Cabezas' reaffirmation of the Civilization versus Barbarism paradigm, as Saldaña-Portillo points out, the two great organizing tropes of imperial reason are civilization and development (23). Cabezas not only reinscribes this dominant narrative like so many other intellectuals, but also further perpetuates it. For example, he writes, "yo sabía que por tener mayor nivel intelectual podía darle vuelta y sacarle información al campesino sin que sintiera que le estaba sacando información" (*La montaña* 74). [I knew that because I had a higher intellectual level, I could go around the issue and get information from the peasant without him knowing.] Or, "porque los urbanos somos más complejos, somos más abstractos, más sofisticados, más complicados" (95). [Because us urbanites are far more complex, we are more abstract, more sophisticated, more complicated.] The paternalistic and deterministic attitudes that correspond to the developmentalist approach find their maximum expression in the following quote: "Cuando el campesino te llega a querer, cuando te llega a amar, es algo extraordinario, aman no solamente con la razón, sino también con la fuerza del instinto. Porque también son medio salvajes por el medio, entonces aman con la razón, aman con el instinto también" (120). [When the peasant gets to like you, when he gets to love you, it is something extraordinary; they not only love with reason but with the force of instinct. Since they are also half wild because of their environment, then they love with reason and also with instinct.] And so, the ideological content of Cabezas' testimonio reveals, perhaps, the shortcomings of the revolutionary project.

Sobalvarro's memoir depicts a different ideological tension. From the beginning, an emotive distance exists between the narration and the unfolding circumstances that the narrator experiences. He explicitly mentions this distance in temporal terms. In reference to the dynamics between recruits, he notes that "Ahora, con la distancia temporal que me separa de los hechos, se me hace incomprensible que me haya sentido intimidado por la agresividad de ellos" (Sobalvarro 20). [Now, with the temporal distance that separates me from the facts, it is incomprehensible for me to understand that I could have felt intimidated by their aggression.] This distance raises pertinent questions regarding not only the testimonial memoir as a genre, but also the ideological content latent in the story. At first, this detachment can simply be interpreted by the lapse of time between the events themselves and their time of enunciation. On a deeper level, the distance could also be understood as a narrative strategy made to reproduce the aloofness of an 18-year-old. This remoteness could be seen as an attempt to not fall into bourgeois sentimentalism.

However, as the narrative develops, the narrator expresses his frustration and disillusionment toward the civil war while trying to maintain his ideological commitment to the revolutionary project. By reproducing this distance, the author successfully conveys the difficulty of questioning political practices while maintaining his ideological commitment. For example, after extending his medical leave for a wound received in the arm, he describes his imprisonment for avoiding military service. After nine months of not reporting back to duty, the narrator is arrested along with other young men who were avoiding the war. While imprisoned in a makeshift structure, the boys begin to scream to get the attention of journalists who might be outside and be able to report their plight: "Y aunque yo era uno de los que gritaba no dejaba de preguntarme si lo que hacía era correcto, si no estaba traicionando mi compromiso con la revolución, que aunque siempre lo manejé de manera muy privada y sin retórica, era muy sincero" (92–93). [And even though I was also yelling, I kept asking myself whether what I was doing was right, whether I was not betraying my revolutionary commitment, which, even if I kept very private and without rhetoric, was very sincere.] This sentiment is due to the fact that he never felt like a victim of his circumstances as a conscript precisely because he believed in the revolutionary ideals, unlike the other boys yelling along with him (93). In complete opposition to Cabezas' enunciatory impulse that reinforces a developmentalist ideology performing a revolutionary transformation, for Sobalvarro, solidarity with the poor means "ideas que dejan de ser retórica si uno los integra a sus actos" (93), that is, ideas that cease to be rhetoric if one integrates them into their actions. In his testimonial practice rhetoric does not form a part of the revolutionary action. The tragedy of Sobalvarro's testimonio is integrating those ideals while participating in an armed military against his will.

In this framing of the narrative, the recounting of memories serves a cathartic function to convey and exorcize anger and frustration in the face of those historical circumstances turned personal, yet collective. Sobalvarro's ideological tension becomes a measuring device with which the narrator implicitly compares himself to figures such as Cabezas, and in turn, Ché, who championed the heroism of war. Ultimately, Sobalvarro's stance remains critical of war in general, no matter who wages it. In the epilogue, the author states, "Como la mayoría también creo que lo peor de aquella década fue la Guerra, una de sus peores partes fue el servicio militar, pero también lo fue la contra, porque la contrarrevolución también derivó en un servicio militar obligatorio para aquellos campesinos que por vivir en aquellos campos de batalla, no podían quedarse al margen" (Sobalvarro 261). [Like the majority, I also think that the worst of that decade was the military service, but likewise it was *la Contra* because the counterrevolution also ends up in mandatory military service, obliging peasants who lived in the battlefields to participate because they could not just stand by in the margins.] Guerrilla fighting does not always mean triumph and cannot be mythologized as such. Whereas Cabezas' earlier testimonio emphasizes the political transformational potential of fighting, Sobalvarro reminds us that the very means (guerrilla warfare) that can make political change happen can also unravel that change.

To conclude, Omar Cabezas' testimonio narrates the construction of the self as a *guerrillero*, while emphasizing the transcendental character of that epical transformation (Rodríguez 5). In hindsight, this endeavor can be understood as a means to solidify the Sandinista revolutionary project by linking it to the grand narrative of revolution established by the Cuban experience. This endeavor can also be understood to emphasize the egalitarian and hence legitimate character of the project. Sobalvarro constructs an historical memory—understood as a counter-hegemonic narrative—that recounts the loss of childhood and revolutionary idealism precisely by shaping (in a voluntary way or not) that self as a *guerrillero*. He narrates the ideological tension established by contradictory political practices such as military recruitment and revolutionary commitment. Sobalvarro believed in revolutionary principles, but was not willing to die for them. Has the time passed to read Sobalvarro's accounts? If so, then, why was it written? Is it no longer of interest because it does not recount an armed insurrection but rather a failed civil war? Can we conceive of a testimonial narrative as having a localized political/historical objective removed from what happens in the North American academy? If by definition a kaleidoscope is an observer/producer of beautiful forms, and guerrilla narratives create a kaleidoscopic effect upon history, then time, as seen through that narrative lens, allows us to see the ethical-dialectical character between failures and disillusionments. Moreover, this lens reveals a commitment, yet also portrays the lost hope left behind in the historical possibility that guerrilla narratives represent.

Notes

1. Although the EZLN (Zapatista Army of National Liberation) utilizes some of the visual codes related to the guerrillas, it is well known that it is not a guerrilla but rather a political movement, with its weapons signifying preemptive measures of self-defense.
2. Beverley notes that testimonio began as an ancillary component of armed liberation struggles, although "its canonization was tied even

more, perhaps, to the military, political and economic force of counterrevolution in the years after 1973" (Beverley 77). He further states: "But testimonio's moment, the originality and urgency—to use Lacan's phrase—the 'state of emergency' that drove our fascination and critical engagement with it, has undoubtedly passed, if only by the logic of the aesthetic familiarization" (77).

3. Sobalvarro's text has not been translated into English; all translations are my own unless otherwise noted.
4. For a discussion of guerrilla literature, see Juan Duchesne's "Las narraciones guerrilleras: configuración de un sujeto épico de nuevo tipo." Regarding the place of testimonio within the category of resistance literature, see Barbara Harlow's *Resistance Literature.*
5. Discussions regarding testimonial narratives can be traced through Barnet, "The Documentary Novel"; Beverley, *Testimonio: On the Politics of Truth;* Yúdice, "Testimonio and Postmodernism"; Sklodowska, "Spanish American Testimonial Novel: Some Afterthoughts"; Gugelberger, *The Real Thing: Testimonial Discourse and Latin America,* and many others.
6. In his seminal essay "The Margin at the Center: On *Testimonio,*" Beverley defines testimonio as a printed form "told in the first person by a narrator who is also the real protagonist or witness of the event he or she recounts, and whose unit of narration is 'life' or a significant life experience" (31). Beverley explains that such texts may include: "autobiography, autobiographical novel, oral history, memoir, confession, diary, interview, eyewitness report, life history, *novela-testimonio,* nonfiction novel or 'factographic' literature" (31).
7. In addition to the article referred to here, Delgado Aburto's book *Márgenes recorridos: Apuntes sobre procesos culturales y literatura nicaragüense del siglo XX* (Surveyed margins: notes about cultural processes and Nicaraguan literature of the 20th-century) includes an insightful chapter, "Proceso cultural y fronteras del testimonio nicaragüense" (The borders and the cultural process of the Nicaraguan testimonio), that traces the critical genealogy of testimonial narrative to provide an intricate reading of this form and of its reception in the Nicaraguan context.
8. Delgado Aburto points out that Urtecho's characterization of Cabezas corresponds to his insistence upon maintaining the divide between a literary canon and nonliterary production ("Proceso" 114).
9. The writers who participated in politics and/or the politicians who participated in writing were, for example, Andrés Bello and Domingo Faustino Sarmiento, both of whom characterized the nineteenth century in Latin America. Twenty years after participating in the struggle and writing his testimonio, Omar Cabezas would serve a five-year term (2004–2009) as Human Rights Commissioner in Nicaragua; this tenure was not free of controversy.

10. In March 2009, the presidential candidate for the FMLN, Mauricio Funes, won the elections after two decades of conservative rule in El Salvador. The political party emerged as a part of the peace treaty accords signed that same year. In 1980, the FMLN was established as an umbrella group of different guerrilla organizations and participated in the civil war until the peace accord was reached.
11. To contextualize the Nicaraguan civil war in terms of cold war politics, see David Dent: *The Legacy of the Monroe Doctrine: A Reference Guide to U. S. Involvement in Latin America and the Caribbean.* The second edition of Walter LaFeber's *Inevitable Revolutions: The United States in Central America* also provides a historical synopsis of the civil war.
12. Unlike Duchesne's claim that Cabezas' linguistic strategy provides a different voice for a new consciousness through the use of colloquialisms, my reading claims that the exaggerated use of the local vernacular emphasizes a performative gesture of nationalism.
13. Significantly, within the context of testimonial production in Latin America, the publication of Cabezas' text coincides with Rigoberta Menchú recounting her experience to Elisabeth Burgos-Debray in what would become the prototypical text and epicenter of testimonio discussion.
14. Ileana Rodríguez and María Josefina Saldaña-Portillo offer suggestive readings of guerrilla narratives/testimonios.
15. Although Cabezas' text has been translated into English (1985), I am using and translating text from the 4th edition published in Nicaragua (1987).
16. In Nicaragua, the minimum voting age is 16 years. A change was implemented in 1987 when the age of legal recruitment for military service was lowered from 18 to 16. The compulsory military service (SMP, or Servicio Militar Patriótico) (Patriotic Military Service) was established by the EPS (Ejército Popular Sandinista) (Sandinista Popular Army) in 1983 and lasted until 1990. Although the law mandated that 18–25 years was the age of conscription, boys as young as 14 are reported to have been recruited.
17. As if Cabezas had written for a U.S. audience and had contradicted himself about the ideological content of the text, the review by Steven Kinzer in the *New York Times* states: "Fire from the Mountain *does not deal much with ideology* or international relations, but it contains valuable lessons for Americans. Among other things, *it shows the strength of Sandinista ideology* and the risk that it will be reversed by pressure or the passage of time" (emphasis mine).

Works Cited

Arias, Arturo. *Taking their Word: Literature and the Signs of Central America.* Minneapolis: U of Minnesota P, 2007. Print.

Barnet, Miguel. "The Documentary Novel." *Cuban Studies/Estudios Cubanos* 11.1 (1981): 19–32. Print.

Beverley, John. *Testimonio: On the Politics of Truth.* Minneapolis: U of Minnesota P, 2004. Print.

Benjamin, Walter. "Theses on the Philosophy of History." *Illuminations: Essays and Reflections.* Ed. Hannah Arendt. New York: Schocken, 1969. 253–64. Print.

Cabezas, Omar. *La montaña es algo más que una inmensa estepa verde.* 4th ed. Managua: Nueva Nicaragua, 1987. Print.

——. "Testimonio de mis testimonios (sobre preguntas de Edward Waters Hood)." *Hispamérica* 64.65 (1993): 111–20. Print.

Coronel Urtecho, José. *Libro de conversaciones sobre libros.* Managua: Editorial Nueva Nicaragua, 1994. Print.

Delgado Aburto, Leonel. "Proceso cultural y fronteras del testimonio nicaragüense." *Istmo: Revista Virtual de Estudios Literarios y Culturales Centroamericanos* 2 (2001): n. pag. Denison U, June 26, 2001. Web. March 20, 2011.

——. *Márgenes recorridos: apuntes sobre procesos culturales y literatura nicaragüense del siglo XX.* Managua: Instituto de Historia de Nicaragua y Centroamérica, 2002. Print.

Dent, David. *The Legacy of the Monroe Doctrine: A Reference Guide to U. S. Involvement in Latin America and the Caribbean.* Westport: Greenwood, 1999. Print.

Duchesne-Winter, Juan R. "Las narraciones guerrilleras: configuraciones de un sujeto épico de Nuevo tipo." *Testimonio y literatura.* Ed. René Jara and Hernán Vidal. Minneapolis: Institute for the Study of Ideologies and Literature, 1986. 85–137. Print.

Gugelberger, Georg M. "Introduction: Institutionalization of Transgression: Testimonial Discourse and Beyond." *The Real Thing: Testimonial Discourse in Latin America.* Durham: Duke UP, 1996. 1–21. Print.

Kinzer, Steven. "Organizing the Revolution." Rev. of *Fire from the Mountain: The Making of a Sandinista*, by Omar Cabezas. *New York Times*, June 30, 1985. Web. March 5, 2011.

LaFeber, Walter. *Inevitable Revolutions: The United States in Central America.* 2nd ed. New York: Norton, 1993. Print.

Mantero, José María. "La mitificación de la Revolución Sandinista: El caso de Omar Cabezas y *La montaña es algo más que una inmensa estepa verde.*" *Revista de Estudios Hispánicos* 30.2 (2003): 47–57. Print.

"Memorias y relatos de una *Perra vida.*" *El Diario de Hoy.* Vida. Elsalvador.com, April 20, 2006. Web. Feb. 15, 2011.

Moreiras, Alberto. "The Aura of Testimonio." *The Real Thing: Testimonial Discourse and Latin America.* Ed. Georg Gugelberger. Durham: Duke UP, 1996. 192–224. Print.

Rodríguez, Ileana. *Women, Guerrillas and Love: Understanding War in Central America.* Minneapolis: U of Minnesota P, 1996. Print.

Saldaña-Portillo, María Josefina. *The Revolutionary Imagination in the Americas and the Age of Development.* Durham: Duke UP, 2003. Print.

Sklodowska, Elzbieta. "Spanish American Testimonial Novel: Some Afterthoughts." *The Real Thing: Testimonial Discourse and Latin America.* Ed. Georg Gugelberger. Durham: Duke UP, 1996. 84–100. Print.

——. *Testimonio hispanoamericano: historia, teoría, poética.* New York: Peter Lang, 1992.

Sobalvarro, Juan. *Perra vida: memorias de un recluta del servicio militar.* Managua: Lea Grupo Editorial, 2005. Print.

Yúdice, George. "Testimonio and Postmodernism." *Latin American Perspectives* 18.3 (1991): 15–31. Print.

CHAPTER 5

BEARING FALSE WITNESS?
THE POLITICS OF IDENTITY IN ELSA OSORIO'S
MY NAME IS LIGHT (A VEINTE AÑOS, LUZ)

Nancy J. Gates-Madsen

Are some stories too difficult to tell? Recent scholarship on testimonio has questioned everything from its truth-value to its potential to effect social change, while its central premise has remained unchallenged: testimonial narrative aims to bear witness to a silenced or unacknowledged story of trauma, to give voice to the voiceless. Yet what are the implications if the story of suffering is only partially told? If, as Lawrence Langer has suggested regarding literary representations of the Holocaust, we should be wary of narratives that "make us feel better," rather than "help us *see* better" (12), Elsa Osorio's novel *My Name Is Light* reveals the difficulty of bearing witness to the painful living legacy of the children of the disappeared in Argentina.[1]

My Name Is Light follows Luz, a young woman who discovers she was born in captivity during the 1976–83 dictatorship and given to a military family. Using narrative strategies pertaining to fairy tale, thriller, and *telenovela* (soap opera), the novel portrays Luz's search to understand her country's history and her true identity as a suspenseful and relatively uncomplicated process of discovery, thereby embodying the catchphrase of the Grandmothers of the Plaza de Mayo, "La identidad no se impone" (Identity cannot be imposed). Nevertheless, by romanticizing the experience of the youngest victims of the dictatorship, Osorio's text effectively silences the extraordinarily complex issues surrounding the politics of identity. While on the one hand the narrative aligns with the testimonial impulse to tell the story of children born in captivity and denounce the military's actions, on the other hand it reduces the victims' plight to a simple tale of discovery, thereby undermining testimonio's imperative to tell the full story.

Fiction and Testimonio

It may seem surprising to consider the fictional tale *My Name Is Light* as a testimonial narrative. Although there is disagreement regarding the exact definition of testimonio, many leading theorists including John Beverley, René Jara, Marc Zimmerman, and Elzbieta Sklodowska, to name a few, define the genre as a first-person, mediated text, in which a member of a subaltern group shares a story with an interlocutor in order to provide testimony of an event or significant life experience that might otherwise be silenced or forgotten. Whether they emphasize the importance of testimonio's truth-value (Beverley), its urgency (Jara), its claim to witness (Beverley and Zimmerman), or its collaborative nature (Sklodowska), these theorists do not consider fiction to be part of the testimonial genre. After all, testimonio, like autobiography, invokes a "pact of truth" so the reader will assume the events are true, while fiction requires a "suspension of disbelief" so the reader will unquestionably accept unbelievable events in the narration.[2]

Yet the division between testimony and fiction is rarely straightforward, especially in contexts of trauma. Jacques Derrida argues in *Demeure: Fiction and Testimony* that testimony cannot help but be fictional, because the boundaries between the two are fluid and ever-changing. As he states, "if the testimonial is by law irreducible to the fictional, there is no testimony that does not structurally imply in itself the possibility of fiction, simulacra, dissimulation, lie, and perjury—that is to say, the possibility of literature, of the innocent or perverse literature that innocently plays at perverting all of these distinctions" (29). In other words, because testimony depends upon faith that the eyewitness is telling the truth—there is no other way of empirically verifying its validity—it must always remain "haunted" by the possibility of fiction (30). For Derrida, there is no such thing as a pure, nonfictional testimonial account of an event, for testimony always is implicated by fiction.

Regarding trauma narrative in particular, Shoshana Felman and Dori Laub have emphasized the difficulty of fully articulating horrific events, for such moments simultaneously demand and resist witnessing. In *Testimony: Crises of Witnessing in Literature, Psychoanalysis and History*, they claim that often literary or artistic witnessing becomes a necessary element of the trauma narrative. Cathy Caruth similarly argues that traumatic events must be "spoken in a language that is always somehow literary: a language that defies, even as it claims, our understanding" (5). Trauma defies expression, therefore its articulation by necessity incorporates fictional modes of telling.

Given the imprecise distinction between fiction and testimony, especially in the context of historical trauma, Kimberly Nance proposes a broader definition of testimonio based primarily on the goal of such writing, rather than the mode. In *Can Literature Promote Justice? Trauma Narrative and Social Action in Latin American Testimonio*, Nance defines testimonio as "the body of works in which speaking subjects who present themselves as somehow 'ordinary' represent a personal experience of injustice, whether directly to the reader or through the offices of a collaborating writer, with the goal of inducing readers to participate in a project of social justice" (7). Although Nance's definition indicates the nonfiction quality of testimonio, the emphasis on the texts' purpose (a representation of trauma that aims to promote action) rather than mode of expression (a first-person, mediated narrative) allows for a much broader inclusion of works under the umbrella of testimonial representation.

A definition based on purpose avoids the issue of truth value that has plagued much of testimonial theory. For despite the differences of opinion regarding its definition, the central purpose of testimonial narrative remains constant: testimonio speaks truth to power; it seeks to break a repressive silence regarding a traumatic event. Furthermore, putting Nance's definition in conjunction with Derrida's theory implies that texts do not have to be first-person eyewitness accounts in order to fall into the realm of testimony—*any* fictional tale that engages the legacies of real victims of trauma should be considered part of a testimonial project. While Derrida, Felman and Laub, and Caruth approach the blurry boundary between fiction and testimony from the side of testimony, it can be equally useful to approach the boundary from the fictional side when examining works such as *My Name Is Light*. In short, just as testimony is always "haunted" by fiction, fictional representations of historical trauma are, in turn, always "haunted" by testimony. By treating the sensitive subject of babies born in captivity and aiming to not only shed light on but also condemn the widespread practice of appropriation of children by the military during the Argentine dictatorship, *My Name Is Light* situates itself in the realm of testimonio.

The Ethics of Witnessing

The novel's engagement with the reality of state terrorism in Argentina implicates the text in a larger ethical dilemma regarding fictional representations based on historical events. Elizabeth Swanson Goldberg outlines the problem in *Beyond Terror: Gender, Narrative, Human Rights*: "How not to do further violence to these humans, their loved ones, or their descendants by spectacularizing, eroticizing, or otherwise *getting wrong* the representation of pain inflicted by the grave violation of human rights" (14). Through an analysis of several contemporary literary and cinematic representations of recent human rights abuses in places ranging from Latin America to Iraq, Goldberg outlines a possible ethics for fictional witnessing of atrocity that involves avoiding facile or generic narrative codes. By eschewing simplistic treatments of complex issues, one begins to approach an ethical representation of historical horror.

Such an ethics of representation proves especially appropriate in the case of *My Name Is Light*, given the difficult subject matter. Any text that engages the complex legacy of the children of the disappeared must be sensitive to the lived experience of the youngest victims of the dictatorship. The novel portrays Luz as a determined woman who searches for her true identity despite numerous obstacles, thereby serving as an heroic example to others who may doubt their origins. By interspersing references to known clandestine detention centers, the systematic practice of torture and disappearance, and the legal aftermath of the dictatorship, *My Name Is Light* exposes the crimes of the military and serves as a fictional witness to past atrocity. Nevertheless, by choosing to portray a relatively straightforward recovery of a missing child, the narrative risks simplifying the complexities of the politics of identity and may also be viewed as a further violation to the legacy of appropriated children.

Fictional Witnessing Part I: How the Novel Calls Attention to Past Crimes

At the time of its publication in 1998, *My Name Is Light* called attention to a lesser known practice of the dictatorship.[3] Although the Grandmothers of the Plaza de Mayo had been searching for their missing grandchildren since 1977, the military's "pact of silence" regarding the systematic practice of baby-stealing had proved remarkably effective. Yet the children of the disappeared were coming of age. In 1995, H.I.J.O.S. (Sons and Daughters for Identity and Justice against Forgetting and Silence) was founded, comprised of young people whose parents were victims of the dictatorship and others dedicated to the cause of bringing perpetrators to justice and continuing the struggle for human rights.[4] The Grandmothers also launched several informational campaigns in 1997 to draw young people who might have doubts as to their identity to the organization. Osorio's novel similarly served to break the silence surrounding a brutal aspect of the dictatorship that had yet to gain the same level of national and international attention as the plight of the *desaparecidos*.

Divided into five sections, *My Name Is Light* moves between time periods and geographical spaces in order to assemble the scattered pieces of Luz's complicated life story. The prologue takes place in Spain in 1998 and relates a conversation between Luz and Carlos Squirru, the man she suspects is her biological father. The remainder of the text relates Luz's journey from an appropriated child unaware of her origins to a politically active mother in search of her true parents, interspersing portions of Luz and Carlos' conversation into the narrative of other characters involved in Luz's life. These include Miriam, the former prostitute who spent time with her biological mother Liliana in the days after Luz's birth, Eduardo, the man who raised her as a daughter and was murdered for investigating her origins, and Dolores, a childhood friend of Eduardo who educates him as to the horrors of the dictatorship.

Nance's observations regarding the rhetoric of testimonial narrative can help illuminate how Osorio's novel sheds light on a dark episode in Argentina's history. According to Nance, authors of testimonio employ Aristotle's three categories of rhetorical strategies to tell the tale of trauma: forensic, epideictic and deliberative. Forensic speech describes past events as just or unjust, epideictic speech categorizes present actions as either noble or shameful, while deliberative strategies employ a rhetoric of persuasion and dissuasion to compel a listener to determine whether he or she should take action (23–31). Nance's analysis reveals that many testimonial narratives (and critics of the genre) privilege the forensic and epideictic categories. Indeed, Osorio's text aligns with these two strands of testimonio, for it seeks to condemn the past actions of the military as well as pass moral judgment on the present actions of the characters as they define their relationship vis-à-vis the past.[5]

One strategy Osorio employs to call attention to past injustice is her use of representative characters to condemn the military's behavior and uphold that of the *desaparecidos*. Sergeant Pitiotti, a.k.a. "el Bestia" (the Beast), stands out for his unwavering dedication to his job as a torturer in one of the camps.⁶ He lives up to his name in many respects: prone to violent outbursts in his domestic life, he tortures with efficiency and discretion, and subsequently benefits from the favors of his superior officer, Lieutenant Colonel Dufau. Dufau, the father of Luz's "adoptive" mother, "was the type who believed that the more subversives they liquidated, the better," for "the only good subversive was a dead one" (230). While *el Bestia* and Dufau represent the military and its atrocities, Liliana (and her baby) embody the human face of suffering and serve to demonstrate the worthiness of the cause of the *desaparecidos*. Through Miriam's eyes, the reader sees Liliana as a victim of the dictatorship's brutality. Liliana explains to Miriam that she and other militants simply "wanted a just society" (69), and her dying words to Miriam—"Save her, and tell her about... [her parents]" (95)—represent a call to remember what was done to her and her child.⁷

The novel also seeks to demonstrate the profound injustice of the military's practice of kidnapping babies by appealing to the reader's emotions, often through the juxtaposition of the violence of the time period with the innocence of childhood. In a key scene of awakening for Miriam, Liliana recounts the horrors of the camp, while Miriam holds the baby in her arms, singing her a soothing lullaby. The words of the lullaby are interspersed within Liliana's narrative, as Miriam attempts to shield the baby from the violence and lighten Liliana's burden. As she states, "I'm trying to hide behind the nursery rhyme, [...] I want [Liliana] to keep spewing up all that stuff I'd no idea about, [...] even if it turns my stomach, and makes me sick, and splashes all over me, and covers me in horrible stinking stuff, I just want Liliana to feel better" (69). The juxtaposition of the innocent lyrics of the lullaby ("the littlest one brought a bouquet of flowers, ahití ahitá, rataplán") (68)⁸ with "those blood-curdling words" (69) underscores both the extent of the violence and the innocence of the victims.

Nance explains that often the forensic and epideictic strategies preclude any type of deliberative action, for they ultimately distance the reader from the text. In her words, "such modes do not actually call upon their readers to do anything beyond categorizing an act as just or unjust, or assigning praise or blame" (30). Although this is the case for the most part in *My Name Is Light*, Osorio does employ narrative strategies that seek to engage the reader directly in the tale, to bring him or her closer rather than create distance. Most strikingly, at key moments in the text, the narrative employs the second person rather than first or third person narration. Although the use of *tú* (you) ostensibly demonstrates Eduardo's internal conflict, in effect these select moments address the reader directly, thereby implicating him or her in the crimes of the past.

It is no accident that the narrative begins to employ the second person singular when Eduardo—the man who raised Luz and loved her as a daughter—begins to realize the extent of the military's violence. These moments of second person narration often take the form of pointed questions, and in this way they situate the reader in relationship with the violence. For example, after hearing Dolores' tale of her brother and sister-in-law's disappearance, Eduardo reflects that Dolores has "good reason" to hate the military: "Wouldn't you, if Javier and Laura [Eduardo's brother and sister-in-law] had disappeared?" (155). Although the question is ostensibly addressed to Eduardo, it forces the reader to consider how he or she might feel if a loved one was taken.

Although the use of the second person brings the reader closer to the text, ultimately these pointed questions or statements regarding Eduardo's inability to "see" the truth respond to the epideictic strategy of categorizing present actions as either shameful or noble. After listening to Dolores's tale, Eduardo laments "What country, what world have you been living in while all this was going on, all these things Dolores is telling you?" (159). As Diana Taylor explains in *Disappearing Acts: Spectacles of Gender and Nationalism in Argentina's "Dirty War,"* the Argentine military's combination of erasure and intimidation meant that the general public suffered from "percepticide" (10), an inability or refusal to see what was happening in front of their eyes. *My Name Is Light* emphasizes the duality between blindness and seeing in order to highlight the gradual awakening of the characters, starting with the main character, Luz, whose very name implies illumination. As she states, "I knew I had to shed light into all the dark corners of this story, to find out the truth" (8). Similarly, Eduardo marvels at his own inability to imagine the possibility that Luz could be the child of *desaparecidos*: "But did you really want to find out the truth?" (167).[9] Eduardo's agonizing question—also addressed to the reader—implicates the broader society in this self-imposed blindness and encourages censure of those who choose to remain in ignorance. The use of "you" in selected moments of the text thereby serves to emphasize the reader's compromise with the epideictic—the reader must judge his or her *own* actions as either noble or shameful, as well as those of the characters.

In sum, to use Nance's terms, *My Name Is Light* proves effective on the level of forensic and epideictic rhetorical strategies—depicting the military's past actions as unequivocally unjust, their present actions as shameful, and the present actions of characters such as Eduardo and Miriam, who literally risk their lives to uncover the truth, as laudable. Osorio's text thereby succeeds in bringing past atrocity to light and, given its worldwide success, educating a broader public about the dictatorship's systematic appropriation of children.[10]

Fictional Witnessing Part II: How the Novel Engages with Complexity

Not only does Osorio's novel fulfill the testimonial impulse to tell a silenced story, but it further recognizes some of the inherent emotional complexities of Luz's plight. Although the text ultimately falls short in depicting the full nuance of Luz's situation, it does highlight the tension between love and politics in several ways: through showing the complicated relationship between Luz and her two "fathers," Carlos and Eduardo, and by questioning simplistic moral codes in the context of state terrorism.

The narrative portrays Luz's encounter with her biological father as unquestioningly complicated and at times uneasy. Carlos exhibits a range of emotions, including surprised delight to discover that Liliana's baby survived, intense jealousy regarding Luz's close relationship with Eduardo, and profound self-criticism for his negative feelings toward the man who loved Luz like a daughter. The narrative emphasizes these contradictory emotions and complicated familial relationships through the brutally honest conversation between Luz and Carlos. Her repeated lament that "No one searched for me" (111) both highlights her emotional struggle and implicates Carlos as guilty of abandoning her to her fate, of not doing everything he could to help her. When he criticizes Eduardo for marrying a daughter of a military man and collaborating in the appropriation of a child that was not his, she counters: "Listen, the man who married Mariana lost his life finding out who I was. [. . .] But you're my flesh and blood, and what did you do for me?" (283). Luz's sharp reproach effectively underscores the nuances of family—Carlos's position as biological father does not necessarily make him her best advocate—and also points to the challenge of making an emotional connection given the circumstances.

The way in which Carlos and Luz reflect upon the words "mamá" and "papá" also speak to the complexity of family relationships. Carlos is bothered by the tenderness he hears in Luz's voice when she speaks of Eduardo, and the way she calls him "papá" (153). His emotions demonstrate an understanding of her difficult situation—love and family are not simply determined by biology. Regarding her use of "mamá" to refer to her "adoptive" mother Mariana, with whom she had a conflicted relationship, Luz demonstrates an ambivalence that points to the loaded nature of such signifiers. She muses, "It's a word you only come to appreciate with time [...] [Mariana] was the person I'd called Mum ever since I started connecting that sound with a person" (186). Such a statement implies a certain flexibility in the terms "mamá" and "papá" and prompts the reader to consider what characteristics determine the connection between the sounds and the person: Biology? Love? Living together under the same roof?

Perhaps the best example of how *My Name Is Light* engages the difficulty inherent in Luz and Carlos's relationship is Luz's criticism of Carlos and Liliana's motives for having children. Speaking as the ultimate innocent victim of the dictatorship, Luz confronts Carlos for deciding to bring a child into the world during perilous times, accusing him of "selfishness" at best and dangerous irresponsibility at worst. As she pointedly claims: "Children weren't given the chance to decide whether they wanted to run that risk for the sake of their beliefs, the way their parents were. [...] it was the military regime that made me disappear, but it was my own parents who exposed me to the nightmare of disappearing—and surviving" (84).[11] By juxtaposing Carlos and Liliana's decision to have a child with the military's practice of disappearance, in this emotionally charged moment the narrative implicates the militants in the lasting effects of the violence. This bold assertion in a text that otherwise praises the revolutionary struggle responds to the complex legacy of the dictatorship.

While Carlos's struggle to understand the multilayered repercussions of his new family situation highlights the complicated reality of the militants, Eduardo's struggle demonstrates the equally intricate reality of the "adoptive" families. Once Eduardo begins to suspect that Luz may be the child of *desaparecidos*, the narrative depicts his inner conflict, his dawning awareness that what is best for Luz (finding her true identity) might have devastating consequences for his family. Like Carlos, he is criticized for his "selfishness" (291), of wanting to pretend that Luz's presence in his life has no greater political repercussions. His divided loyalty between his family (his love for Mariana, his desire to keep Luz) and his duty to the truth clearly demonstrates the possibility for love *and* complicity to reside in the same person and makes it clear that not all of those involved in the appropriation of children base their actions on questionable moral grounds.

In fact, the novel repeatedly criticizes any type of easy categorization of people as "good" or "bad." Every time Carlos passes judgment on Eduardo or Miriam, Luz demonstrates how the intricate situation precludes any simplistic moralizing. For example, when Luz insists that Eduardo too was a victim, prompting Carlos to explode, "How can you defend someone who stole your identity like that?" (159), she fixes him with a look of rage and replies "I would prefer it if you listened more and stopped being so judgmental" (160). Miriam also serves to undermine the usual expectations regarding moral behavior. Supposedly tainted by virtue of her profession, Miriam's behavior proves more exemplary than those who occupy a more respected position in society, in particular the military and the privileged upper class. In sharp contrast to *el Bestia*, who blindly parrots the rhetoric of the military regarding the patriotic duty to rid the country of subversives, Miriam makes her own decisions regarding the right course of action during this time of "war," ultimately risking her life several times in order to reunite Luz with her biological father. While the character of the "prostitute with the heart of gold" fulfills an expected role in this sentimental tale, she also serves to question easy categorizations, thereby highlighting the complexities of the political situation.

Finally, the narrative is especially critical of those characters who view the world in terms of black and white, emphasizing the importance of "shades of gray" in this complicated post-authoritarian society. Once he becomes aware of the truth regarding the disappearances, Eduardo criticizes Mariana's "infantile" worldview: "For Mariana those kind of people were the baddies, as simple as that" (154). Mariana's insistence that they raise Luz with the "correct" ideas about right and wrong also serves as a critique of such dogmatic thinking (169). By underscoring the importance of nuance, the narrative roundly critiques the military's rhetoric of subversives who needed to be eliminated and speaks to the complexity of the post-dictatorship context.

Although on many levels the novel recognizes the nuanced situation of appropriated children, *My Name Is Light* ultimately falls short in its attempt to fully engage the nature of the tragedy. In his article "Identidad robada y anagnórisis: De *Nunca más* a *Quinteto de Buenos Aires*" ("Stolen Identity and Anagnorisis: From *Nunca más* to *Quintet of Buenos Aires*"), Marco Kunz argues that Osorio's text, like many others that treat the subject of disappeared children, chooses to profile a situation that is far from representative of the majority of cases, but which allows for greater drama (181).[12] Recognizing the "ethical dilemma of not straying too far from reality and at the same time satisfying the reader's expectations for suspense and emotion" (180), Kunz believes that *My Name Is Light* errs on the side of too little reality. He criticizes the text for employing "an excess of fabulation" and creating an intricate, unbelievable plot that resorts to trite stereotypes and heightened drama at the expense of verisimilitude (187). Kunz argues that this lack of verisimilitude discredits any testimonial value the work may possess, a position that seems overstated. Nevertheless, the novel proves highly sentimental, and the central theme of "love conquers all" can easily be viewed as one of the "facile or generic narrative codes" Goldberg refers to in her consideration of an ethics of representation. Furthermore, although the situation of a young woman raised in a family that is not her biological one allows for emotional complexity, *My Name Is Light* conveniently arranges both plot (Eduardo, Luz's loving parent, is killed when she's a young girl) and character (Mariana never really loves Luz) in order to avoid the potential messiness of the politics of identity.[13]

The Politics of Identity Part I: The Rhetoric

When it comes to the politics of identity, *My Name Is Light* echoes the language employed by the Grandmothers of the Plaza de Mayo, in particular their slogan "La identidad no se impone" (Identity cannot be imposed). Put simply, biology is destiny. As a baby, Luz suffers from nightmares stemming from the brutal transition from her biological mother to Eduardo and Mariana, and she invokes these early memories in her conversation with Carlos. Although she was taken from her mother when she was only two weeks old, the novel intimates that she preserves some memory of that time, memories that come to the surface when she touches the artificial plastic of the baby bottle Mariana gives her in order to feed her own baby, Juan. The touch of the plastic nipple provokes a physical reaction in Luz that catalyzes her search, "As if I'd touched a spider or a scorpion" (316); in short, her body knows what her mind has yet to understand.

The novel emphasizes the importance of this "natural" type of knowing. As Gema Palazón Saez explains in her article "Reconstrucción identitaria y mecanismos de memoria en *A veinte años, Luz*" ("The Reconstruction of Identity and the Mechanisms of Memory in *My Name Is Light*"), much of Luz's knowing is internal—"she feels in her body the stigma of the dictatorship, because she is also a victim" (479).[14] Examples in the text abound where Luz's intuition, intimately connected to her body, guides her toward discovering her true identity. For example, she explains to Carlos that living with Mariana and her new husband Daniel always felt "unnatural" (264). In a similar fashion, she falls in love with her husband Ramiro through dancing—their bodies just "know" they are right for each other. Palazón explains Luz's corporeal knowledge in terms of silence and speech ("the body registers what cannot be said") (479), yet the emphasis on her body also points to a biological determinism that aligns with the rhetoric of the Grandmothers regarding what constitutes a "true" identity.

The narrative sets up a contrast between what is seen as "natural" and what is not, exemplified by Luz's relationship with her son. Luz possesses a fierce desire to breastfeed Juan and insists upon being with him at all times, despite Mariana's insistence that she bottle-feed instead. Her strong physical reaction to the touch of the bottle on one hand underscores the violence of her appropriation, yet on the other hand it also serves to prioritize what is natural in family relationships—babies should not be taken away from their mothers, and the connection between Liliana and Luz (symbolized by breastfeeding) represents the most natural bond between mother and child. Any other type of connection—seen in Luz's fraught relationship with Mariana—is unnatural, and therefore a perversion of her real identity.[15]

Another way in which the novel incorporates the rhetoric of the Grandmothers is the repeated reference to the stolen babies as "botín de guerra" (spoils of war). Sergeant Pitiotti refers to the child he hopes to receive for Miriam as "a sort of war trophy" (44); meanwhile, Carlos bitterly remarks that for the military, "those babies were just things, plunder" (55). The Grandmothers have long used the term "botín de guerra" to call attention to the way the military considered their missing grandchildren simply one more valuable "thing" that could be taken from the disappeared, and for this reason they also advocate a policy of restitution that entails recovering these appropriated children and returning them to their original families. The repeated mention of the language related to the Grandmothers' struggle, as well as the eventual reunion between Luz and her biological family, indicates how *My Name Is Light* supports the rhetoric of the Grandmothers: appropriated children have been denied their "true" (biological) identity and must be recovered and restored to their biological families.

The Politics of Identity Part II: The Complex Reality

In this fictional account, like many others that treat the subject of the children of the disappeared, there is no space for a loving military family.[16] Luz's (loving) adoptive father ends up dead when he tries to discover her true identity, and her (unloving) stepmother drives her away, thereby avoiding any potential conflict when Luz eventually reunites with her biological father. Yet the reality of the plight of the missing children is much more complicated, and ultimately more tragic, than most fictional narratives—or even the rhetoric of the Grandmothers—allow, for it points to a crime that has both lasting consequences and, in more cases than one might want to admit, no possibility for reparation.

The Grandmothers estimate that there are between 400 and 500 appropriated children—to date, approximately 100 have been located.[17] Some cases of recovery demonstrate a similar type of "happy ending" seen in *My Name Is Light* and are often highlighted by the Grandmothers in order to promote their cause of recovering these stolen children.[18] Yet the range of responses to the work of recovering these missing grandchildren and restoring their identity is much more varied and nuanced, as seen in a 2008 collection of testimonies of appropriated children compiled by the journalist Analía Argento titled *De vuelta a casa: historias de hijos y nietos restituidos (Home Again: Stories of Recovered Children and Grandchildren)*.[19] The complexity of these cases points to some difficult (and at times irresolvable) issues regarding the politics of identity. Clearly the military considered these children as "war booty," things to be distributed as they saw fit.[20] Yet it is precisely because people are not spoils of war that the process of recovery becomes complicated. If the actions of the military demonstrate their belief that these living beings were possessions that could be appropriated or given away, the rhetoric of the Grandmothers with its emphasis on recovery and restoration unwittingly reproduces this same attitude. Referring to the children as "stolen" or "appropriated," although true, implies that to a certain extent they are still considered objects—as victims, they remain "spoils of war" that need to be returned to their rightful families.

The testimonies in *De vuelta a casa (Home Again)* demonstrate that family ties are more than simply biological, and the process of appropriation does not necessarily preclude love. The majority of the individuals who shared their stories with Argento felt conflicted about the process of discovering their biological identity. While some like being welcomed into another family, and others changed their names to reflect their new identity, still others choose to maintain their given name or have resisted any contact with their biological families. Some still live with or maintain very close relations with the parents who raised them, even when these individuals were implicated in the disappearance of their birthparents.[21] From the perspective of the grandparents, a grandchild's refusal to voluntarily submit to DNA testing and to know his or her birth family represents an incredible disappointment; as Argento explains, "It was as if they had stolen [the grandchild] from them again, or worse" (171). Several stories included in *De vuelta a casa (Home Again)* highlight the complications that arise precisely because children are not "spoils of war."[22]

The intricate problem of the politics of identity can be viewed as a struggle between overlapping groups of victims, in this case the biological family (most often the grandparents) and the children themselves. While in many cases the goals of the Grandmothers and the children may align, unfortunately in some cases the needs of one group diverge from those of the other. What the Grandmothers demand—restoring the child to his or her biological family—may not be what the child wants, or necessarily what is best for the child. Although the Grandmother's rhetoric regarding the "right to an identity" represents a worthy claim and is seen as in the child's best interests, in some cases mandating a connection with the biological family may constitute a further violation to these victims.[23] While at times the Grandmothers and the children work toward a common goal, in others instances the clashing needs create a tragic situation in which nobody feels as if their rights are valued, and which may even appear fundamentally unjust.[24]

Identity, indeed, cannot be imposed—yet this works both ways. For the Grandmothers, a "false" identity imposed on a child stolen from his or her parents can never be imposed; yet because these are living human beings and not war booty, a "true" biological identity cannot be imposed either. This is the tragedy that needs to be told as the legacy of the systematic appropriation of children, for this particular crime against humanity has devastating, permanent effects that in many cases have no remedy or possible reparation. The grandmothers continue to suffer with the continued absence of their grandchildren. Meanwhile, the children may suffer if and when they are recovered—there is no easy way out. The bonds of love do not align with the needs of justice or reparation, and to present these complicated stories of identity as simple tales of discovery silences the real tragedy of this particular crime.

Fiction versus Testimony

Of course one could easily argue that fictional representations create spaces where historical truths can be suspended or set aside. Novelists, after all, have the right to portray history not as it actually happened but as it could or should have happened. However, representing an easy way out of the labyrinth of the politics of identity, through a false "happy ending," ultimately can be viewed as a further violation, for it silences the real crime, thereby undermining the goal of any type of testimonial narrative. Furthermore, one can view Osorio's use of these victims' experiences as another form of appropriation—in this case, their stories.[25] Since their stories comprise part of their identity, using their experience as inspiration for a popular novel risks not only silencing the real tragedy of the appropriation of children but also objectifying these victims once again.

The attempts to bury any evidence relating to the systematic appropriation of children during the dictatorship years is referred to as a "pact of silence" by the military. Yet while *My Name Is Light* serves to break this particular pact of silence, it unwittingly contributes to another. In her consideration of testimonial narrative, Nance refers to the power of the "socially sayable," "specific and formulaic speech acts" utilized by testimonial speakers "that comprise the socially acceptable channels for the narration of trauma" (106). Noting that "[i]n the literatures of trauma, the restrictive force of the socially sayable is extremely strong" (107), Nance argues that many times speakers are unable to articulate trauma in a way that will provoke any action. Applying Nance's idea to the fictional realm, the socially sayable seems to affect the types of stories that can be told about past trauma. Unlike many other trauma narratives, the story of appropriation does not defy linguistic expression; rather, the inability to tell the complete tale reveals a reluctance to fully engage with the tragedy. Nevertheless, if we only tell the good stories, the ones with the happy endings, we are also contributing to a pact of silence that suppresses the truly tragic tales. Furthermore, the ramifications of such silence remain and must be addressed if we are to come to a full understanding of the depth of the trauma and the horror of this particular crime against humanity.

My Name Is Light aims to call attention to the plight of children born in captivity during the Argentine dictatorship and denounce the military's actions. By emphasizing the criminality of Luz's appropriation and the importance of her search for identity, the narrative indeed sheds light on this difficult subject. Nevertheless, while Osorio's novel succeeds in documenting the initial crime of stealing children, by reducing Luz's situation to a simple tale of discovery, it silences the lasting effects of such atrocities, thereby undermining testimonio's imperative to tell the "real" or complete story. Put another way, shining more light in one area paradoxically creates deeper shadows in another. Furthermore, the erasure of the difficult issues related to the politics of identity does not point to the challenge of representing trauma, but rather a reluctance to fully bear witness to painful truths. Although Osorio's text purports to help the reader "see" better, ultimately the reader only ends up "feeling" better at the end of the tale. In the final analysis, the failed witnessing in *My Name Is Light* implies that sometimes the obstacles to telling the whole story stem not from the impossibility of finding appropriate words but the unwillingness to articulate them.

Notes

1. All quotes come from Catherine Jagoe's translation of Osorio's novel, unless otherwise indicated.
2. For a discussion of the autobiographical pact of truth, see Nancy K. Miller's "Facts, Pacts, Acts."
3. After Horacio Verbitsky and Adolfo Scilingo appeared on television talking about the now-infamous "death flights," Argentina began to experience what Claudia Feld has termed a memory "boom," a blossoming of documentaries and testimonials aimed to raise awareness of the widespread practice of torture and disappearance during the dictatorship. (See *Del estrado a la pantalla: Las imágenes del juicio a los ex comandantes en Argentina*. Madrid: Siglo Veintiuno de España; Social Science Research Council, 2002).
4. It should be noted that the members of H.I.J.O.S. are not all appropriated children, for not all children of the disappeared were appropriated. Furthermore, many appropriated children remain unconnected to H.I.J.O.S. even after discovering their biological identity.
5. Although Nance does not include fiction in her analysis of testimonio's rhetorical strategies, given the broader definition of testimonio outlined above, I find her categories useful when analyzing Osorio's novel.
6. The English-language translation of the novel refers to *el Bestia* as "Animal." For the purposes of this essay, I preserve the Spanish for this character's name.
7. Pablo represents the noble militant who rejects his upper-class background to fight for the working poor. His conversations with his sister Dolores demonstrate his dedication to provide "a life of dignity to all" (146). Liliana, Pablo, and Dolores all serve to educate the reader as to the goals of the militants.
8. Translation is mine.
9. Translation is mine. The quote is from page 192 in the Spanish edition.

10. Although the novel focuses on one particular fictional case, it makes clear that Luz represents one of many babies born in captivity and given to military families as part of an organized system of appropriation.
11. The original Spanish refers to being "desaparecido... con vida" (disappeared... alive) (97), a reference to the calls for "aparición con vida" (reappearance alive) by the family members of the disappeared.
12. All translations are mine.
13. The interests of space preclude a prolonged discussion of Mariana, but she is portrayed as an evil stepmother who never loves Luz and drives her to find her biological family, neatly preventing Luz from becoming trapped between two loving families.
14. All translations are mine.
15. The novel also includes many direct references to the "right to an identity" as defined in Articles 7, 8 and 11 of the International Convention of the Rights of the Child, also known as the "Argentine clauses" (United Nations Convention on the Rights of the Child, New York, 1990).
16. The *Teatro x la identidad* (Theatre for Identity) play cycles are perhaps the best-known fictional representations of appropriated children. The characters of military parents are often named "appropriators"—in other words, they are defined by their actions. These plays thereby emphasize the impossibility of any type of loving relationship in a family created out of violence and appropriation.
17. For updated numbers, refer to the official website of the Grandmothers of Plaza de Mayo, abuelas.org.
18. Such are the cases of Juan Cabandié and Carla Rutila Artés, both abused by the families who appropriated them. Cabandié speaks of his discovery of his true identity in glowing terms, and Rutila Artés eventually testified against her appropriator in August of 2010 when he was put on trial for crimes committed during the dictatorship.
19. *De vuelta a casa: Historias de hijos y nietos restituidos*. All translations are mine. Until recently, few voices of these appropriated children have been heard. Some cases have been featured in documentaries, and selected testimonies of recovered grandchildren can be found on the Grandmother's website, yet for the most part the story of the youngest victims of the dicatorship has been told by the Grandmothers or others closely aligned with this organization. Argento's work represents a notable exception, especially because it was published by a press with no connection to the Grandmothers.
20. See, for example, Daniel Blaustein's documentary *Botín de guerra (Spoils of War)* (2000) and Estela Bravo's *¿Quién soy yo? (Who Am I?)* (2007), as well as the *Spoils of War* text published by the Grandmothers.
21. The story of Evelin Karina Vásquez is especially striking. She refuses to this day to consider the parents who raised her as anything other

than loving; furthermore, she considers the legal action taken against them, and the effort to restore her biological identity, as a violation in itself rather than an act of justice (162).

22. Another complicated story is that of Matías Reggiardo Tolosa, one of the twins involved in what became a very high-profile case of appropriation (mentioned in *My Name Is Light*). The man who raised them, Samuel Miara, was a Federal Police chief who was involved in the disappearance of their biological parents, yet when the Miaras were sent to jail, the twins were still quite young. Matías describes the way in which he and his brother were taken from their "parents" as very traumatic, and he still maintains a very close loving bond with Beatriz Miara, the only mother he ever knew. In his words, "We had a happy childhood, in our ignorance or whatever you want to call it, but in a home in which they raised us with love" (209).

23. The way in which the judicial system has mandated the verification of identity—police entering homes to search for documents, separating children from the only parents they have ever known—eerily echoes the violent practices of the military during the years of state terrorism, and lawyers representing children who refuse to voluntarily submit to testing have noted this parallel. Evelin's lawyer argued that the Grandmothers "couldn't strip her of her identity, of the person she was and of her name because without them she would lose all of her rights [. . .] she would become an NN walking the streets," a reference to the graves of the disappeared marked with NN, *ningún nombre* (unnamed) (172).

24. At the time of this writing, there is currently another high-profile case of appropriation working its way through the court system in Argentina. Marcela and Felipe Noble-Herrera, the adoptive children of the media magnate Ernestina Herrera de Noble, have categorically refused to submit to DNA testing, even after receiving a court order. Their refusal aligns with the idea that a "child" should not have to testify against a "parent"; the Grandmothers counter that they hold evidence of a crime in their bodies and have an obligation to present it. According to statements made by Estela Carlotto, President of the Grandmothers of the Plaza de Mayo, during January of 2011, although it may not be deliberate, "the adoptive children of Ernestina Herrera de Noble are part of the cover-up of a crime" and therefore have the obligation to offer the evidence they carry inside their bodies ("Son parte del ocultamiento" *Página 12*. January 21, 2011).

25. In the prologue to *De vuelta a casa (Home Again)*, Juan Cabandié states that he was initially suspicious of Argento's motives for interviewing appropriated children. He complains that earlier representations of their situation have treated them "as *objects* of sociological study, like *the elements* of a social experiment" (emphasis added, 15).

Works Cited

Argento, Analía. *De vuelta a casa: historias de hijos y nietos restituidos*. Buenos Aires: Marea, 2008. Print.

Beverley, John. *Testimonio: On the Politics of Truth*. Minneapolis: U of Minnesota P, 2004. Print.

Beverley, John, and Marc Zimmerman. *Literature and Politics in the Central American Revolutions*. Austin: U of Texas P, 1990. Print.

Botín de guerra. Dir. Daniel Blaustein. Cinemateca, 2000. Film.

Cabandié Alfonsín, Juan. Prólogo. *De vuelta a casa: historias de hijos y nietos restituidos*. By Analía Argento. Buenos Aires: Marea, 2008. 9–15. Print.

Caruth, Cathy. *Unclaimed Experience: Trauma, Narrative, and History*. Baltimore: Johns Hopkins UP, 1996. Print.

Derrida, Jacques. *Demeure: Fiction and Testimony*. Trans. Elizabeth Rosenberg. Stanford: Stanford UP, 2000. Print.

Feld, Claudia. *Del estrado a la pantalla: Las imágenes del juicio a los ex comandantes en Argentina*. Madrid: Siglo Veintiuno de España; Social Science Research Council, 2002. Print.

Felman, Shoshana, and Dori Laub. *Testimony: Crises of Witnessing in Literature, Psychoanalysis and History*. New York: Routledge, 1992. Print.

Goldberg, Elizabeth Swanson. *Beyond Terror: Gender, Narrative, Human Rights*. Princeton: Rutgers UP, 2007. Print.

Jara, René, and Hernán Vidal, eds. *Testimonio y literatura*. Minneapolis: Institute for the Study of Ideologies and Literature, 1986. Print.

Kunz, Marco. "Identidad robada y anagnórisis: De *Nunca más* a *Quinteto de Buenos Aires*." *Violence politique et écriture de l'élucidation dans le basin méditerranéen*. Ed. Ambroise Claude and Tyras George. Grenoble: Université Stendhal, 2002. 179–93. Print.

Langer, Lawrence L. *Versions of Survival: The Holocaust and the Human Spirit*. Albany: State U of New York P, 1982. Print.

Miller, Nancy K. "Facts, Pacts, Acts." *Profession* (1992): 10–14. Print.

Nance, Kimberly A. *Can Literature Promote Justice? Trauma Narrative and Social Action in Latin American Testimonio*. Nashville: Vanderbilt UP, 2006. Print.

Nosilia, Julio E. *Botín de guerra*. 3rd ed. Buenos Aires: Abuelas de Plaza de Mayo, 2007. Print.

Osorio, Elsa. *A veinte años, Luz*. Buenos Aires: Grijalbo Mondadori, 1999. Print.

———. *My Name Is Light*. Trans. Catherine Jagoe. New York: Bloomsbury, 2003. Print.

Palazón Saez, Gema. "Reconstrucción identitaria y mecanismos de la memoria: *A veinte años, Luz*." *Río de la Plata* 29–30 (2004): 475–85. Print.

¿Quién soy yo? Dir. Estela Bravo. Bravo Films in association with the National University of San Martín. Co-production of the *Encuentro* Channel. 2007. Film.

Sklodowska, Elzbieta. *Testimonio hispanamericano: historia, teoría, poética.* New York: Peter Lang, 1993. Print.

"Son parte del ocultamiento." *Página 12.* January 21, 2011. Web. February 6, 2011.

Taylor, Diana. *Disappearing Acts: Spectacles of Gender and Nationalism in Argentina's "Dirty War."* Durham: Duke UP, 1997. Print.

United Nations. Office of the United Nations High Commissioner for Human Rights. *Convention on the Rights of the Child.* New York: United Nations, 1990. Print.

Part III

Connected Communities: Emerging Contexts and Merging Mediums

CHAPTER 6

TESTIMONY IN TRUTH COMMISSIONS AND SOCIAL MOVEMENTS IN LATIN AMERICA

Lynn Stephen

This essay explores the role of oral testimony in truth commissions and social movements in Latin America. A majority of indigenous, rural, and urban inhabitants in Latin American countries receive news and culture through oral and visual media: radio, television, videos (commercial and self-produced), and sites like YouTube. Oral testimony is a long-standing form of political participation in indigenous and rural communities. Most basically, testimony refers to a person's account of an event or experience as delivered from the lips of that person through a speech act. It is an oral telling of a person's perception of an event. It signifies witnessing, from the Latin root *testis*, or witness. In the discussion that follows, however, I am also very interested in the performative and public aspects of oral testimony.

Oral testimony allows people to bear witness, archive the memory of wrongs committed, and represent lived personal histories within complex identity categories of race, ethnicity, gender, and class. My examination here of the role of oral testimony in Latin American truth commissions and social movements relates to important larger questions about memory and the ways that history and truth are multiply understood and interpreted. These larger questions include: Who defines legitimate speakers? Who defines history? Who controls and legitimates social memory and how? How do we understand and interpret "truth" whether in a legal context, in the construction of local, regional, or national histories, or in identity and social movement construction? I first explore the role of testimony in truth commissions, focusing on the agency that testifiers have in a broader social context—not just in testimonial courtrooms—and on the multiple forms of knowledge that testimonials bring that permit the complication of national histories and ideas about finding one agreed-upon truth. I then contemplate the role of testimonials in social movements, with a particular focus on their place in indigenous social movements where language has historically been oral, written, and performative. Next, I move to a discussion of Diana Taylor's ideas about archive and repertoire and her method of the "scenario" as a framework for analyzing testimony in social movements. The last section of the chapter uses the elements of Taylor's "scenario" to analyze the testimonial of a teacher in the Oaxaca social movement of 2006 at a specific press conference and beyond, showing how testimony builds and travels through multiple channels and can motivate concrete actions.

Testimonials in Latin American Truth Commissions

The practice of the oral testimony has been broadly defined by Shoshona Felman and Dori Laub as a form of retrospective public witnessing of shattering events of a history that is " 'essentially not over' and is in some sense brought into being by the (itself interminable) process of testimonial witnessing" (Felman and Laub xv–xvii; Sarkar and Walker 7). Modern Latin American truth commissions since the 1980s have placed individual oral testimonies focused on specific cases, individual victims, and individual perpetrators in tension with the collective social motivation and experiences of victims that are related to structural and systemic violence (J. Taylor 197; Grandin and Klubock 4–6). The contemporary truth commission form, as documented by Grandin and Klubock, begins in 1982 in Latin America with the establishment of Bolivia's Comisión Nacional de Desaparecidos (National Commission of the Disappeared), followed by the Argentinean Comisión Nacional sobre la Desaparición de Personas (National Commission on Disappeared People) in 1983 (1). Later commissions added the terms "reconciliation" and "historical clarification" to their titles, suggesting not only the documentation of human rights abuses, but also a process of forging healing, forgiveness, and national unity, ideas that are included under the concept of transitional justice.[1] The latter, of course, usually came with impunity for perpetrators of violence. "Truth commissions" have functioned in Argentina (1983), Bolivia (1982), Chile (1990), Ecuador (1996), El Salvador (1992), Guatemala (1994), Peru (2000), and Uruguay (2000) (Arias and del Campo 9).

The impact of these commissions in eight different countries over almost two decades cannot be underestimated in terms of their role in rewriting national histories. As such, truth commissions are important archives of historical materials that are and will be continually drawn upon to interpret periods of brutal violence and dictatorships as well as the "democratic transitions" that followed, usually with neoliberal economic development policy as part of the healing process. As characterized by Grandin and Klubock, "truth commissions work, at least in theory, similar to other myths and rituals of nationalism, to sacramentalize violence into a useful creation myth" (3). Thus truth commissions can work to paper-over past atrocities in the name of "getting over it" and "moving on" to "prioritize catharsis and forgiveness over punishment" (5). In sum, they may not function to punish the perpetrators of human rights violations.

While I do not disagree with this analysis, in this study I focus on a different dimension of truth commissions that centers on the testifier as an active social agent who is engaged in a personal and collective performative act that can potentially broaden the meaning of truth, and also serve to advance alternative and contested understandings of history. The focus here is on what the act of testifying inside and outside of the official forums of truth commissions does for survivors of human rights abuses, their families, and larger communities. While Grandin and Klubock rightly point out that "in the case of commissions whose charge is both truth and reconciliation (Chile and Peru, for example) and forgiveness in the case of South Africa, it might be argued that the goal of reconciliation imposes profound obstacles to the production of historical truth" (6), we might also question whether any process can produce a homogeneous historical truth equally believed and understood by all. Part of what happens in the process of truth commissions with the inclusion of people who have been literally silent and invisible in officially sanctioned spaces of legality is that they and others close to them have the experience of speaking and being heard. As suggested by Kimberly Theidon, one of the important purposes of truth commissions is the rewriting of national narratives so that they are more inclusive of groups that have been historically marginalized (456). Theidon rightly points out that such forums usually have a focus on victims, are victim friendly and victim centered—producing a narrative standard that many may feel compelled to follow (see Nance on this point as well). Fiona Ross has made similar observations in her analysis of the South African Truth and Reconciliation Commission ("Using Rights" 178–79) as has Julie Taylor in her discussion of Argentina's truth commission. Taylor argues that truth commissions tend to transform individuals, political activists, and others into "innocent or transgressing individuals with individual rights and obligations" or as "victims" (J. Taylor 197–98). But victim narratives in court may be recast elsewhere with very different meanings.

In her analysis of focus groups and public assemblies conducted by the Peruvian Truth Commission in Ayacucho in 2002, Theiden found that while there was a preponderance of witness testimony about rape and sexual violence that primarily followed a victim narrative in public arenas, when the same women entered into conversations with Theidon and her research team outside of official venues, they located sexual violence within broader social contexts. "They detailed the preconditions that structured vulnerability and emphasized their efforts to minimize harm to themselves and to the people they cared for. With their insistence on context, women situated their experience of sexual violence—those episodes of brutal victimization—within womanly narratives of heroism" (265). In other words, we cannot read the larger social impact of people's statements in truth commissions simply in terms of what is said within the courtroom or the official forum. The same people circulate their testimonials in different forums outside of the courtroom where they may be expressed and interpreted quite differently. For this reason it is important to consider testimonials given during truth commissions in a broader context.

Testimony giving does affect those people who provide them both in and outside of the courtroom. Because truth commissions function within national legal systems and rely on both eyewitness and third-person testimonies—particularly, for example, in terms of women's extreme reluctance to report on rape in Guatemala, Peru, and South Africa (Theidon 458; Mantilla 3)—the courtroom becomes a platform for speaking and juridical recognition of voices of victims and their right to talk both inside and outside of the courtroom (Jelin and Kaufman 94). As stated by Rachel Seider, "the legal system is converted into a contested site of meaning over state accountability and citizens' rights as the dominant ideas and values that underpin the law provide the framework for advancing alternative understandings"—of history, democracy, rights (204). In his magisterial trilogy, *The Memory Box of Pinochet's Chile* (2004, 2006, 2010), Steve Stern argues for "the study of contentious memory as a process of competing selective remembrances, ways of giving meaning to and drawing legitimacy from human experience.... In the approach I have taken, the social actors behind distinct frameworks are seeking to define that which is truthful and meaningful about a great collective trauma" (*Remembering Pinochet's Chile* xvii). The point of oral history for Stern and the testifying process within that is not simply to establish the "factual truth or falsehood of events... but to be able to understand what social truths or processes led people to tell their stories the way they do, in recognizable patterns" (xviii). If truth commissions are looked at as important arenas for oral expression bound to larger contexts, then we can broaden our view of the impact of testimonials.

In the trial of nine junta members who ruled Argentina from 1976 to 1983 and who were accused of "organizing and ordering massive kidnappings, torture, and killing of anonymous individuals" (Jelin and Kaufman 93–94), testimony was a crucial part of the process, particularly in the absence of high levels of material evidence. Testimony in the court room was clearly connected to the kinds of discourses that had been circulating in families, neighborhoods, and organizations for some time. As Jelin and Kaufman point out, because the construction of juridical proof was based on the testimony of victims since military records had been mostly destroyed, "this implied juridical recognition of their voices and their right to talk" (94). In the courtroom, testimony is broken down into specific components that fit into the judicial framework: "the requirement of personal identification, the pledge to tell the truth, the description of circumstances, and relationship with the case" (94). Testimony in court legitimizes those testimonies that are moving around in society. While the disappeared, for example, can cease to exist as subjects of rights since they are not present in the court as "victims" who are converted into witnesses, the testimony in court of those who have been searching for them is legitimized through its entrance into the legal record and through this receives recognition.

In this process, oral testimony thus became a vehicle for broadening historical truth through opening up who legitimately speaks and is heard. It is interesting to note that in truth commission court hearings, the evidentiary standards are flexible. This in turn requires a flexing of the notion of truth, moving away from strictly empirical, material evidence to incorporating other forms of information. As pointed out by Theidon, "while legal standards of proof might disallow 'hearsay' or anecdotal evidence, truth commissions can work with other evidentiary standards to establish historical truth" (458).

In Peru, third-person testimonies were permitted and Theidon notes that the majority of information about rape and sexual violence came through third-person testimonies where women talked about what they had heard or seen happen to others—not to themselves. Theiden (458) and others (Ross, "Using Rights" 169–70) have interpreted this as evidence of the self-censorship and community gender policing that have permeated many public hearings in truth commissions.

Recent discussions regarding the role of testimony in documentary films also center on what kind of "truth" is captured through testimonials in film. This discussion is useful for interpreting testimony in courtrooms and other venues as well. In implicit dialogue with the "Rigoberta Menchú" controversy of the late 1990s launched by David Stoll's book *Rigoberta Menchú and the Story of All Poor Guatemalans,* José Rabasa suggests that all "forms of collecting testimony are by definition forms of engaged dissemination of truth" (234).[2] In an article that analyzes different documentaries about the massacre of 45 indigenous Tzotzil men, women, and children by paramilitaries in Acteal, Chiapas, in 1997, Rabasa's analysis suggests that simply including a testimonial in a documentary "necessarily involves recognition of its veracity...testimonial documentaries are therefore political interventions in the context of a disputed truth" (234). Instead of returning to the overworked conversation about Stoll's book, Rabasa turns to a different critique of testimony written by Beatriz Sarlo (2005), who suggests the epistemological limits to knowing the past in Argentina through the use of testimonies in Argentina's truth commission. While Sarlo's critique comes from a deconstructionist framework in which the certainty of all knowledge is questioned (whether from an empirical point of view calling for "evidence" or belief in the truth of testimony), Rabasa suggests that we not enter into the trap of determining "the truth." Instead he suggests that we "observe that testimony partakes of other forms of knowledge besides those based on fact and falsification or even on experience...the point is that mistaken memories, amnesias, and other such aproria should not entail the dismissal of testimony, but rather a redefinition of epistemological terms that would no longer call forth factuality as the ultimate criterion" (Rabasa 235). He suggests that testimonial film can sidestep the framework revisionists attempt to impose about "fact checking," not by an immediate, innocent, and iconoclastic expression of truth, but by taking full advantage of what he calls the "fabric of testimonial film" (235). His strategy for interpreting documentaries about the Acteal massacre comes from Bruno Latour. Interpreting Latour, he states:

Belief is bound to the iconoclastic destruction of the icon: "'Fetish' and 'fact' can be traced to the same root. The *fact* is that which is fabricated and not fabricated.... But the *fetish* too is that which is fabricated and not fabricated.

Rather than seeing these audio-visual texts as truthful representations of the community of martyrs (which they are) we ought to underscore that these documentaries... *fabricate* and *not fabricate* the truth of Acteal.... The truths produced in the documentaries should be understood as *factishes*, rather than just the facts."

(236–37)

If we take Rabasa's insights back into the courtroom of truth commissions, then we can think of testimonials as producing partial insights that broaden the range of perceptions and experiences included in the historical record, thus complicating the texture of national histories and truths. Rabasa's suggestion, like that of Theidon, is that we evaluate testimonials not in terms of themselves but as part of broader social and historical contexts. When we do, then our definition of "truth" is necessarily multiple and complicated. I now turn to the role of testimonials in social movements by beginning with a discussion of the historical role of language in indigenous communities, which necessarily focuses our attention on the interrelatedness of written, oral, and performative language.

Testimonials and Social Movements

Prior to the Spanish conquest, indigenous peoples had several types of writing found in codices and in glyphs on architecture. As discussed by Linda King and others, this means that such societies were literate societies, even if commoners were unable to read the writing as it was primarily elites who learned how to write, read, interpret, and perform these texts (Faudree 49). While native scribes and intellectuals learned to write in Spanish as well as in Nahuatl, Quechua, and other languages in alphabetic literacy through orthographies in western script, by the end of the colonial period native language literacy and literatures had ended. By Independence, literacy came to mean almost exclusively literacy in Spanish. The use of indigenous languages was vibrant at independence in Mexico and elsewhere, but "their circulation became almost exclusively oral" (Faudree 56). As stated by Faudree, following independence and the creation of nationalist cultures in Latin American countries like Mexico, Guatemala, Peru, Bolivia, and Ecuador with large indigenous populations, "indigenous languages became oral in a new way, defined not only by their oral transmission practices but also in contrast with Spanish.... Ideas that indigenous languages were just dialects and hence 'cannot be written down' found increasing traction" (61). The transmission of history, local knowledges, and the administration of indigenous rituals, and systems of governance and law, however, continued to be done orally in hundreds of indigenous languages in Latin America.

In fact, one could argue that the archiving of knowledge and history took place orally not only for indigenous peoples, but for many others as well for a significant part of the twentieth century in Latin America. In Mexico, for example, only about 15 percent of the population was literate in 1910. By 1940, literacy campaigns raised this rate to 41.7 percent overall. But literacy rates in the heavily indigenous south remained lower. For significant numbers of people—particularly women and those in heavily indigenous parts of Latin America—oral knowledge transmission continued to be important.

Given the long history of oral knowledge transmission in Latin America and its continued importance, the role of oral testimony in more contemporary social movements should come as no surprise. What is interesting, however, is a lack of analytical discussions about the ways in which oral testimony functions in contemporary Latin American social movements. One of the most useful sources of analysis comes from performance studies, which focuses on testimonials as an event joining together memory and knowledge replication. Dori Laub states that "knowledge in the testimony is... not simply a factual given that is reproduced and replicated by the testifier, but a genuine advent, an event in its own right" (62). Sarkar and Walker observe that testimonials are performative "with regard to the truths and memories of testifying and witnessing" (10).

My argument here with regard to the role of testimony in Latin American social movements—particularly those bound to indigenous contexts directly or indirectly—is that because of the long history discussed above in which indigenous languages were used simultaneously orally, performatively, and until the mid-1800s in writing at least by elites, we need to center an analysis of testimonials in a space that considers them in all of these dimensions. The work of Diana Taylor in performance studies is particularly useful here.

Taylor locates part of her discussion in the strain between the concepts of the archive and the repertoire. According to her:

> The archive includes, but is not limited to, written text. The repertoire contains verbal performances—songs, prayers, speeches—as well as nonverbal practices. The written/oral divide does, on one level, capture the

archive/repertoire difference I am developing in so far as the means of transmission differ, as do the requirements of storage and dissemination. The repertoire, whether in terms of verbal or nonverbal expression, transmits live, embodied actions. As such, traditions are stored in the body through various mnemonic methods, and transmitted "live" in the here and now to a live audience.

(D. Taylor 24)

In moving away from the notion that writing is equivalent to memory and knowledge—an idea developed during the sixteenth century as a part of colonial regimes in relation to writing and printing (Anderson 67–82; de Certeau)—Taylor proposes that performance studies allow us to "take seriously the repertoire of embodied practices as an important system of knowing and transmitting knowledge" (D. Taylor 26). In indigenous and other social movements tied to contexts in which knowledge production and transmission happen partially or even primarily through oral testimony and transmission, Taylor thus suggests that we look at the performance of repertoires as forming part of knowledge archives. Pushing against the idea prevalent in some strains of cultural studies to turn everything into a text, she suggests that we pay attention to the repertoire. How should we do that?

Taylor proposes that instead of privileging texts and narratives we look at what she calls "scenarios" as meaning-making paradigms (D. Taylor 28). For our discussion here, she suggests a new methodology for helping us understand testimonials as they are narrated in real time and space. If we think of testimonials in truth commissions as well as in social movements within the framework of scenarios as defined by Taylor (below) then we can better understand the emotional and social power of oral testimonials in these two contexts.

Taylor suggests six characteristics of a scenario, which I summarize here (D. Taylor 29–32). First, a scenario involves a scene as a physical environment such as a stage or place. Second, it requires viewers to deal with the embodiment of the social actors. Third, by including both action and the formulaic structure of performance, scenarios suggest certain outcomes yet allow for reversal, parody, and change. Fourth, because of the multiplicity of forms of transmission (telling, reenactment, mime, gestus, dance, singing), a scenario can draw from written and oral archives and/or repertoire. Fifth, the frame of the scenario forces us to situate ourselves in relationship to what is going on as participants, spectators or witnesses, to "be there." Finally, the scenario usually works through reactivation of past situations and memories to make them present, constituting a "once-againness."

In the remainder of this article, I apply Taylor's method of the scenario to the testimony of Elionai Santiago Sánchez, who was a part of the 2006 social movement in Oaxaca, Mexico.

THE SCENARIO OF ELIONAI SANTIAGO SÁNCHEZ: TORTURE AND IMPUNITY IN THE OAXACA SOCIAL MOVEMENT OF 2006

The state of Oaxaca in southern Mexico has the largest percentage of indigenous population of any state in Mexico—32.5 percent of its population is indigenous (there are 14 different indigenous languages spoken there)—and is often ranked as one of the poorest states in Mexico with a per capita average income of $3,351 per year in 2006, less than half the national average (SIPAZ; de la Rosa Medina). Oaxaca has a long history of indigenous and other social movements. Building on this legacy, hundreds of organizations came together in the summer of 2006 to form one of the most significant social movements in contemporary Mexico.

During the summer and fall of 2006, what began as a large group of teachers exercising their right to bargain for higher salaries through the occupation of Oaxaca City's historical colonial square erupted into a widespread social movement after state police violently attempted to evict the teachers. Mega-marches of thousands, the creation of a popular assembly known as the APPO or the Popular Assembly of the Peoples of Oaxaca, occupation of state and federal buildings and offices, the takeover of the state's television and radio station, the construction of barricades in many neighborhoods, and regional movements throughout the state questioned the legitimacy of the state government and resulted in a massive assertion of rights by many. The APPO interrupted the usual functions of the Oaxaca state government for six months and began to construct a parallel police force, constitution, and a state assembly structure geared toward a more inclusive and participatory political vision for the state. They were met with strong repression. In the course of just six months (June-November of 2006), at least 23 persons were killed, hundreds of people were arrested and imprisoned, and over 1,200 complaints were filed with human rights commissions. Elionai Santiago Sánchez was one of hundreds arrested and imprisoned. He was tortured during his detention. What follows is a partial transcript of his testimonial given on July 17, 2007 to me on video and audio. He is discussing events that took place in August of 2006. His narrative closely follows a testimonial given publicly on August 12, 2006, both to a human rights organization and at a press conference (see LIMEDDH for a summary and Stephen "Elionai Santiago Sánchez" for a partial video recording of the testimonial).

Elionai is a 25-year-old teacher who is a member of the Local 22. His mother, also a teacher, is from the city of Putla, an indigenous cultural and political center in the western part of the state. Elionai lives on the outskirts of the state capital of Oaxaca. He was teaching elementary school in the southern part of the state in 2006. He was an active participant in the teachers' union known as Local 22 of CNTE (Coordinadora Nacional de Trabajadores de la Educación) (National Committee of Education Workers), a democratic current within the national educational workers' union known as the SNTE (Sindicato Nacional de Trabajadores de la Educación) (National Union of Education Workers). He had supported the teachers' occupation of the zócalo in May and June of 2006. He got caught in the state police attempts to evict the teachers from the center of the city and went on to support other actions the teachers and the APPO undertook. Elionai helped to guard the transmission towers of the Oaxaca Corporation of Public Radio and Television (COR-TV) after it was taken over by several hundred women on August 1, 2006, and he also attended conferences, marches, and other activities. While not a leader in the teachers' movement and the APPO, he felt confident of his ability to participate freely. He said of the months of June and July of 2006:

After the attempt to remove the teachers from the zócalo a lot of activities started. But our spirits were very, very high because we (the teachers) had tremendous support from the people. People would arrive in the zócalo with blankets, with food, with money to support us. This kind of experience really made a difference and motivated us. We realized that our struggle was supported by the people of Oaxaca. There were marches that came down from the different neighborhoods in the city and people came to tell us that we were not alone. Little by little there were more and more activities like conferences, talks, other things. I was really into it because my family was participating too. My mother, my sister, we had grown up in this atmosphere because my mother is a teacher too and she had suffered a lot in the past as well. We were also really angry about what had happened with the attempted eviction and how people were treated.

(Stephen, "Elionai Santiago Sánchez")

Confident that he could freely exercise his rights to free speech and free assembly, and interact with all of the people who were participating in a flood of activities organized by the teachers and the

APPO, Elionai spoke with the people who had congregated daily in the zócalo. Many groups from a wide range of leftist and progressive perspectives had set up booths in the zócalo. Thousands of teachers were sleeping and living in and around the zócalo in what had become a tent city. Hundreds of meetings, exchanges, cultural events, and activities were taking place. Many of the groups who established a presence there also set out books, brochures, DVDs, CDs, and other materials for sale or for small donations. Elionai bought a book and was distributing flyers for an APPO march. When several men detained Elionai along with his brother-in-law Ramiro Aragón and friend and fellow teacher Juan Gabriel, they found a biography of Stalin and an APPO flyer on Elionai. He was immediately tagged as "suspicious," and treated as if he had no civil or human rights. Elionai stated in his testimonial in July of 2007 and similarly on August 12, 2006 (Stephen, "Elionai Santiago Sánchez," see also Bellinghausen; LIMEDDH):

They had Ramiro on one side and Juan Gabriel on the other and they pushed me up against the side of a truck with hands up in the air. They patted me down, like a routine check, and then they stop and say, "What's this?" They found my teacher's I.D. and a book, a biography of Joseph Stalin that I had bought from a stall in the zócalo. I saw a red book that said "Life and Works of Joseph Stalin" and I bought it. I had this with me and I was also passing out the last accords of the APPO which said that they were going to have a march for children.... So I had these documents and when they found them, their attitude changed. One of them said to me, "What are you doing with Stalin? Now you are going to really get fucked up teacher. What are you doing here? What are you looking for?"

They took my cell phone, all of my documents, my credit card, only leaving me my teacher's I.D. Then they tied us up with really heavy rope.

They were beating me really hard in the front of my body and another person was beating me on the neck. The blows were really hard and I asked for help, but who was going to help me.... Then they started to pull on a rope. The one who was behind me began to strangle me. I tried to grab it with my hands... for a while I was able to use my hands on the rope to keep them from strangling me... Talk, talk, talk, they kept saying. They were telling me that I was guilty of something. I don't know what their intentions were.... Then they grabbed me by the hands and then I heard them break a bottle. They said, "Now we are really going to fuck over the three of you"... Then I heard Ramiro and Juan Gabriel screaming and I felt really bad. I started to get really very, very nervous, hysterical, and I started to scream. Their screams were really terrible... After they broke the bottle that is when I thought, now they are going to kill me. And they said to us "Now you are going to die."

I thought they were going to cut my throat or something. But, no. I started to feel an intense pain in my ear and I felt lots of blood flowing. I said, oh, no, they are going to cut my ear. I started to scream because the pain was unbearable. That's all I remember because after that I received a blow that rendered me unconscious.... Then I remember that Ramiro was beside me. I touched his hand and he moved. The three of us were there. I remember thinking "well, at least all three of us are alive."

(Stephen, "Elionai Santiago Sánchez," my translation)

Elionai Santiago Sánchez and Juan Gabriel Ríos were captured with Ramiro Aragón. They were jailed with him and served with false charges of possession of weapons that are for exclusive use by the Army. These are federal charges that put them in the custody of the Federal Attorney General's office. Finally Elionai and Juan Gabriel were released on 12,000 pesos bail each (about 1,200 U.S. dollars) on August 12, 2006. Elionai and Juan Gabriel were later convicted of the charges levied against them after they exhausted all of their appeals. They paid a large fine and have a three-year suspended sentence. If they are ever arrested again for any other offense, the three years will be added to whatever new jail time they receive. This has effectively silenced them and kept them from going to any political demonstrations or events. Ramiro Aragón was freed in November of 2006 but all charges against him were left in legal limbo. He fled the country with his family and received political asylum in the United States in July of 2009.

Eloinai's Testimonial in Action—Analysis of August 12, 2006, Press Conference

In this section, I take the six elements of Diana Taylor's "scenario" as a basis for analyzing the press conference where Elionai first gave his testimony. The photographs referred to in my analysis may be found at: http://espora.org/limeddh/spip.php?article48. Hours following his release, he and Juan Gabriel appeared at a press conference in the central plaza or zócalo of Oaxaca to publicly testify about what had happened to them and to ask for help in securing the release of Ramiro Aragón, who was still being held in jail. Before more than 100 people and surrounded by television, radio, and print journalists, they shared their stories. They were accompanied by Yessica Sánchez Maya, a human rights worker, and Ruth Guzmán, Elionai's sister and wife of Ramiro Aragón. Award-winning journalist Herman Bellinghausen covered the story. He wrote the following description about their appearance and people's response to their testimonials at the press conference:

The teachers were severely beaten on the face and on their bodies. Their eyes were swollen, and they had wounds on their faces and signs of lacerations on their backs. They had cut Elionai's ear with glass so much that it was almost mutilated. He had dozens of sutures from various wounds in his ear. It looked as if they had sewn it back together in a big hurry. They [Elionai and Juan Gabriel] showed their clothing with huge blood stains on them. Their blood. In their testimony, the teachers said that besides severely beating Ramiro as they did them and even worse, they also burned his forehead with cigarettes.

[Elionai stated]: "One of them grabbed me from the back seat and grabbed my ear and I didn't know what happened until I felt that blood that filled up my throat." He raised the jacket he was wearing, with a blood stain that covered almost half of it. He raised his shirt and showed his torso. He showed his ear. His face already said everything. "What bad people they are!" exclaimed a voice from the public that had gathered in front of the old city hall.

(Bellinghausen, my translation)

Physical Environment

The press conference took place in the zócalo of Oaxaca, in front of the old city hall that had been taken over by the APPO movement. In their occupation of major city buildings, the APPO had converted the zócalo into their logistical center with a press tent, a medical tent, a media tent, and other public spaces. News was often shared for the first time with reporters and the public in this area. Late night strategy sessions took place there and in dozens of locations surrounding the zócalo in the streets occupied by thousands of teachers and others. The zócalo is a traditional gathering place where crowds often gather to watch performances, listen to music, and meet family members. During 2006 it was the news and event center for the APPO. The website features pictures from the press conferences. Elionai is in the first, second, third, and fourth photographs, and Juan Gabriel appears to the right of Elionai in the third photograph.

Embodiment

As the photographs suggest, this is a case of a corporeal as well as a verbal testimony regarding the torture that Elionai and Juan Gabriel suffered. They are showing their physical wounds to the press with gestures and facial expressions as well as verbal descriptions. The third photograph illustrates the cojoining of verbal and nonverbal elements.

Structure of Performance

The press conference follows a format that people expect. This includes oral and visual testimonies of what happened, additional testimony from Ruth Guzmán, and the sharing of a letter signed by intellectuals and nonprofit organizations addressed to then president Vicente Fox, calling for the release of Ramiro Aragón. The event moves out of the structure of a press conference and into a rally at the end when Juan Gabriel cries, "There have been others before us and there will be others. This is what we cannot permit anymore" (Bellinghausen, my translation). In this way, the structure of the press conferences morphs into an emotional rally that then motivates people to work to free Ramiro and other political prisoners. Although Kimberly Nance has argued that traditional written testimonio does not necessarily move readers to act and become personally involved in struggles for social justice, here we can see that public oral testimony can motivate people to act in specific ways. This suggests that we need to reconsider how oral testimony can redefine the relationship between knowledge production, knowledge reception, and praxis.

Multiplicity of Forms of Transmission

In the event of the press conference, transmission of Elionai's testimony is oral and corporeal. Subsequently, however, the testimony in this one event gives rise to multiple forms of transmission through different press outlets via the national TV network Televisa, Radio Cacerola Radio Station (a station run by APPO at the time taken over from the state public radio and TV network, see Stephen 2011), *La Jornada* national newspaper, *Las Noticias* local newspaper, and via those who attended talking to others. The testimonial, partially textualized by the LIMEDDH and put up on a website (LIMEDDH 2006), is repeated again in various publications of Amnesty International ("Oaxaca") and other human rights organizations (see United Nations General Assembly 209–16) and then re-video recorded and put on a website "Elionai Santiago Sánchez"). The initial scenario not only brings together multiple forms of transmission but gives birth to others, bringing together the repertoire of knowledge that Elionai and Juan Gabriel provide and then serving as the basis for different forms of oral, visual, and textual archiving. The repertoire used at the press conference becomes a part of the archive.

Observers/Readers/Listeners Situated as Witnesses

The people at the press conference were clearly situated as witnesses and testifiers. Bellinghausen's written account of the press conference includes two remarks by audience members and provides a sense of presence. The retelling of what happened to them connects audience members to Elionai and Juan Gabriel and motivates some listeners to act as the press conference transforms into a rally and then also results in the formation of a commission to free Ramiro Aragón. This commission functioned at a high level for several months and resulted in dozens of activities and actions aimed at freeing Ramiro and other political prisoners. In this sense, "being there" is highly emotive for observers (see Juris). This connection continues for those who read Elionai's testimony and watch it on video.

Reactivation of Past Events

Related to the "witnessing" dimension of the scenario of Elionai's testimony at the press conference, the retelling of past events here brings them into the present, constituting what Taylor calls a "once-againness." Testimony has the ability to reactivate not only past events, but emotions linked to them and to attach those past emotions of the tellers to the present emotions of the listeners. In social movements, this can be a particularly powerful dimension of testimonies as they reconnect listeners/readers/observers to events that have already happened but which become alive again through the telling of testimony and can motivate some to want to act.

The analytical and methodological framework of the scenario as suggested by Taylor permits us to see how testimonials function in particular contexts and to also begin to see how they are connected to broader social contexts. Here we have observed how a testimonial can be linked to organizing actions in social movements, such as the commission to free Ramiro Aragón from prison in 2006. Elionai's testimony may also be connected to providing new and more complex versions of Oaxacan history about the social movement of 2006. Until December of 2010, the state government of Oaxaca was completely unwilling to take seriously or even listen to testimonies such as that of Elionai and hundreds of others, including the families of 23 people who were killed during 2006. The governor dismissed the reports of Amnesty International and other human rights groups as "tainted" and took no action to investigate murders and abuses. Currently, the state of Oaxaca has elected and installed a new governor, Gabino Cué, who pledged during his campaign to investigate the assassinations and human rights abuses committed in 2006 and to punish the guilty (Galo Samario). There are senators in the state legislature and social movements calling for an "Oaxacan Truth Commission" to investigate the crimes and assassinations that occurred during the social movement of 2006. Upon occupying the governor's seat on December 1, 2010, Cué discarded the idea of a truth commission. He did, however, state that he thought it was better to turn the job over to "someone with the necessary economic and investigative resources so that we can arrive at the political truth" ("Si no hay justicia"). While it is still unclear who that someone would be and what "political truth" means, it seems reasonable to assume that an investigative process will be undertaken and those who suffered human rights abuses will perhaps finally have an officially sanctioned legal forum for being heard. In the case of Elionai's testimonial, engaging in a scenario analysis with the elements suggested by Taylor permits us to see how the life of testimonials extends far beyond one event, one telling, or one text in terms of how they travel, work, and may resignify "the truth" and official and unofficial versions of history.

Conclusions

Structural analyses of the role of testimony in truth commissions suggest the limits to testimony and the tendency of truth commission culture to produce uniform narratives that de-emphasize larger political, economic, and social inequalities and emphasize individual victims. A focus on the experience of testifying for those who do it, the ways in which their testimonies function in broader social contexts, and the possibilities offered by broadening the official historical record can lead us to a more optimistic reading of the impact of testimony in legal venues and beyond. Part of this analytical refocusing requires rethinking the epistemological assumptions we bring to the table in terms of what counts as evidence and what we actually learn from testimony in terms of how and why people remember events in certain ways, and valuing the insights we gain from contested and multiple histories and truths. If we explore the role of language and testimony historically in Latin America, particularly in indigenous communities, we see that testimony functions through multiple channels—written, oral, and performative. I have suggested here that a performance studies approach, such as that of the scenario proposed by Diana Taylor, can yield fruitful insights into how testimonials function in social movements. This approach allows us to see how people deploy their repertoire of knowledge and memory through testimony in particular events and also how testimonies deployed in specific events are then transmitted and archived in multiple forms that may influence processes of organization, identity creation and contestation, and official and unofficial discourses and ideas about history and society.

Notes

1. United Nations Secretary-General defines transitional justice as "the full range of processes and mechanisms associated with a society's attempts to come to terms with a legacy of large-scale past abuses in order to ensure accountability, serve social justice and achieve reconciliation. These may include judicial and non-judicial mechanisms, with differing levels of international involvement (or none at all) and individual prosecutions, reparations, truth seeking, institutional reform, vetting, and dismissals or a combination thereof" (Parmar et al., xviii).
2. In his book, Stoll suggested that Menchú had not personally witnessed or experienced directly all that she wrote about in her 1983 testimonial and that this raised questions about the objective truth value of her testimonial.

Works Cited

Anderson, Benedict. *Imagined Communities: Reflections on the Origin and Spread of Nationalism*. London: Verso, 1983. Print.

Arias, Arturo, and Alicia del Campo. "Introduction: Memory and Popular Culture." *Latin American Perspectives* 36.5 (2009): 3–20. Print.

Bellinghausen, Hermann. "Torturó la policía a dos maestros acusados de portación de armas. Reaparecen en Oaxaca dos profesores con huellas de torturas." *La Jornada*. DEMOS, Desarrollo de Medios. Aug. 13, 2006. Web. Nov. 2010.

Certeau, Michel de. *The Writing of History*. Trans. Tom Conley. New York: Columbia UP, 1988. Print.

de la Rosa Medina, Tómas. "PIB per cápita de mexicanos en 21.5 dólares diarios: Oaxaca tiene un ingreso por persona igual a Argelia, Bielorrusia, Serbia o Túnez." *El Semanario*. Prensa de Negocios. Nov. 23, 2006. Web. Oct. 2010.

Farriss, Nancy. *Maya Society under Colonial Rule: The Collective Enterprise of Survival*. Princeton: Princeton UP, 1984. Print.

Faudree, Paja. *Singing for the Dead: The Politics of Ethnic Revival in Mexico.* Durham: Duke UP, forthcoming. Print.

Felman, Shoshona, and Dori Laub. *Testimony: Crises in Witnessing in Literature, Psychoanalysis and History.* New York: Routledge, 1992. Print.

Galo Samario, Agustín. "Se indagarán asesinatos cometidos en el conflicto de Oaxaca de 2006: Gabino Cué." *La Jornada.* DEMOS, Desarrollo de Medios. July 10, 2010. Web. Sept. 2010.

Grandin, Greg, and Thomas Miller Klubock, eds. "Truth Commissions: State Terror, History, and Memory." Spec. issue of *Radical History Review* 97 (2007): 1–184. Print.

Greer, Thomas. "An Analysis of Mexican Literacy." *Journal of Inter-American Studies* 11.3 (1969): 466–76. JSTOR. Web. Nov. 2010.

Jelin, Elizabeth, and Susana G. Kaufman. "Layers of Memories: Twenty Years after in Argentina." *The Politics of War Memory and Commemoration.* Ed. Ashplant, Dawson, and Roper. New York: Routledge, 2000. 89–110. Print.

Juris, Jeffrey. "Performing Politics: Image, Embodiment, and Affective Solidarity during Anti-Corporate Globalization Protests." *Ethnography* 9.1 (2008): 61–97. Print.

King, Linda. *Roots of Identity: Language and Literacy in Mexico.* Stanford: Stanford UP, 1994. Print.

Latour, Bruno. *Pandora's Hope: Essays on the Reality of Science Studies.* Cambridge: Harvard UP, 1999. Print.

Laub, Dori. "Bearing Witness or the Vicissitudes of Listening." *Testimony: Crises of Witnessing in Literature, Psychoanalysis and History.* Ed. Shoshona Felman and Dori Laub. New York: Routledge, 1992. 57–74. Print.

LIMEDDH (Liga Mexicana por la Defensa de los Derechos Humanos). "Relato de Tortura en Oaxaca: Relato de Elionai Santiago Sánchez y Juan Gabriel Ríos." *Liga Mexicana por la Defensa de los Derechos Humanos.* espora.org. Aug. 13, 2006. Web. Dec. 2010.

"List of Mexican States by Literacy Rate." *Wikipedia.* Wikimedia Foundation, March 10, 2010. Web. Oct. 2010.

Mallon, Florencia. "Bearing Witness in Hard Times: Ethnography and Testimonio in a Postrevolutionary Age." *Reclaiming the Political in Latin American History: Essays from the North.* Ed. Gilbert Joseph. Durham: Duke UP, 2001. 311–54. Print.

Mantilla Falcón, Julissa. "The Peruvian Truth and Reconciliation Commission's Treatment of Sexual Violence against Women." *Human Rights Brief* 12.2 (2005): 1–4. Print.

Nance, Kimberly A. *Can Literature Promote Justice? Trauma Narrative and Social Action in Latin American Testimonio.* Nashville: Vanderbilt UP, 2006. Print.

"Oaxaca: Clamor for Justice." *Amnesty International Canada.* Amnesty International, July 31, 2007. Web. Sept. 2010, http://www.amnesty.ca/amnestynews/upload/amr41312007.pdf.

Parmar, Sharanjeet et al. "Introduction." *Children and Transitional Justice: Truth-telling, Accountability and Reconciliation*. Ed. Parmar et al. Cambridge: Human Rights Program-Harvard Law School, 2010. xv–xxvi. Print.

Rabasa, José. *Without History: Subaltern Studies, the Zapatista Insurgency, and the Specter of History*. Pittsburgh: U of Pittsburgh P, 2010. Print.

Ross, Fiona. *Bearing Witness: Women and the Truth and Reconciliation Commission in South Africa*. London: Pluto, 2002. Print.

——. "Using Rights to Measure Wrongs: A Case Study of Method and Moral in the Work of the South African Truth and Reconciliation Commission." *Human Rights in Global Perspectives: Anthropological Studies of Rights, Claims, and Entitlements*. Ed. Richard Ashby Wilson and Jon P. Mitchel. London: Routledge, 2003. 163–83. Print.

Sarkar, Bhaskar, and Janet Walker. *Documentary Testimonies: Global Archives of Suffering*. New York: Routledge, 2010. Print.

Sarlo, Beatriz. *Tiempo pasado: Cultura de la memoria y giro subjetivo. Una discusión*. Buenos Aires: Siglo Veintiuno, 2005. Print.

Seider, Rachel. "Rethinking Citizenship: Reforming the Law in Postwar Guatemala." *States of Imagination: Ethnographic Explorations of the Postcolonial State*. Ed. Thomas Blom Hansen and Finn Stepputat. Durham: Duke UP, 2001. 203–20. Print.

"Si no hay justicia no habrá paz en Oaxaca: Cué." *SDPnoticias.com*. SDPnoticias.com, December 1, 2010. Web. Dec. 2010.

SIPAZ. "Oaxaca en Datos. San Cristóbal de las Casas, México." *Sipaz.org*. Sipaz.org, April 24, 2010. Web. Aug. 2010.

Sommer, Doris. "No Secrets." *The Real Thing: Testimonial Discourse and Latin America*. Ed. Georg M. Gugelberger. Durham: Duke UP, 2006. 130–57. Print.

Stephen, Lynn. "Elionai Santiago Sánchez: Video Testimonial." July 7, 2007. *Making Rights a Reality: The Oaxaca Social Movement, 2006–Present. Digital Ethnography*. Chap. 3. U of Oregon, 2009. Web. Sept. 2010.

——. "The Rights to Speak and to be Heard: Women's Interpretations of Rights Discourses in the Oaxaca Social Movement." *Gender and Culture at the Limit of Rights*. Ed. Dorothy Hodgson. Philadelphia: U of Pennsylvania P, 2011. 161–80. Print.

Stern, Steve J. *Battling for Hearts and Minds: Memory Struggles in Pinochet's Chile, 1973–1988*. Durham: Duke UP, 2006. Print.

——. *Reckoning with Pinochet: The Memory Question in Democratic Chile: 1989–2006*. Durham: Duke UP, 2010. Print.

——. *Remembering Pinochet's Chile: On the Eve of London 1998*. Durham: Duke UP, 2004. Print.

Stoll, David. *Rigoberta Menchú and the Story of All Poor Guatemalans*. Boulder: Westview, 1999. Print.

Taylor, Diana. *The Archive and the Repertoire: Performing Cultural Memory in the Americas*. Durham: Duke UP, 2003. Print.

Taylor, Julie. "Body Memories: Aide-Memories and Collective Amnesia in the Wake of Argentine Terror." *Body Politics: Disease, Desire, and the Family.* Ed. Michael Ryan and Avery Gordon. Boulder: Westview, 1994. 192–203. Print.

Theidon, Kimberly. "Gender in Transition: Common Sense, Women, and War." *Journal of Human Rights* 6 (2007): 453–78. Print.

UNESCO Institute for Statistics. "World Adult Illiteracy Rates 2000: Latin America and the Caribbean (Selected Countries)." *UNESCO Institute for Statistics.* UNESCO, July 2002. Web. Dec. 13, 2010, http://www.uis.unesco.org/en/stats/statistics/ed/g_lit_amerique%20latine.jpg.

United Nations General Assembly. "Report of the Special Rapporteur on Extrajudicial, Summary, or Arbitrary Executions." By Phillip Alston. *Project on Extrajudicial Executions.* Addendum. Center for Human Rights and Global Justice, New York University School of Law, March 12, 2007. Web. Oct. 2010, http://www.extrajudicialexecutions.org/application/media/A_HRC_4_20_Add_1.pdf.

Chapter 7

Rumors as Testimonios of Insile in *La mujer en cuestión* (The Woman in Question) by María Teresa Andruetto

Corinne Pubill

During the 1976–1983 military regime in Argentina, many stories circulated about shocking violence and human rights violations, causing its citizens to become paralyzed by fear. Uncertainty and paranoia also created intense anxiety throughout Argentina's society.[1] Rumors began to circulate so wildly that people began to accuse each other of various heinous acts. Whereas rumors are often seen as insignificant, unreliable, and untrue, during this period in Argentina no rumor was insignificant. People were murdered, imprisoned, tortured, and disappeared merely on the basis of a rumor. While from an historical perspective we can now see how rumors played such a significant and often tragic role for the Argentinean people, curiously, contemporary scholars have overlooked this critical issue. Recently, the Argentinean writer María Teresa Andruetto used rumor as the central narrative device in her 2003 *La mujer en cuestión* (The Woman in Question).[2] In this essay, I present the double articulation of the anti-testimonio (rumors) as a collective representation of Argentinean memory (narrative text). I demonstrate how this complex dichotomy offers a new perspective on testimonio and how those rumors attest to the phenomenon of insile as an individual rather than a collective experience.

La mujer en cuestión consists of a series of *informes* (interviews) conducted by an investigator to establish what Eva Mondino did during the years of the military dictatorship. On a first reading, the text is presented as what could be called a parody of testimonio since it questions the aforementioned genre. The text fails to provide a unified and coherent code, and thus refuses to offer a cohesive vision of the woman in question. Many voices become rumors that contradict one another because the more that is said, the less is known. These polyphonic voices remain highly subjective, sometimes intentionally false or naively inaccurate, though sometimes probably true. The form of the narrative is consistent with the logic of rumors, unsettling the reader throughout the text due to the impossibility of finding "the" truth and by giving him or her the task of deciphering hidden messages. Through a subversive and underground form, the text creates a space that includes different voices and implicit suggestions. Upon creating a fragmented reality, the novel becomes even more confusing through its use of the clichés and stereotypes circulating within the social imaginary. These clichés and stereotypes, however, provide insights into the ideologies of various community members.

In these ways, the absence of clarity attracts attention and therefore interpolates the reader. The protagonist, Eva Mondino, has virtually no agency in the text. She appears in very few interviews and is primarily represented through mini-testimonios provided by people who have shared moments from her past or present. Whether it be from afar, or up close, those who have heard about her repeat what they have heard, thereby echoing rumors of rumors and creating more rumors ad infinitum. The end result is that the woman in question becomes doubly erased in the text. In this way, the testimonial condition is erased since she does not participate from a position of solidarity. She is not in charge of her representation and moreover is silenced by rumors. Based on the fragmented mini-testimonios that construct her trajectory, the woman seems to have distanced herself from society's expectation of her as a woman, the time in which she lived, her social class, and her Judaic background. The narrative voices attempt to condemn her as they present multiple interpretations and representations of Eva Mondino. Although mostly accused of being "subversive," she is also condemned as an accomplice of the military regime.

Turning to Georg Lúkacs's *Theory of the Novel*, he affirms that protagonists of the novel are inseparable from the narrative totality and the community they reflect. The hero gives sense to that reality thereby creating an ideal that he/she will pursue: "The inner form of the novel has been understood as the process of the problematic individual's journeying towards himself" (Lúkacs 80). We can imply from this that Eva Mondino does not comply with the classical category of the hero because, even though it is implied that she had dreams of freedom, she is unable to pursue that ideal since she is erased by the people who surrounded her. In this way, María Teresa Andruetto positions this mechanism of rumors as the main protagonist of her narrative. In this sense, *La mujer en cuestión* does not offer a traditional vision of Lukacs' definition of a novel, but rather offers distinctive voices of what can be seen as a testimonial narrative of insile.[3]

Rumors are fragmented and cannot be strictly considered testimonios of the reality they represent because they are not a written document, are ephemeral, and oftentimes conflictive since they serve to harm others. In written form and as a narrative device, rumors become the main character in the novel, and also, paradoxically, they provide an (anti) testimonial perspective. In order to better understand how Andruetto uses rumors, we must first examine how rumors function from an ideological standpoint.

The military government tried to counteract the proliferation of any political and cultural diversity that threatened their conservative ideas.[4] The news that later circulated in the media appeared encoded, and the recipients did their best to decode the information being reported on television, in newspapers and magazines, and on the radio. From this moment on, rumors proliferated as intertexts and, as such, these narratives managed to avoid censorship and archiving. The rumor encapsulated a secret that was revealed as it began to circulate among the populace. Dismantled by this rumor-making process, the coercive mechanisms of power failed to control the usually well-managed dominant cultural production field. This does not mean that these rumors depart ideologically from their origin; rather, they now fall into another category. Given these dynamics, rumor, along with its conspiratorial origins, changes status from classified to declassified, breaks silences, transforms, contradicts, and reproduces itself to create other informative texts. With the intention of discovering an indicator that explains what Eva Mondino has done and what "she would have never done" (Andruetto 100), the *informe* (report), which becomes the narration of the very same text, compiles testimonios that contradict themselves and therefore distort reality.[5] Unlike John Beverley's definition of testimonio as "a novel or a novella-length narrative in book or pamphlet form, told in the first person by a narrator who is also the real protagonist or witness of the events he or she recounts" (31), the narrative discourse, through rumors, acts as an anti-testimonio.

In order to delve into a more nuanced reading of the text, one must participate as an active reader, a sort of detective who reconstructs these stories in order to differentiate between the facts and the decoys given as much by the informants as by the investigator himself. The text in itself does not provide answers and we reach the end without knowing with certainty the protagonist's crime. The investigator lies and states that, on the one hand, he lacks "a complete and truthful image" of the protagonist, while on the other hand he states that he proposes to make "an adequate and complete image of the woman in question" (Andruetto 43). Here, the contradictions supplied by the investigator become clearer to the reader. In this regard, as Paul Ricoeur suggests, the text needs to be read with suspicion (27). Instead of questioning the validity of rumors, the narrative gives them a central role because they are a part of the power dynamics. This multiplicity of facts presented in *La mujer en cuestión* refers to the experiences lived by Argentineans during the military dictatorship. In this way, it becomes evident that no single past remains fixed in everyone's memory, but rather memory transforms during a process of collective construction in which testimonios intervene through rumors, impressions, objective information, and subjectivities.

It is important to reiterate that not only fear, but also envy, resentment, or the need for revenge perpetuate rumors. Rumors take on new forms since they are social phenomena accompanied by an emotional tension of relief and a justification for all that has transpired. They become a way to appease the consciousness of those who perpetuate rumors and allow them to understand the events unfolding before them. It also seems that in order for rumors to be effective, a certain level of complicity is needed. This complicity remains apparent in the person who generates the rumor or the one who receives it, or simply in the plausible connection between the speaker and the initiator of the rumors. The report does not expose horror and fear in either a direct or a graphic way, but instead it implies them.

Eva worked between 1975 and 1976 for a newspaper and attempted to show that she "was thinking in a different way" than she actually did for fear of being accused as subversive (Andruetto 18), demonstrating that those who disagree with the politics of the moment had to live in a "state of camouflage" (Pubill, "Insilio femenino" 146) if they wanted to continue working and not put their lives in danger. Instead of explaining that the woman in question lives in constant fear of being discovered, in insile, the textual voices attempt to justify her fear with unconvincing reasons, such as having to work late hours and travel home at night through the red-light districts. These rumors, delivered by the interviewees, try to assuage this anxiety by substituting it for the daily fears as understood by the general public. In other words, the real dread tends to be minimized by a large segment of society that prefers to accept any explanation for what it does not understand—as long as the clarification fills the void created by a government that hides from the public. In this way, these voices serve to exorcise uncertainty and evoke a sense of relief.

Only one voice, lucid and critical, stands out in the text and shows that fear is a consequence of the terror imposed by the "Falcón de la Federal" (The Federal Ford Falcon); that is, military power (Andruetto 19).[6] Lila, one of Eva's friends and her defender, explains "yes, once she confessed to me that she was petrified with fear" (18). Eva's ex-husband, Rodriguez, offers a counterpoint through an inappropriate and disconcerting comment when he says, "Fear? But she was never afraid of anything [...] when she slept with that guy she had no fear, and when she told me that night, they knew very well that I could have lost my temper, break her face into pieces, and still she had no fear" (19). This meddling by a character hostile towards Eva does not provide anything relevant for the understanding of the story, and instead serves to annoy the reader with a sexist viewpoint—a discursive strategy ubiquitous in the report. On the one hand, Eva is the direct victim of the tension between masculine and feminine, and, on the other, she represents those in danger of being suspected of subversion, who risk their lives to be unmercifully judged by those surrounding them.

In order for rumors to circulate, the person who articulates them assumes that the individual accused of these rumors is guilty and therefore this justifies what is happening to him or her. In order to find a common interest in the diffusion of rumors, scholars have identified a process called "the leveling" through which certain details are eliminated in order to emphasize the prejudices and the slogans circulating around the country (Allport and Postman 75). In other words, rumors feed on other rumors, like aphorisms that continue reproducing without the speaker or the receiver needing to find out the facts in the matter. They instead consider them as indisputable and they count them as givens. A passive complicity devoid of critical thinking is, in this way, ultimately exercised.

An example of this notion of leveling concerns Eva's partner, Aldo Banegas, who joins the Navy and disappears in March of 1976. The voices explain that "algo habrá hecho" (he must have done something) to deserve disappearance (Andruetto 113). Here again it is preferable to blame the Other rather than bring up the question of guilt. It is not important to know what Aldo Banegas did, nor what happened to him once they made him disappear, as evidenced by the textual shift to the discursive voices of society instead of focusing on issues of blame and victimization. The Argentinean expressions "algo habrán hecho" (they must have done something) or "por algo será" (there must be a reason) work to temporarily erase the fear that disappearances create in the collective consciousness. This perverse technique is used to justify unfolding events. Thus, rumors spread by the fault of those who passed them along to others. We should remember that the voices of the text, starting with the title and the first few pages of *La mujer en cuestión*, portray a conservative viewpoint and depict the main character suspiciously. This perspective serves to reinforce the idea that the rumors are based, once again, on the prejudices attributed to otherness, thus producing an appearance of knowledge as manipulated by power.

Following this line of questioning, in the beginning of 1976, after Aldo's disappearance, Eva has a violent altercation with a neighbor. Although not detailed in the text, this fact serves to highlight the danger posed by these types of confrontations (36). The various voices explain that "Maybe for the desire to fall into good graces of the authorities" there were those who "did all they could so that she would lose her job, her husband and her son" (41). In other words, the phenomenon of denouncing the Other clears their own name of any suspicion. During this period of military government repression, and just like other totalitarian regimes such as the Franco dictatorship, or Nazism, fear exists precisely because of society's participation in acts of violence such as denunciation, accusations, insults, and instigation of hatred towards diversity. The armed forces manipulate large social sectors such that the supposedly "good people" participate convincingly in the construction and the maintenance of the dictatorial state. Thus, rumors function like testimonios, but have the opposite effect in representing the other, since there is no space for the Other to speak.[7]

The topic of denunciation complements that of collaboration. If we return to the moment when Eva was desperately searching for Aldo, her first partner who disappeared, we find that she asked for information from a professor who was associated with the army and who agrees to her wishes under the condition that she sleep with him. As described earlier, competing textual voices call into question Eva's actions and make us doubt her integrity. These conflicts highlight her marginalization instead of foregrounding the importance to the professor's appalling behavior. Later, Eva starts seeing Rodriguez, who will become her husband in 1979. At first, it is understood that he had been in Campo de la Ribera (Ribera Camp).[8] Later Eva realizes that he knows too many details about her detention and therefore she begins to suspect his involvement with the torturers. Speculation arises as well that he had been extracting information from her during their marriage (105). Eva's friends explained that Rodriguez was a social climber who ascended too quickly in the 1980s, which means that once again Eva is victimized and betrayed by those around her. Regardless, other voices doubt Eva's innocence and depict her as an accomplice to her husband's actions. It is important to highlight what Fernando Reati says when referring to Andruetto's work:

> Her supposed betrayal pales in the face of the acts of mini-collaboration with the regime carried out by many of those same, ordinary citizens who now condemn her as a traitor, once democracy has returned. Among them are the fearful neighbor who wouldn't let her hide in her house, the lawyer who denounced her to the authorities, the professor who wanted her to sleep with him in exchange for information, and even her own parents, who wouldn't lend her money to flee the country.
>
> ("Torture and Abuse" 8)

In other words, as a means to maintain the channels of power, these voices condemn Eva and fail to consider the environment in which she was living. These social voices cast her aside once as a "fucking communist" because of her relationship with Aldo and then again as a "traitor or denouncer" (Andruetto 34), thus rejecting her on both fronts, emphasizing, again, the state of ostracism (insile) to which she must resort for her own survival.

Given that the protagonist is constructed by the interviewees, who suggest that she may or may not have done something without making direct accusations, the reader focuses on the motives for her actions. The conditions of Eva's life are presented throughout the report, especially her poverty and hunger. Some voices claim that lack of money justifies what she might have done. Others prefer to justify her acts of collaboration out of a need to know (in the sense of the Spanish verb, *saber*, to find out). For example, Lila, Eva's friend, concentrates on the state of panic surrounding her and explains that her cooperation with the current report is due to the fact that she still wants to know what happened, especially regarding Eva's son. Multiple and contradictory voices now focus on her son. To some, the boy was never born; for others, he died at birth; still others say he was kidnapped.

In order for these rumors to exist, they must be plausible. Later, for the rumor to continue, it must grow with information. To do this, some of the versions can be pragmatic, others moderately optimistic and hopeful, but all must be devoid of any factual foundation. The text becomes obscure because defenders and detractors of the issue at hand are mixed together. The facts presented, uncorroborated and imprecise, complicate any understanding that what matters is not what actually happened to Eva or her son, but rather refer to the different interpretations of what could have happened to many of the children born in captivity. All rumors tend to be denied, qualified, or alter primary information. If the main point of the rumor was accepted as indisputable, then the rumor would disappear and the facts would surface as confirmed and validated. The report ends with the following:

> According to the number and the study of the numerous testimonios and documents that have been obtained and evaluated during the course of the current investigation, this informant [the investigator] finished the current publication with a few truths: In effect, Eva Mondino had a son (N. of I.: this informant assumes the risk in considering that indeed she did have one since the witnesses in her defense on the matter are sufficient in number) and this son, still following the same hypothesis, came into the world on the night of October 29, 1976, four days after she was detained.
>
> (111)[9]

In this way, the text validates Eva Mondino's struggle, closing with a key element that squelches the rumor.

Rumor takes part in an oral or written text that predates it and then constantly updates itself through acts of enunciation. In order to spread rumors, one must believe that the information provided is true and therefore attempts to convince the recipient of its validity. Rumor is not necessarily negative or false since it seeks "a" truth and interprets it in order to create new enunciations, which are different from the initial rumor. In this respect, one must again consider the power of rumor. It can displace official versions and create new social and subaltern spaces that resist power, criticize the system, and can become, once transformed, fuel for hope. Gayatri Chakravorty Spivak points out that "It is more appropriate to think of the power of rumor in the subaltern context as deriving from its participation in the structure of illegitimate writing rather than the authoritative writing of the law" (214). Since the subaltern cannot speak, one must strategically read the syndrome of rumor as a heterogeneous or subversive technique. In this context, the power of the spoken word outweighs the written word. Rumors can be understood as anti-testimonial in that they are mainly oral, have no clear agent of enunciation, and lead to the alienation of the Other, as seen in *La mujer en cuestión*.

As such, rumors can be understood as a condition or representation of insile and the text itself becomes a testimonial narrative. The abstract concept of insile becomes literal for, once out of Campo de la Ribera, Eva remains under surveillance and lives in constant fear:

"Freedom is a way of saying it," because she was "under conditional freedom" [...] and "they required her to confine herself to her house," [to stay for] ... months without stepping outside of the door, with an atrocious fear of everything and everyone [...] but she did not want to talk, she was silent, hours on end watching from the window of her patio without saying a word.

(80–81)

In other words, she suffers displacement from prison to insile. In order to survive and control the horrific terror imposed by the military, she resorts to self-ostracization, a state of silence, and permanent hiding. She could not fight in an active way nor share her pain with anyone since she was isolated from society. Rumors, which led to her detention and torture, had a strong impact on her condition of insile. Eva's isolated condition brings to mind Fernando Reati's study of former exiles or former detainees of the 1990s: "once in democracy, they lived with their memories, unable to adapt to their new post dictatorship lives, giving the impression of estrangement, alienation and of not belonging" ("Exilio" 185). After separating from Rodriguez in 1984, Eva lives in a state of isolation and confinement, unable to live in a global world, preferring to buy from small shops rather than the supermarket. She even sells from home and harvests her own food. Once disconnected from the world and retired to the countryside, she lives a simple life and stays on the outskirts of society. She opts for forgetting, hiding in herself "to erase from her life what happened that afternoon" (Andruetto 33). Betrayed by many of her friends, her neighbors, her own family, and even her husband, she seems to have changed and "no longer understands the world in which she lives" (112).

Insile comprises people who live under difficult conditions, such as being hungry, disconnected from their familiar environment, losing their job for ideological reasons, suffering the loss of a loved one because of the military dictatorship, feeling obligated to be someone else, hiding political opinions, and living hidden away for fear of insults and the sheer terror inspired by denunciations. We can clearly state that Eva, alienated from the evolution of society, lived and continues to live in a state of trauma and disillusionment. Moreover, her emotional pain and psychological state are difficult to measure since she cannot share these aspects of self. Confronted with her own solitude, silence and invisibility become her only weapons for survival and resistance. The central idea of this work can be summarized in the following quote from the text: "before, when I was with Aldo, I was happy, because we were young, because we had plans... because we believed in a better world... but all of this is over. After what happened, we had to suffer what is not written" (113).

It is exactly in what is not written that we must read *La mujer en cuestión*. Throughout this work, the investigator manipulates information by intercalating sequences of confusing facts about the protagonist, contradictory voices, mixing up flashbacks, imposing textual gaps, and distributing silences that upset a coherent meaning about the woman in question. In this "no saber" (not knowing), one must accept the impossibility of achieving any certainty of meaning. Orlando Mondino, Eva's brother and informant, commented that Eva "[b]uilt, to put in one word, a character that said she did not know what she knew, forgot what was necessary to forget, invented names and places" (81). The dilemma of "el decir o no decir" (to speak or not to speak) within a civil society regarding what they know or do not know corresponds to the incomplete image of the protagonist. Eva is "multifaceted and changing" and "gives the impression of having lived various lives" (32). Through multiple voices, and more specifically through rumors, Eva embodied different versions of reality. The phrase, "She is one person but in reality she is many," shows that Eva's memory is added to Argentina's collective memory (31). This sentence reflects Rigoberta Menchú's affirmation that "[m]y personal experience is the reality of a whole people" (1). As Beverley states, Menchú's text is written from the classical testimonial "I" perspective and "[e]ach individual testimonio evokes an absent polyphony of other voices, other possible lives and experiences. Thus, one common formal variation on the classic first-person singular testimonio is the polyphonic testimonio, made up of accounts by different participants in the same event" (34).

María Teresa Andruetto offers an alternative form of testimonio. Her text erases the presence of a narrator and eliminates the voice of her fictional protagonist, who remains silenced. Here the testimonial voice takes place through Eva, the victim of denunciation. Rumors take the place of a narrative voice in order to represent a fractured and marginalized reality that seeks to be recognized and acknowledged. In this way, stories of insile are inscribed and finally represented thanks to the fact that a testimonial impetus requires "an ironic distancing on the part of both novelist and reader from the fate of the protagonist" (Beverley 35). Nevertheless, this testimonial text gives voices to the unheard civilians who had to live under insile, oppressed and invisible under other dominant forms of representation, while also portraying the shame that these anonymous voices had evoked from the insiled person.

Beverley notes that "[w]hat gives form and meaning to those events, what makes them *history*, is the relation between the temporal sequence of those events and the sequence of the life of the narrator, articulated in the verbal structure of the testimonial text" (4). Even if rumors give voice to others and function as anti-testimonio, silence constitutes the narrative text and testifies to the personal experience of María Teresa Andruetto's insile. Of note is that María Teresa Andretto started studying literature at the University of Córdoba in 1971, where she also was a militant student. In 1975, she had to live in insile until after the dictatorship, hiding for four years in the backroom of an hotel. She was not able to see the light and therefore lived in an inside prison, secluded from the outside world in order to save her own life and protect herself from denunciation and the constant fear of the likely possibility of being detained.

La mujer en cuestión, written through fragmented discourses that can disturb and unsettle the reader, becomes a political narrative of resistance that shows the urgency of knowing one part of Argentina's past, since official history still overshadows the case of the "insiliados" (insiled ones). As we have seen, the text problematizes the traditional spectrum of the definition of the novel and uses the format of a "true" report. This report blends rumors and confusion—half way between real and imaginary—in order to emphasize the structure of rumors over literary effects, thereby transforming the text into a "pledge of honesty," as Beverley understood it (33). In this case, the effect of fiction is erased to convert itself into a new testimonial form since it is the only way that the story can be told.

To conclude, this essay has unveiled a discursive space to speak for a reality that has not been examined in Argentina. María Teresa Andruetto, in *La mujer en cuestión*, questions, through the use of rumors, the veracity of testimonio and validates the notion of different truths and authenticities. In this sense, the text responds to Beverley's statement that "testimonio certainly has the effect of making subaltern experience and voice into something that 'matters'" (xvi). *La mujer en cuestión* shows the complexity of living in a permanent state of fear and suspicion, and offers a new way of imagining the identity and the agency of those who have not yet had a voice in society.

Beverley also notes that "[w]hat is at stake in testimonio is not so much the truth *from* or *about* the other as the truth *of* the other. What I mean by this is the recognition not only that the other exists as something outside ourselves, not subject to our will or desires, but also of the other's sense of what is true and what is false" (Beverley 7). In the novel, rumors convey different life experiences, present marginalized voices, do not have a fixed narrative creator, and are orally transmitted from one person to another. Rumors distance themselves from various power structures and successfully represent a number of silenced voices that are marginalized within certain sectors of society.

If we follow this logic, we can certainly consider that Andruetto's text, through rumors, becomes an active testimonio in constant mutation, one that questions the notion of literature and provides a slice of the reality lived by a large part of Argentinean society in an era marked by extreme violence. Pilar Calveiro notes that "[s]ociety is multiple and within it the powers of submission and resistance circulate" (97). Along these lines, the person who lives in insile becomes an alienated "yo" (I), disassociated and broken, ultimately becoming an object of the unrelenting dynamic of rumors.

Rumors represent a means of transgression since they evoke disagreement and resistance, but also adhesion and conformity, as they are trapped between two antagonistic discourses. Each person who spreads rumors maintains a different relationship with power and the history of what they contain, since everyone provides his or her own vision, ideologies, and creates a new version of the facts. These interdiscourses exist in a process of continuous construction and exceed the discursive in representing the social imaginary.[10] *La mujer en cuestión* appears as an "extraliterary or even antiliterary form of discourse" that contests the dominant system (Beverley 42) and shows how rumors are the means with which *insiliados* convey their reality. Although those voices have not yet found an official place in history, María Teresa Andruetto's narrative conjures up memories of an oppressed and marginalized group of insiled people who seek social change through an innovative permutation of testimonial writing.

Notes

1. One can only understand the author's use of rumors, so central to this narrative, by placing Andruetto's text within the historical and political context of the Argentinean military regime during the years 1976 to 1983. The military junta used terror to dismantle groups that they considered "terrorists" but also murdered civilians who,

according to them, represented a "danger" to the security of the country (CONADEP 480). It was under this oppressive climate that more than 360 concentration camps were created all over the country. Many Argentineans had no other option than to remain silent, live in insile or exile, or collaborate with the regime. The state armed itself with repressive techniques, and invented a discourse that "denied, justified, transformed, and lied with the intent to distance citizens from the horrific circumstances under which they were living" (Lopez Laval 99). State terrorism fueled fear mainly through the press. The government used a very explicit and official language to justify the introduction of a supposedly healing and spiritual plan; the true purpose of which was to purify and cleanse the country of dissidents. This mistaken discourse reflected the hypocrisy of a manipulative government for whom the end justified the means. The junta never mentioned that they were partly guilty of so much horror, and instead maintained that in a dysfunctional country the blame lies with the *Other*, the so-called subversive (44). For more information, see Lopez Laval's *Autoritarismo y Cultura*.
2. The Argentinean María Teresa Andretto was born in 1954 in Arroyo Cabal in Córdoba. She published her first novel, *Tama*, in 1992. In 2009, *La mujer en cuestión* was republished. A Cordoban branch of the famous theater troupe called Teatro por la Identidad (Theater for Identity), the Balbuceando Teatro (The Babbling Theater), adapted her text for the stage in 2009 in a play called "Diría nadie la última palabra" ("Nobody Would Say the Last Word"). The Theater for Identity is an active group of actors, writers, and directors who perform plays in order to help the Grandmothers of the Plaza de Mayo (May Plaza) find children who were disappeared under the dictatorship.
3. I defined the word insile in an article published in *Romance Notes*, "Insilio femenino y la representación de la memoria en la obra de Andruetto" ("Feminine Insile and the Representation of Memory in the Work of Andruetto"). An interview with María Teresa Andruetto can also be found in *Hispamérica* (2009) where she explains that "[a]n 'insiliado' is a person who hides and lives in an 'auto-prison,' like Julia in *Lengua Madre* (*Mother Tongue*) who had to hide in a confined space for years. There are also those who hide in social anonymity, people who are aware of what is going on in the country and with some political visibility, and who have to live a very limited secluded life, very limited, full of scarcities, since they lost or abandoned their jobs, their dreams, their social life, and so many things, for years" (57).
4. It should be noted that the military junta indeed expressed the thinking of an important sector of society: a social class that made a clean sweep of the country's resources in order to become rich. In this sense, the military junta was doing the dirty work for this social class, as represented by certain circles of the farming oligarchy and the neoliberal bourgeoisie.

5. All translations of *La mujer en cuestión* are mine.
6. The "Falcon" refers to the green Ford Falcon automobiles used by the federal agents.
7. See Gayatri Chakravorty Spivak's, "Can the Subaltern Speak?"
8. Campo de la Ribera was an illegal detention center on the outskirts of Córdoba, Argentina. In this "chupadero" (secret military prison) the military practiced torture, illegal executions, as well as taking babies from imprisoned mothers. Since 2010, this space has been a museum called *Space for Memory*.
9. "N. of I." means "Note of Informant."
10. Michel Foucault analyzes these kinds of interdiscourses in *Archeology of Knowledge* (66). Additionally, Jean-Noël Kapferer in *Rumeurs* posits that researchers do not study rumors but rather the memory that has been left on people by rumors (11). Kapferer contradicts previous studies on rumors and concludes that rumors are "not necessarily false, but are necessarily non-official," since they sometimes contest the official reality and offer another reading of this reality (303).

Works Cited

Andruetto, María Teresa. *La mujer en cuestión*. Buenos Aires: Alción, 2003. Print.
Beverley, John. *Testimonio: On the Politics of Truth*. Minneapolis: U of Minnesota P, 2004. Print.
Calveiro, Pilar. *Poder y desaparición: Los campos de concentración en Argentina*. Buenos Aires: Colihue, 2006. Print.
CONADEP. *Nunca más*. Buenos Aires: Eudeba, 1999. Print.
Foucault, Michel. *Archeology of Knowledge*. New York: Pantheon, 1969. Print.
Kapferer, Jean-Noël. *Rumeurs: Le plus vieux média du monde*. Paris: Seuil, 1987. Print.
López Laval, Hilda. *Autoritarismo y cultura*. Buenos Aires: Fundamentos, 1995. Print.
Lúkacs, Georg. *The Theory of the Novel*. Cambridge: MIT, 1971. Print.
Menchú, Rigoberta. *I, Rigoberta Menchú: An Indian Woman in Guatemala*. Ed. Elisabeth Burgos-Debray. Trans. Anne Wright. New York: Verso, 1984. Print.
Pubill, Corinne. "Insilio femenino y la representación de la memoria en la obra de Andruetto." *Romance Notes* 49.2 (2009): 143–53. Print.
———. "Interview: María Teresa Andruetto." *Hispamérica* 111 (2009): 63–74. Print.
Reati, Fernando. "Exilio tras exilios en Argentina: vivir en los noventa después de la cárcel y el destierro." *Aves de paso: autores latinoamericanos entre exilio y transculturación (1970–2002)*. Ed. Birgit Mertz-Baumgartner and Erna Pfieffer. Madrid/Frankfurt: Iberoamericana/Vervuert, 2005. 185–96. Print.

———. "Torture and Abuse as a National Art Form: *Auschwitz*, by Gustavo Nielsen." *Violence in Argentine Literature and Film (1989–2005)*. Ed. Carolina Rocha and Elizabeth Montes Garcés. Calgary: U of Calgary P, 2010. 3–17. Print.

Ricoeur, Paul. *Freud and Philosophy: An Essay on Interpretation*. New Haven: Yale UP, 1970. Print.

Spivak, Gayatri Chakravorty. "Can the Subaltern Speak?" *The Post-Colonial Studies Reader*. Ed. Bill Ashcroft, Gareth Griffiths, and Helen Tiffin. New York: Routledge, 1995. 24–28. Print.

Valdés Deluis, Francisco. "Psico-Sociología del Rumor." *Revista Mexicana de Sociología* 22.1 (1960): 77–88. Print.

Chapter 8

Accomplishing "Tellable-Tellings": Managing Displays of Faith on Live Radio

Melissa Guzman

Many scholars have employed the study of testimonio as a critical method for examining and understanding the relationship between narrative and social change (Beverley, "Testimonio" 547). Although there is no universal definition of testimonio, it can be characterized as a "novel or novella-length narrative" in "printed form" told by a narrator who has directly experienced or witnessed a significant life situation (Beverley, "The Margin" 12–13). Testimonio is also a "narración de urgencia" (an urgent narrative) to the extent that it involves "a problem of repression, poverty, marginality, exploitation, or simply survival that is implicated in the action of narration itself" (Beverley, "Testimonio" 556). Yúdice, for instance, describes testimonio as "authentic narrative, told by a witness who is moved to narrate by the urgency of a situation" (17). This treatment of testimonio implies a particular relationship between the textual narrative and its reader. In effect, testimonio invites its audience to become ethically and epistemologically involved in recounted struggles.[1] Testimonio, as a social project, entails that speakers break out of external and governmental containment strategies that determine what they can say, when, how, and to whom (Nance 570). Simultaneously, in the study of testimonio, readers and analysts are confronted with an agent who is involved in a "transformative project" of gaining a voice and a sense of representation (Beverley, "Testimonio" 548).

Testimonio has been understood to be a mediated narrative—the result of a speaker who tells her story to an interlocutor, an intellectual or professional, who then edits and textualizes the account (Beverley, "Through All Things" 4; Nance 586). This has led scholars of testimonio to contend that the process of mediating, gathering, and editing testimonial narratives is fraught with complications.[2] Still, the collaborative nature of testimonios can have the potential for interrogating "the hierarchical structures of power implicit in literature as a cultural institution" (Harlow 11). Testimonio involves the scratching out of the function and thus also of the powerful presence of the "author" that to a large extent defines most major forms of Western literary and academic writing (Beverley, "Testimonio" 548). Ultimately, testimonio has the capacity to challenge dominant conventions of what constitutes literary value and discourse "as such."

My perspective on testimonio complements existing approaches by employing sociology and the findings of conversation analysis (CA) to explore the process through which a telling is produced between a speaker and her interlocutor. In this way, this work enriches what many scholars of testimonio have acknowledged about testimonios: their rootedness in everyday language. Eliana Rivero, for instance, has noted that "the act of speaking faithfully recorded on the tape, transcribed and then 'written,' remains in the *testimonio* punctuated by a repeated series of interlocutive and conversational markers" (220). Similarly, Rebeca Atencio's work on *escritura da exclusão* (writing of exclusion) contends that one of the hallmarks of the testimonial genre is the "inherent orality of the narrative" (279). The text that becomes the object of analysis for scholars of testimonio consists of an edited transcript of a recorded oral narrative that retains some of the features of everyday, spoken language (Atencio 279). The spoken mediations between a testimonio's speaker and its "editor," then, have a significant role in the narrative project of testimonio, especially in shaping how it is responded to by its audience (Nance 572). This essay examines how speaking subjects and their interlocutor manage the telling of religious testimonios told on a live, Spanish-speaking, religious radio program called *Cambiando Vidas*.

Cambiando Vidas (Changing Lives)

Cambiando Vidas is a radio program broadcast on a network called Radio Nueva Vida (New Life Radio), the first 24-hour religious

Spanish-language station in California. *Cambiando Vidas* represents the religious narratives of Latina/os in Evangelical Christian and Catholic faiths. Although the show is sponsored by a nonprofit Evangelical Christian media network, it also attracts many Catholic Latina/o audiences throughout the United States—especially in California. The religious testimonios people tell as part of this radio community provide a social institution within which people build, negotiate, patrol, and otherwise manage boundaries, standards, and values important to them. In their testimonios, callers share stories about illnesses, emotional affliction, bureaucratic paperwork, attaining legal status in the United States, deportation, driving broken cars, unemployment, et cetera. In certain respects, the troubles reported in the testimonios are universal to all human experience. However, many of the troubles reported by callers are predominately based in the precarious legal/socioeconomic status of Latino/as in the United States—that is, having financial problems, being undocumented, not having a driver's license or bank account, and not having access to health care.

Evaluating the narrative process that occurs within *Cambiando Vidas*, this essay pays close attention to both the actions that callers launch in telling their testimonios and how the host, in turn, negotiates these interactions. I have first compiled a body of recorded, testimonial narratives told on a live radio program, then transcribed the mediations between callers and the host.[3] This essay employs sociology and CA to analyze the mediation processes (as a set of talk interactions) that occur within the radio program. In turn, it provides a turn-by-turn transcript of five recorded extracts of interactions occurring between the host and callers on *Cambiando Vidas*.

Sociology, CA, and Religious Testimonios

Theological approaches to religious testimony identify many of the same elements noted by scholars of testimonio. Theologians have primarily analyzed religious testimonies by focusing on their content, in which people correlate their personal experiences with their understanding of their faith and its presuppositions (Pedraja 10). For theologians, testimonies are vehicles for articulating religious experiences and God's presence in one's life. This perspective treats testimonies as a finished textual object with which people make analytical judgments (Dorfman 134; Pedraja 16). Theology argues that religious testimonies are not mere accounts of events, but descriptions of how a person lives. As such, they can have an immense impact on both the life of the person doing the telling and her audience—the broader religious community (Aponte et al. 200). In theological accounts, testimonies have an active potential for expressing people's faith in God, are central to a community's worship practices, and have the power to articulate a lived sense of theology (Gonzalez 53). The validity of religious expressions in the form of testimonies is based primarily on their ability to help maintain the faith of those who listen, as well as to motivate hope and witness the role of the Holy Spirit in a religious community through a telling (53). This theological account of religious testimonies, like much scholarship on testimonio, leaves the actual interactional contexts in which testimonies are produced, and the social processes through which they are monitored and responded to, relatively unexamined.

The following sections describe how sociology can contribute to our understanding of testimonio. One fundamental concern in sociology has been to study people through social institutions and interactions between individuals and social structures (Durkheim 245). Social interactions matter because they measure how systems of norms organize identities, values, and roles in normative contexts such as the family, government, and religion. Erving Goffman observed that the social organization of interaction constitutes a sui generis social institution (13). This makes the social organization of interaction a significant matter for sociology because it is a main point of production for most other social institutions and other social phenomena (Raymond 939). Consequently, how people use language in interaction becomes one of the most important resources for understanding social action (939).

On *Cambiando Vidas,* the actual telling of a testimonio is relevant for displaying religious belonging. Thus, I examine a set of different methods by which participants of this religious community patrol the telling of religious testimonios. The monitoring of religious tellings on this radio program subtly shapes how speakers conform to the visible boundaries of their religious communities. The real-time production of religious testimonios as a site for managing and patrolling their validity is crucial to understanding their import for the everyday practices of the religious communities in which such testimonios are produced and used by members. I draw out the implications by tracking how participants manage the practices by which testimonios are organized on a live broadcast and by examining the ways in which people accomplish "tellable tellings."

A crucial starting point for analyzing the testimonios told on *Cambiando Vidas* is to frame the program as an institutional context.

Applying the findings of CA to better understand how institutional settings work shows how participants' practices produce various features of institutionality (Drew and Heritage 3). A major feature of institutionality is its goal orientedness (Drew and Heritage 23; Schegloff 102). The "institutionality" of this show involves the actions of speakers who can achieve "tellable tellings" or can tell testimonios that appropriately convey God's presence in their lives and manage the host's assessments, appreciations, and interventions in relation to this goal. The situations that callers report in their testimonios vary in relation to how these are understood and negotiated by the host. In this sense, she serves as an official representative of this institutional context and mediates the interactions by which callers tell their testimonios on this show (Drew and Heritage 24). Simultaneously, callers also have particular goals—giving thanks and seeking help—and in this way, actively participate in the reception of their testimonios.

Cambiando Vidas remains unique as an institutional domain of interaction in that the telling of testimonios in this context invokes the everyday struggles of people who are seeking help from the divine. *Cambiando Vidas* provides its participants with the opportunity to engage in actions that negotiate how to appropriately and legitimately talk about the role of God in human life. Although these negotiations can be launched in a range of ways, the subsequent sections emphasize three main points: (1) the kind of actions testimonios are launching; (2) the types of experiences callers attribute to God; and (3) the report of trouble as an indication of having a strong faith or doubt. This essay explores how speakers, as they interact with the host of this radio program in telling their testimonios, manage the constraints set by the show as an institution with particular goals for the content and delivery of live testimonios. Speakers must negotiate a range of constraints as they give thanks and seek help from God in their testimonios. With few exceptions, the radio program largely consists of callers who use the occasion for reporting a resolved trouble in their lives, to give thanks to God, and display a strong religious faith. Testimonios, however, are also employed to report unresolved situations of struggle. This discussion of the interactional context of testimonios features five excerpts of different tellings in which callers give thanks to God on air and request help from the host of *Cambiando Vidas*. Focusing on the interactional contexts of testimonios reveals how "tellable tellings" result from the narrators' management of their speech in relation to how they might be assessed, namely, as adequate and legitimate participants of particular religious ways of sense-making.

Testimonio Organization

This first case illustrates the principal way that callers and the host participate in organizing a testimonio within the context of *Cambiando Vidas,* exemplifying how a successful testimonio is formulated. Elena thanks God for healing her heart problems. One of the primary interactional features in Extract One is that after Elena's main report, the host's brief follow-up responses confirm the act of gratitude found in her testimonio.[4] Elena's testimony is composed as a story. This narrative recounting is designed to give praise and thanks for God's work in her life, as projected in its preface and as reflected in the story's conclusion in which the caller reports the restoration of her health.

E: So God has been wonderful, good with me.

H: Yes.

E: He brought me to this country and gave me the residency, and then gave me citizenship, right. And he has been so good, so merciful and has healed me so many times. Recently he's healed my heart because they told me it was too big and since I went went with a heart specialist but since I was being charged too much right so I put everything in God's hands and I gave, part of what I was going to give in my second visit, I gave it to the church where I go right, I gave it to God for his deed and God healed me sister. I have a healthy heart, I don't feel anything.

For callers, religious practices like telling testimonios facilitate a deeper understanding and awareness of the societal conditions they face as immigrants in the United States. Testimonios not only make speakers aware of their conditions as immigrants in the United States, but also provide an opportunity to make sense of these conditions in that being a legal citizen is, indeed, a divine blessing. Elena's certainty regarding her interpretation of events like coming to the United States and attaining her residency and citizenship papers treats these experiences as a default understanding that God is responsible for the outcomes in her life. Elena's report of heart trouble treats the situation as already resolved and reports this resolution as part of the telling. In this way, Elena's narrative conveys thanks for the help she has received for a series of events and circumstances beyond her control. In her response, the host's idiomatic expression recognizes the completion of Elena's testimonio (Drew and Holt 117), while her selection of a religiously oriented idiom specifically ratifies the spiritual element of her testimonio.

H: Glory to God.

E: No bothers like before.

H: Good.

E: Yes sister, God has healed me and has been very good and very merciful with me and with all my family.

H: That's nice Elena. And God will keep doing greater things in your life.

...

H: Especially for those who trust and who believe in him.

Elena agrees with the host's recognition of her story's gratitude and elaborates by extending the scope of her thanks for God being merciful. The host provides further appreciation via a summative evaluation of Elena's story and an assessment that casts a future orientation to further blessings.

In the telling of testimonios, both the host and the callers assume responsibility for articulating and negotiating God's intervention in resolving certain matters. The articulation of God's intervention, however, entails specifying which outcomes can be treated as resolved due to God's involvement. In Extract Two below, although the caller thanks God for a resolved issue, the host's response consists of both praise and advice.[5] At first, the host accepts María's formulation of God's intervention and agrees with her framing of the car stalling at a stop as a miracle.

M: And today I saw God's powerful hand because my car right on Van Nuys turned off at a stop sign. *God fixed everything so that it would be there* and I asked God, the car turned back on; I got to my house without having any accidents and I was able to take my daughter to school.

H: Glory be to God that's good, and good, it still turned off at a stop sign. Much better than running in the middle of traffic, María.

M: Yes.

The participants of this show must not only know how to convey God's power in spiritual matters, but also in the secular and common sense troubles of everyday life. What is most important about this excerpt is that we can observe the host's alignment with María's resolution. That is, the host glorifies God for María's car stalling at the stop sign (and not in traffic). María's car stalling at a stop sign under secular circumstances could not be treated as a resolved situation, but under a spiritual and religious framework of interpretation, that stalling was taken by the caller and host as a consequence of God's action. Yet, at the end of the call, the host begins to give advice when the resolution of María's reported problem can be fully assessed and reformulated at the end of her testimonio (Jefferson 220).

H: God is good but I think that we have to be wise and attend to the calls of attention, you have to fix that car.

M: Yes.

H: You have to do it. May God keep blessing you María, thank you for sharing with us.

As a second element to her response, the host reframes her response by indicating the car stall as a "call of attention" and not as a genuine resolution to driving a car that stalls. While reminding María that "God is good," the host reformulates María's articulations of God's power by casting the outcome of her story in common sense terms. Thus, through giving María practical car advice, the host casts her report of God's intervention in terms of personal responsibility and tells María to fix her car. After María's weak uptake of her initial advice, the host produces an upgraded statement by ordering Maria that she "has to do it." In responding to testimonios, the host may reformulate certain parts of the telling to mark what types of matters can be attributed to God. Although the host ratifies María's formulation of God's role in resolving a problem, she also modifies her praise by indicating the limits of seeing God's power in everyday problems. In this case, the host treats what the caller had attributed to God as a personal responsibility. This case is particularly important because the host produces advice and modifies the caller's testimonio in order to assert that people's faith must not blind them to their personal responsibilities.

These brief summaries demonstrate the organized practices through which religious testimonios are routinely produced and embodied in interaction within the context of *Cambiando Vidas*. The telling of resolved issues in their testimonios enables people to engage in a highly specialized type of activity: the giving of thanks for troubles that could possibly require God's help or intervention while allowing the host to manage callers' responses. In the next section, three cases report unresolved problems and show how both the host and the caller must adapt to the ensuing contingencies.

REQUESTS FOR HELP

The testimonios aired on *Cambiando Vidas* overwhelmingly achieve one action: giving thanks to God. However, the testimonios also report unresolved matters which consequently become an occasion for achieving a different action: asking for help. Below is an example of an unresolved situation in which both the host and caller must manage how faith in God gets displayed in a testimonio. This third extract is Alba's request for prayer for a son who is incarcerated and about to be deported.[6] Callers share narratives about their unresolved troubles while seeking spiritual help. Alba's request for help is positioned and given in addition to her ongoing testimonio. That requests for help are told along with an initial story shows that they have a status different from the action of giving thanks.

A: And I have a great faith in God that each time I feel something in my body, I kneel and I ask with all my heart, and he replies sister.

H: Amen, how nice.

A: Yes, and another thing sister, I wanted to ask, because they have just gotten my son, they've got him locked up in Houston, I wanted to request a prayer for him for the love of God.

H: What's his name, don't say his last name, but give me the name.

A: Yes, his name is David, and they're going to deport him.

By requesting Alba to provide her son's first name, the host prepares the ground for accepting Alba's prayer request—as prayers are individualized and specialized for the situation and person in question. Furthermore, Alba's prayer request consists of two justifications of why her son needs prayer. In many cases, callers warrant their requests for help by justifying their needs and the host responds accordingly. In this way, callers request confirmation from the host about whether their requests will be affirmed or rejected.

H: Yes of course, Alba. We will be praying for David and we will ask our father who knows each of our futures, if it's best that David remains here (in the U.S.).

A: Yes.

H: He may allow him to stay, and if not, may God's will be done but we will believe God and whatever he decides is what's best for David.

A: I know sister.

H: And I hope he consoles you and gives you peace in your heart of a mother so you can have that hope in God, Amen?

A: Amen sister.

The host's "yes of course" in the response counters any doubts that the caller may have about her request being fulfilled. What is most unique about this case is that after providing advice, the host offers her own petition for Alba. In this interaction, the "Amen?," a religiously-oriented marker verifying one portion of the caller's testimonio, indicates that the host's religious and spiritual advice was produced on her behalf. In turn, this "Amen?" requests a specific response from Alba, mainly to accept future blessings.

In Extract Four, Rosalinda has just thanked God for resolving an illness. Like Alba, she uses the opportunity of giving thanks to initiate a request.[7] The host however, approaches Rosalinda's distress about her daughters as a sign of doubt in God's promises.

R: And we are always thanking God for this miracle and I want to ask you sister to pray for my daughters, their names are Silvia and Gabriela Lona and I wish that they could accept God.

H: They accepted God?

R: No, they haven't, but they are good girls, but...

H: So wait, don't get upset or afflicted because you are doubting a promise that God has given us Rosalinda. And you are a woman of God. God's promises will occur. You will be saved, you and your house.

A: Well I hope so sister.

The host's initial question prompts Rosalinda to elaborate or clarify what her reported trouble implies. Indeed, there is no praise and no blessing, and her response interprets the caller's prayer request as a sign of affliction and doubt. Through these statements, the host recasts Rosalinda's feelings as "affliction" and being "upset." She can then set boundaries around what callers and community members can legitimately take as troublesome and worthy of God's relief. In the closing of the testimonio, Rosalinda reverts to giving thanks to God for being saved only after her prayer requests do not get accepted by the host. Once Rosalinda gives thanks, the host's "amen" gives praise.

H: And even more so if they are good girls, decent who don't have a lot of negative influences. You have to doubt less that soon they will come to Christ's feet.

R: That's right sister. I request prayer for them.

H: With sweetness and wisdom.

R: Well, I give thanks to God because he saved me.

H: Amen.

By interpreting callers' feelings, the host can cast testimonios as symptomatic of certain stances of faith. Here, interpreting Rosalinda's feelings about her daughters as signs of spiritual doubt allowed the host to reject her prayer request. In effect, by reinterpreting callers' feelings about a certain troublesome situation, the host makes claims about how prayer requests should be justified. Specifically, this case shows that prayer requests for unresolved troubles may require specific displays of faith in God and particular descriptions of feelings about God's role in one's life.

Callers orient themselves to knowing what sorts of unresolved troubles warrant help from the host. In fact, spiritual troubles, like needing more from God, may be precisely what this show is designed to address. The last extract below initially consists of reporting a set of resolved troubles. God healed Teresa of a cancerous tumor and helped her brother who was supposed to be incarcerated for four years and lose his papers, but his sentence was reduced by one year. Significantly, testimonios designed to request help are constructed of two parts. First, callers requesting help produce a statement that gives God thanks for affecting the outcome of a problematic matter. Second, callers produce a statement that requests help or assistance from the host. In Extract Five, Teresa prefaces her request of prayer from the host by giving thanks.[8] Teresa also testifies to her entitlement for spiritual help when she says "I already received God in my heart sister." Yet the "but" in her request for prayer marks the continuity to her previous statement, while demarcating her need for help.

T: And I am very thankful for you guys too for being here for everyone, listening to us sister, may God bless you always, and that for the honor and Glory of God pray for me a lot because I want to change my life, I want to have, I have already received God in my heart sister, but I need, I need more of Christ, I want you to understand me. I apologize because I don't know how to talk but this is what I feel in my heart.

H: Look Teresa, the word of God tells us that faith comes from listening to the word and it is the word of God that liberates us and transforms our mind and our heart, God just saved you, you are a new creature in Him, but this doesn't mean that you will instantly stop being who you were, He has to work through you through his Holy Spirit to create a new mind, a new heart, a new way of thinking, a new lifestyle, but it's through knowing the instructions. And if you don't study the bible you cannot learn, that is why it is necessary that after you receive Christ, one attends a church, congregate where she can listen, learn the lessons of the Word of God and know the instructions God has there for you and for me, so we can live a life of victory, a life of peace, a life full of joy when we learn to obey His mandate. So it is necessary that you attend a church and study the Word of God because liberty comes from knowing that truth, the truth is the Bible. May God illuminate you and bless you.

Teresa's apology not only justifies her request but indicates that it may not quite conform to the typical way testimonios are told on this show. The host's curt response "Look Teresa" suggests that the host may *not* be orienting to providing praise or approval of Teresa's request. This reply hints that requesting help is an accountable matter for participants. As such, there is a demand for legitimate justifications for asking and offering help (Edwards 2). On closer examination of the host's response, we can see that it is built of at least two separate components. First, she appeals to what the bible says about faith. Second, she offers Teresa advice about making sense of her new relationship with God. Third, the host advises Teresa to attend church and read the bible. Nowhere in her response does the host assure Teresa that the show will pray for her. Instead, Teresa's prayer request and unresolved matter of needing more from Christ is treated by the host as a confusion about how faith is learned and "getting to know the instructions" through reading the bible.

What resources are employed by the host to delineate a caller's faith and doubt? The host has to constantly manage the way callers explain their faith in their testimonios. As we have seen, the host is responsible for holding callers accountable for the requests they make. This accountability teaches the participants of this religious community the particular ways in which they can express their needs—secular or spiritual. Furthermore, it requires the host to be held responsible for the type of help or assistance she can legitimately provide for callers.

CONCLUSION: THE ACHIEVEMENT OF "TELLABLE TELLINGS"

The accomplishment of "tellable tellings" on *Cambiando Vidas* involves speakers' abilities to manage their talk on a turn-by-turn basis and in relation to normative ways of appropriately displaying their faith in God. In turn, the host of *Cambiando Vidas* uses a set of methods to manage the "tellability" of callers' testimonies. Employing religiously oriented idiomatic expressions (e.g., "Amen," "Glory to God," "God bless you") praises and ratifies callers' testimonios. As a representative of this institutional setting, the host is in a position to give callers advice about practical or spiritual matters that, in turn, modify the telling of testimonios. Finally, the host reinterprets callers' feelings about unresolved troubles by determining whether their reported feelings amount to doubt or a strong faith in God.

A sociological and conversation-analytical approach complicates the conceptualization of testimonios by examining the production of testimonios in multiple media and not just as textual objects. Studying publicly broadcast testimonio allows for an elaboration of the interactional contexts in which they are told. Testimonial narratives in their textual form do not give us an opportunity to consider their interactional context in detail. Examining the interactional contexts of testimonios as they are told in real time helps us understand how members of particular communities employ them as tools for the ongoing establishment and maintenance of collective values and concerns (Beverley, "The Margin" 15). Testimonios on *Cambiando Vidas* must be "tellable" as the type of tellings that they are with respect to the demands of the show. That is, tellings in this context are produced, patrolled, and interpreted with reference to a set of religious norms that shape how people speak of their everyday troubles and display their faith in God. More broadly, the empirical analysis of the process of telling a testimonio can potentially garner insight about how the enterprise of building a meaningful world works. In this case, spiritual meaning does not necessarily occur within nor is it tied to formal institutional structures, but emerges through public interactions. Thus, the telling of religious testimonios on a public radio program invites people to engage in certain opportunities that shape the goals and functions of the show and its ties to the broader media network. This approach challenges testimonio scholarship to treat the interactional context in which testimonios take place as indicative of the processes of collective and public negotiation of meaning.

Notes

1. See Beverley, "The Margin" 18; Beverley, "Testimonio" 550; Nance 571; and Harlow 11.
2. In his discussion of testimonio, John Beverley argues that since testimonio relies on voice, it can "challenge the loss of the authority of orality in the context of processes of cultural modernization that privilege literacy and literature as a norm of expression" ("Testimonio" 549). Still, there are difficulties in the process of mediation or the relationship between the narrator and the interlocutor. In producing the testimonio, an interlocutor who is generally from a different ethnic/class background elicits and records the narrative, and ultimately, transforms it into a printed text that is then

published and circulated (549). Difficulties related to the relationship between a narrator and her interlocutor can raise a set of questions regarding the degree of authenticity or legitimacy of the speaker's testimonio. A related difficulty in testimonio has been raised by Elzbieta Sklodowska. Sklodowska argues that the tellings of a speaker or witness in a testimonio cannot be a direct reflection of her experiences (378–79). Rather, as speakers produce their testimonios, their tellings have been shaped by memory, intention, and ideology (379). Although in testimonio, speakers employ certain strategies for securing a sense of authenticity and legitimacy in what they recount, the relationship between fiction and history constantly reappears as a problem ("Testimonio" 549).

3. John Beverley has noted that in testimonio the author's role has been transformed into that of "compiler" or "activator" (Beverley, "Testimonio" 556).

4. Elena: Extract One (nine lines omitted)

   E: Pues el Señor ha sido maravilloso y bueno conmigo verdad.

   H: Sí.

   E: El pues me trajo a este país y me me dio la (1.0) la residencia, luego me dio (1.0) am la ciudadanía, verdad. Y él ha sido tan bueno, tan misericordioso y me ha sanado tantas veces. Últimamente me sanó del corazón porque me dijeron que lo tenía grande y este como fui fui, con una especialista del corazón pero como yo miré que me estaba cobrando mucho verdad, entonces yo puse todo en las manos del Señor y y di este, una parte de lo que yo iba a dar de mi segunda visita? lo di a mi iglesia donde yo asisto verdad, se lo di al Señor para la obra del, y el Señor me sanó hermana. Tengo mi corazón sano, y yo no siento ya nada.

   H: °Gloria=a=Dios°

   E: molestias como antes hermana.

   H: °bueno°

   E: el Señor me ha sanado y=ha sido muy bueno, muy misericordioso conmigo y con toda mi familia.

   H: Que lindo Elena. Bueno, y cosas <u>más</u> grandes seguirá haciendo el Señor en tu vida,

   E: °Sí°

   H: sobre todo aquellos que confían y le creen.

5. María: Extract Two (five lines omitted)

   M: Y hoy ví la mano poderosa del Señor que así fue porque mi carro en plena Van Nuys se apagó en el stop el Señor arregló todo para que fuera ahí y yo pedí al Señor se prendió el carro=llegué a mi casa y no tuve accidentes y pude llevar a mi niña a la escuela (0.3).

H: Gloria a Dios que bueno y bueno, todavía se te apagó en una señal de pare mucho mejor que corriendo en medio del tráfico María.

M: Así es.

H: Dios es bueno pero yo creo que (0.2) debemos de ser sabios y atender a los llamados de atención, debes de arreglar ese carro.

M: °Sí.

H: debes de hacerlo. Que Dios te siga bendiciendo María, gracias por compartir con nosotros.

6. Alba: Extract Three (12 lines omitted)

A: Y tengo una gran fe yo en Dios que cada vez que yo siento algo en mi cuerpo me arro_dillo y le _pido con todo mi corazón y él me responde hermana.

B: Amén, que lindo.

A: → Sí=y=otra cosa hermana=yo quería pedirle que me acaban de agarrar a mi hijo (0.2) me lo tienen preso en Houston (0.2) quería pedirle que oraran por él por el amor de Dios.

H: Cómo se llama, no me dé=el apellido, pero dame el nombre.

A: Sí, se llama David, y me lo van a deportar.

(two lines omitted)

H: Sí claro que sí, Alba. Vamos a estar orando por David (0.3) y vamos a suplicar a nuestro padre que conoce el futuro de cada uno de nosotros, si es lo que conviene que David se quede aquí.

A: Sí.

H: Que él permita que así sea (0.2) y si no, que se haga la voluntad de Dios pero vamos a creerle=a Dios y que lo que él decida es lo correcto, es lo que le conviene a David.

A: Yo sé hermana.

H: Y que ponga consuelo y paz en tu corazón de madre para que tú puedas tener esa esperanza en el Señor= amén?

A: Amén hermana.

7. Rosalinda: Extract Four (nine lines omitted)

R: Y nosotros estamos siempre dándole gracias a Dios por este milagro y →quiero pedirle hermana que (0.2) hagan oración por mis hijas ellas se llaman Silvia y Gabriela Lona y quisiera que (0.3) °ellas >aceptaran al Señor<° (starts to cry)

H: Aceptaron al Señor?

R: No, no lo han aceptado pero ellas son buenas niñas, pero

H: Entonces espérate, no te >acongojes ni te aflijes< porque estás dudando de una promesa que Dios nos dio Rosalinda. Y tú eres una mujer de Dios. Las promesas del Señor se van a cumplir eh tu serás salva, tú y tu casa también.

R: pues espero hermana.

H: Y cuanto más si son muchachas b=buenas, correctas que no tienen tanta influencia negativa=menos porque dudar que pronto van a venir a los pies de Cristo.

R: Así es hermana. Pido oración por ellas y (overlap)

H: Con tu dulzura y sabiduría (overlap)

R: Pues, le doy gracias a Dios porque, porque=él me salvó a mí.

H: Amén

(four lines omitted)

8. Teresa: Extract Five (13 lines omitted)

T: Y le estoy muy agradecida a ustedes también por estar o sea para toda la gente, escucharnos hermana, que Dios los bendiga por siempre, y que para la honra y la Gloria=de=Dios sea mi padre santo hermana oren mucho por mí porque yo quiero cambiar mi vida quiero (0.2) tener=tengo recibí a Dios en mi corazón hermana, pero necesito (0.2) yo necesito más de Cristo yo quiero que usted me entienda. Disculpe que no sé hablar pero es lo que yo siento en mi corazón.

H: Mira Teresa, la palabra de Dios dice que la fe viene por oir la palabra y es la palabra de Dios la que nos libera es la palabra de Dios la que nos hace transformar nuestra mente y nuestro corazón eh, Dios te acaba de salvar, tú eres una nueva criatura en él pero, no quiere decir que al instante tú dejarás de ser lo que eras, tiene que venir a trabajar en ti el Señor atraves de su Espíritu Santo para crear una nueva mente un nuevo corazón un nuevo pensamiento un nuevo estilo de vida pero es a través de conocer las instrucciones. Y si tú no escrudiñas la biblia no puedes aprender, por eso es menester que después de recibir a Cristo la persona atienda a una iglesia, se congregue donde pueda escuchar la enseñanza de la palabra de Dios y conocer las instrucciones que Dios tiene allí para tí y para mí para que vivamos una vida de Victoria, una vida de paz, una vida llena de gozo cuando aprendemos a ser obedientes a su mandato. Así que es menester que tú asistas a una iglesia y estudies la palabra de Dios porque la libertad viene por conocer esa verdad, la verdad es la biblia. Que Dios te ilumine que Dios te bendiga.

WORKS CITED

Aponte, Edwin David, et al. *Handbook of Latina/o Theologies.* St. Louis: Chalice, 2006. Print.

Atencio, Rebecca J. "Dangerous Minds: Brazil's Escritura da Exclusão and Testimonio." *Hispania* 89 (2006): 278–88. Print.

Beverley, John. "Testimonio, Subalternity, and Narrative Authority." *The Sage Handbook of Qualitative Research.* Ed. Norman K. Denzin and Yvonna S. Lincoln. 3rd ed. Thousand Oaks: Sage, 2005. 547–57. Print.

———. "The Margin at the Center: On *Testimonio* (Testimonial Narrative)." *Modern Fiction Studies* 39 (1989): 11–28. Print.

———. "Through All Things Modern: Second Thoughts on Testimonio." *Boundary 2* 18 (1991): 1–21. Print.

Dorfman, Ariel. "Political Code and Literary Code." *Some Write to the Future: Essays on Contemporary Latin American Fiction.* Trans. George Shivers with Ariel Dorfman. Durham: Duke UP, 1991. Print.

Drew, Paul, and John Heritage, eds. *Talk at Work.* Cambridge: Cambridge UP, 1992. Print.

Drew, Paul, and Elizabeth Holt. "Idiomatic Expressions and their Role in the Organization of Topic Transition in Conversation." *Idioms: Structural and Psychological Perspectives.* Ed. Martin Everaert et al. New Jersey: Lawrence Erlbaum, 1995. Print.

Durkheim, Emile. *The Rules of Sociological Method.* Trans. W. D. Hales. Ed. S. Lukes. Glencoe: Free, 1982. Print.

Edwards, Derek. "Introduction." *Research on Language and Social Interaction* 40 (2007): 1–7. Print.

Goffman, Erving. "The Interaction Order." *American Sociological Review* 48 (1983): 1–17. Print.

Gonzalez, Justo L., ed. *Alabadle, Hispanic Christian Worship.* Nashville: Abingdon, 1996. Print.

Harlow, Barbara. "Testimonio and Survival: Roque Dalton's Miguel Marmol." *Latin American Perspectives* 18 (1991): 9–21. Print.

Jefferson, Gail. "Sequential Aspects of Storytelling in Conversation." *Studies in the Organization of Conversational Interaction.* Ed. J. Schenkein. New York: Academic, 1978. 219–48. Print.

Nance, Kimberly. "Disarming Testimony: Speakers' Resistance to Readers' Defenses in Latin American Testimonio." *Biography* 24 (2001): 570–88. Print.

Pedraja, Luis G. "Testimonios and Popular Religion in Mainline North American Hispanic Protestantism." *University of Virginia, The Project on Lived Theology. Resources, Papers, Workgroup Meetings: Race.* U of Virginia, n.d. Web. Feb. 2011.

Raymond, Geoffrey. "Grammar and Social Organization: Yes/No Interrogatives and the Structure of Responding." *American Sociological Review* 68 (2003): 939–67. Print.

Rivero, Eliana. "Testimonio y conversaciones como discurso literario: Cuba y Nicaragua." *Literature and Contemporary Revolutionary Culture* 1 (1984–1985): 218–28. Print.

Schegloff, Emanuel. "On Talk and Its Institutional Occasions." *Talk at Work: Interaction in Institutional Settings.* Ed. Paul Drew and John Heritage. New York: Cambridge UP, 1992. 101–34. Print.

Sklodowska, Elzbieta. "La forma testimonial y la novelística de Miguel Barnet." *Revista/Review Interamericana* 12 (1982): 375–84. Print.

Yúdice, George. "Testimonio and Postmodernism." *Latin American Perspectives* 18 (1991): 15–31. Print.

CHAPTER 9

EMBROIDERED DISCOURSE/S BREAK THE SILENCE: THE CPR-SIERRA OF GUATEMALA (RE)VIVE TESTIMONIO

T. M. Linda Scholz

> Ser indígena es pecado en mi país Guatemala .... Los indios de América sabemos: La idea del exterminio es la solución de países <<desarrollados,>> y desconocen nuestra resistencia por muchos siglos. A los indios de la América no nos han *"vencido como pueblos."*
> (To be Indian is a sin in my country, Guatemala .... We Indians of the Americas know: Extermination is the solution of *"developed"* countries, and our resistance has been ignored for centuries.)
>
> (Calixta Gabriel Xiquín 34)

This was the third time I had been back to Guatemala to visit my sister since I returned to the United States permanently in 1985. It was Christmas of 2007 and Marko and I were shopping at the local tourist stores to bring gifts for friends and family back in the States. As I was looking at a display of weavings, my eyes caught a glimpse of a square piece of material with embroidered writing on it. I cannot remember exactly what the embroidery read, but I remember being overcome with emotion as I realized that the print was about the war, and specified the dates during which my Guatemalan immigrant father took us back to Guatemala to live. I knew that this piece of fabric, along with others alongside of it, symbolized so much more than just the beautiful vibrant colors of reds, purples, blues, and greens that characterize the popular Maya indigenous weavings. By the embroidered writing alone, I knew that somehow this was a subversive message of resistance, survival, and documentation of genocide. I took pause for a moment, trying to negotiate the significant historical documentation that I was witnessing, while wanting to learn more about these pieces of fabric, and realizing that they were on display at a tourist store—"Could they actually be *for sale*?" With physical and emotional discomfort, I asked the merchant if the squares were "purchasable." Much to my satisfaction (and embarrassment because I did not want him to think that I was an "ignorant" tourist) he said "No," but handed me a book where those weavings, and many more, appeared.

'Hilos rompiendo el silencio': Historias sobre las mujeres de la CPR-Sierra de la Guerra Civil en Guatemala ('Threads Breaking the Silence': Stories of the Women of the CPR-Sierra from the Civil War in Guatemala) is a compilation of embroideries sewn by women of the Comunidades de la Populación en Resistencia-Sierra, or CPR-Sierra (Communities of the Population in Resistance-Sierra).[1] The CPR-Sierra is one of the three displaced groups that fled to the mountainous region of Ixil in El Quiché Highlands during the height of the human rights violations, which spanned from 1982 to 1996 (Gonzales 13–24). Paralleling Nobel Peace Prize Laureate Rigoberta Menchú Tum's testimonio,[2] the women of the CPR-Sierra convey to readers how Maya indigenous groups sought refuge in the mountains, having to flee frequent military insurgencies and avoid the Ladino-populated cities because of the structural and systemic racism and discrimination launched against the Guatemalan Maya. Many also sought refuge from the violence of the guerilla soldiers. Others joined the guerilla uprising as a mode of survival.

The use of embroideries as documentation of state oppression and human rights violations is not new to human rights discourses in Latin America. Scholars E. Moya-Raggio, Jacqueline Adams, and Marjorie Agosín have written at length about the Arpillera Movement in Chile, which began in the mid-1970s. Akin to the Arpillera Movement, the CPR-Sierra embroideries document state violence. The importance of the CPR-Sierra embroideries is threefold. First, these embroideries present an opportunity to (re)vive the discussion of this type of art form as counter-hegemonic testimonial texts. Second, the CPR-Sierra embroideries continue the discussion of the Guatemalan Maya indigenous genocide that was overshadowed by the international focus on the Menchú-Stoll controversy. Last, these embroideries challenge scholars in an array of disciplines to (re)visit theoretical approaches that provide more complex understandings of the appeals made in indigenous texts. The multiple indigenous projects identified by Linda Tuhiwai Smith—in addition to Gerard A. Hauser and erin daina mcclellan's treatment of vernacular rhetoric—are reflective of such theoretical approaches.

This essay assumes that the CPR-Sierra embroideries are visual instantiations of testimonios. The context under which the embroideries were created is further understood by the accompanying text-based testimonios and biographies of the women who created them. Together, these form the CPR-Sierra embroidery project, which can be understood as a unifying act of indigenous decolonization and self-determination that reveals and challenges current practices of colonialism (Smith *passim*). In the analysis that follows, I first discuss the interconnectivity of Latin American embroideries to testimonios in human rights discourse, and further address how the CPR-Sierra embroideries are vernacular rhetorics of resistance. Second, I offer an analysis of how the CPR-Sierra embroidery project's style and form illustrate the four characteristics of dissident vernacular rhetoric as well as the indigenous projects of "testimonies," claiming, storytelling, remembering, and survival.

CPR-Sierra Embroidered Testimonios as Indigenous Forms of Vernacular Rhetoric

The Communities of the Population in Resistance formed in opposition to the oppressive military system that ruled Guatemala during the 1980s, thus contributing to the Guatemalan human rights movement. Recognizing the importance of documenting the CPR-Sierra's experiences from 1982 to 1996, U.S. retiree Ramelle (Romelia) Gonzales started this embroidery project with the women in 1998. Gonzales is also the founder of Foundations for Education, Inc., a U.S. nonprofit organization that seeks to support Maya indigenous students' education. The students who received scholarships through Foundations also participated in the embroidery project by interviewing the women about the embroideries they created. The students spoke to the women in Mayan languages, which were first translated into Spanish and then into English. The Spanish and English text-based testimonios and brief biographies are included alongside photographs of each of the women. On the adjacent page appear their embroideries, a short bilingual description of each, and translations for those that are text-based. The embroideries include stitched images of people, natural habitats, words, and full text. The themes that emerge from the translated testimonios and the embroideries include the indictment of the military junta, visual documentation of torture, death, overhead bombings, stories of resistance and survival, and women's political agency.

Like the Chilean arpilleras, the CPR-Sierra embroideries serve a cathartic function. Both groups created the embroideries to document how international and national politics had detrimental effects on their pueblos (communities) and families. Both types of embroideries are forms of cultural resistance and public memory that indict military juntas, document human rights violations, and signify women's political agency. Agosín notes that the Chilean Arpillera Movement reflected women's changing roles in Chilean society from housekeepers to heads of households with primary financial responsibility to political citizens (44). There is no ignoring, as well, that part of the inherent power of the embroideries can be attributed to their stealth tactics. In other words, because feminine art forms such as embroidery, weaving, and other forms of sewing are not readily identified in official discourse as "political," they go undetected as political resistance.

Although the Chilean arpilleras and the embroideries of the CPR-Sierra were created under similar oppressive circumstances, there are also important distinctions. First and foremost, the projects emerged under differing cultural contexts. The CPR-Sierra embroideries have been created by the women of a Maya indigenous pueblo that was largely silenced for well over a decade. The embroideries, then, not only document personal and collective accounts of genocide, but they bring a pueblo to voice. The book in which the embroideries appear is not widely distributed, and so this project is still new to an international audience. In the case of the Chilean arpilleras, their history of circulation since the 1970s has garnered international attention, including the prompting of Amnesty International to publish pictures of them on greeting cards for international distribution during the 1980s (Agosín 10). By virtue of the recognition from human rights organizations, the arpilleras entered into an official human rights discourse. Moreover, the creation of arpilleras progressed into the development of organized workshops that were managed by the Vicariate of Solidarity. However, with the advent of democratization in 1989, the workshops disbanded (60).

The CPR-Sierra cannot rely on these kinds of organizational structures, which also indicates that these embroideries as cultural resistance have not entered into official human rights discourse. Instead, these embroideries are a form of vernacular rhetoric that reveals a nexus between indigenous projects. These different methodologies unearth the multiple appeals in the overall embroidery project that official discourse may prevent us from seeing and understanding.

Vernacular Rhetoric

Testimonio has been theorized and amply discussed by academics in literature, Latin American studies, and anthropology. Communication studies has also made a number of noteworthy contributions to testimonial studies through the works of Avant-Mier and Hasian, Delgado, Huaco-Nuzum, Scholz, and Valdivia, and therefore is well positioned to contribute to this rich academic discussion. Theories of vernacular discourse and vernacular rhetoric were developed by communication studies scholars who have been interested in analyzing discourses that challenge and resist dominant structures (see Hauser, Hauser and mcclellan, and Ono and Sloop). This scholarship also affirms and offers varied understandings of subject positions, such as Calafell and Delgado's notions of Latina/o as depicted through different images. These discourses, which emerge from the everyday discussions of smaller communities, have in-group purposes in mind and are intended for this particular audience (Ono and Sloop, *Shifting Borders* 3). Although these discourses are not circulated by leaders, they still "illumine issues of oppression, dissidence, and power differentials" (Hauser and mcclellan 29). Of these theoretical approaches to the vernacular, Hauser and mcclellan's theory of vernacular rhetoric in relation to social movements is particularly instructive to understanding the appeals in the CPR-Sierra embroidery project.

Latin American social movements formed as a result of economic and political oppression and a demand from citizens for a more democratic and just state. According to Hauser and mcclellan, the common conceptualizations of democracy that involve deliberation, the citizen's right to vote and express opinions, and majority rule are, in short, a fable. Hauser and mcclellan offer a counter view that "regards society, whether democratic or authoritarian, as engaged in the ongoing activity of its own self-production" where "this view depicts society as a continuous struggle over resources, including symbolic resources, between those in and those out of power" (24). The tension over symbolic resources identified here is evidenced in "the dramatic and sometimes violent modes of resistance in liberatory movements opposing colonial and postcolonial powers" (24). The Communities of the Population in Resistance in Guatemala illustrate Hauser and mcclellan's points. As such, Hauser and mcclellan emphasize the need to focus on "the intertextual symbolic exchanges of everyday discourse" (26) or vernacular rhetoric. The CPR-Sierra embroideries, as co-constructed discourse from everyday exchanges, are a form of vernacular rhetoric that performs resistance. Furthermore, they reflect Hauser and mcclellan's four characteristics: polyvocality, evasion of detection, interrogation of authority, and the performance of power. In the following section, I elaborate on how each of these characteristics is illustrated in the CPR-Sierra embroidery project while simultaneously functioning as Smith's broader indigenous projects.

Maya Cultural Resistance

Of the 25 indigenous projects Smith identifies, "testimonies" are most synonymous with testimonio/s. Smith also indicates that multiple indigenous projects may intersect with one another. Latin American indigenous testimonios broadly, and the CPR-Sierra embroidery project specifically, illustrate how this intersection can occur in "testimonies/testimonios" between claiming, storytelling, remembering, and celebrating survival. According to Smith, indigenous testimonies include discussions about painful events, through which "the voice of a 'witness' is accorded space and protection" (144). Drawing on diverse explications and definitions offered by various scholars about testimonios, as well as the Spanish terms used by testimonialistas, I offer the following explanation of testimonios that can help to capture the way they function to appeal to international audiences who read/see them.

The Spanish words used by the more popular testimonios given by Menchú, Alvarado, Tula, and Barrios de Chungara include narrar (to narrate), relato (account), and historia (history). Gleaned from this Spanish terminology is that a testimonio is characterized by the politicized narration of specific accounts that took place, spoken in the first person, but reflective of collective experiences, that also encompasses a reconstruction of personal, collective, and national histories. Together, these descriptions indicate how testimonio texts are composed by the multiple voices of the pueblo and therefore are a form of vernacular rhetoric. This description also illustrates what Hauser and mcclellan term "polyvocality" in vernacular rhetoric where "it reflects a variety of voices that enter a discourse in which everyday objects, acts, and expression, such as food we eat, markets where we shop, greetings we exchange, clothes we wear, dialects we speak, and idioms we share are symbolic re-presentations of social reality"

(30). The polyvocality of vernacular rhetoric assumes multiple interpretations, which, in turn, create "a series of dialectical moments in which the powerful and the powerless contest for relational position and voice" (30). The rhetoricity of this discourse is brought to bear on an international audience when it is "smuggled" outside of its country of origin because of its highly politicized nature. However, it would be amiss to assume that the embroidery project is meant only for an international audience. In fact, the project is directed at two audiences: local and international.

There is no questioning the extent to which the embroideries serve a "therapeutic," or perhaps better stated, a healing process, for the local audience of the CPR-Sierra, but in particular for the women who created the embroideries. This therapeutic function is captured in the Spanish word "desahogar," which connotes an emotional "emptying out" of sorts: "I liked working on this project [the embroideries] because I learned more about how to organize people. For me I made my embroideries with sadness, but at the same time I felt happy because people are going to see what we have been holding inside" (Gonzales 63). Through the process of "desahogando" (emptying out), the women were able to negotiate their feelings of sadness, happiness, and tranquility: "The embroideries were good to make because they cleared our minds of our (memories) that are with us day and night" (101). Beyond what the women directly share, there is no way of knowing the other effects that the project may have on them or on their pueblo. That is best left for the pueblo to discuss and is not the domain of an academic essay.

Claiming

Smith asserts that an effect of colonialism is that indigenous people have been reduced to making claims and assertions regarding injustices. She elaborates by stating that "For some indigenous groups the formal claims process demanded by tribunals, courts and governments has required the conducting of intensive research projects resulting in the writing of nation, tribe, and family histories" (143). The depictions in the embroideries are visual claims against the injustices suffered by the CPR-Sierra at the hands of the PAC and military. In many of the embroideries the women stitched the words "ejército" (military) and "PAC" (Civilian Defense Patrols). They also embroidered human figures in military camouflage carrying rifles and machine guns, standing over bodies, and hanging children from trees. Images of helicopters with bombs dropping from them are also consistently included in the embroideries. The stitched words and the images depict specific stories of various massacres and violent events experienced by the individual women, therefore functioning as separate claims of injustices. In unison, the words and images create the collective story of genocide, and therefore the project as a whole is a claim to such effect. As Smith indicates, the importance of a story is that there is no ending because even when justice prevails, the people's journey will continue (144). Such is the case of the CPR-Sierra as they continue to live in an isolated mountainous region.

In relation to vernacular rhetoric, the project of claiming explains how the embroideries and the women's commentary about them are in a dialectic with the official discourse of the Guatemalan government as well as international governments that influenced the war in Guatemala; in this case, specifically, the United States. By visually depicting helicopters dropping bombs and soldiers hanging children from trees, the women tell the story of genocide while simultaneously indicting the junta—dismantling the official discourse that attempted to keep the mass killings a secret from the rest of the world. Furthermore, the visuality of the embroideries illustrates Hauser's and mcclellan's claims that vernacular rhetoric evades detection. Agosín also addressed how the Chilean arpilleras elude interpretation:

An *arpillera* always surprises, because at first glance it gives the impression that it is an innocent art, but it is not. It is an art denouncing torture, forced disappearances, and violence .... The experiences of the intimate lives of the families of the disappeared unite with the experiences of the nation, that out of fear, has attempted to ignore the oppressive nature of its military force.

(17)

Inherent in the evasion of detection is the ability to construct a pueblo-public memory of the atrocities that occurred and to record the responses to those atrocities.

Stories of Remembering

The stories of remembering combine the indigenous projects of storytelling and remembering, identified by Smith. As indicated previously, testimonios are co-constructions of individual and collective stories of pueblo life. Smith identifies several elements that characterize the appeals in indigenous storytelling. First, in addition to recording a collective story that has historical implications for future generations, many of the embroideries are indicative of Maya indigenous beliefs, values, and norms. These nuances include an expression of an interconnectivity between the people and the land. Second, the storyteller is considered the conveyor and controller of multiple truths (not the researcher). Last, storytelling is dialogic in nature, in that it reflects dialogues and conversations between indigenous people.

The visual stories depicted in the embroideries do not exist separately from national and international politics, as decisions made by the U.S. government during the height of the human rights violations in Guatemala influenced Guatemalan politics, which in turn affected the Maya indigenous people in different regions, but in particular El Quiché. Some scholars would argue that the representation of the stitched weapons and helicopters cannot be understood as separate from the alleged training of Guatemalan soldiers at the School of the Americas. Additionally, the depictions of women hiding behind trees as "lookouts" and of the PACs and soldiers pointing machine guns and rifles at individual people document the collective history for future generations. However, not all of the depictions in the embroideries are of gruesome events.

Depictions include stitched trees and flowers, women weaving and cooking, and images of children in school along with the word "escuela" (school). These visually recounted stories function as public memory for the women, who have created the very art form that documents their experiences. As Smith states, the project of remembering involves "remembering of a painful past, and importantly, people's responses to that pain" (146). This process of remembering may also involve coming to terms with people's responses to pain, including abuse in the family, alcohol addiction, and other forms of self-destruction. In the case of the embroideries, the women do not depict the direct impact of human rights violations on men and women's intimate relationships. In testimonios given by Menchú, Alvarado, Tula, and Barrios de Chungara, this is the case. The embroideries documenting women's role as lookouts simultaneously depict women's participation with the Guerilla Movement. It is important to note that this was David Stoll's contention with Menchú's testimonio in his widely discussed book, *Rigoberta Menchú and the Story of all Poor Guatemalans*. Most interesting, however, is that in women's processes of storytelling and remembering, they explain how the act of taking up arms was their primary mode of defending themselves against military attacks and surviving starvation: "In 1982, the army started to cut our cornfields, (property) of the population in resistance. We died of hunger because of suffering so we looked for a way to defend our lives and formed a group of the guerillas" (Gonzales 108).

A few embroideries show women holding rifles, and of these many are accompanied by stitched text. For instance, one translates as "Life is a fight and one fights always with arms. We can fight for our rights as women. I participated in the armed war with the guerillas of the EGP (Army of the Poor) in Guatemala. There is exploitation, inequality, and discrimination" (114). Other embroideries do not show women holding rifles, but instead *articulate* their probable involvement in guerila violence as a means of self-defense, as Inocenta Cuyuch Báten shares in her text-based embroidery: "In 1980 the army started the repression of more than 400 villages in the Ixil Triangle in Quiché, Guatemala, Central America. To defend our lives we carried arms with the guerillas, because of the fear and death on the part of the army" (64). This embroidery, along with the others, exemplifies the process of storytelling and remembering women's involvement in the guerila movement. Additionally, because the women are "sewing" their experiences with subversive acts, their admission "evades detection" while simultaneously debunking official discourse that silenced the Maya indigenous and the reasons why some people took up arms: self defense.

Similar to the arpilleras, these embroideries not only reflect women's involvement as political citizens, but also directly document their involvement as political citizens in the guerilla uprising. Additionally, because these experiences are depicted in a storytelling format, they are not easily and openly read as subversive. Furthermore, because the embroideries are handwoven and likely not read as "professional quality," they go easily undetected as subversive.

THEIR SURVIVAL IS POWER

The final theme that is reflected in the CPR-Sierra embroideries is that of survival. This project also illustrates how vernacular rhetoric performs power. Writes Smith,

> celebrating survival accentuates not so much our demise but the degree to which indigenous peoples and communities have successfully retained cultural and spiritual values and authenticity.... Events and accounts which focus on the positive are important not just because they speak to our survival, but because they celebrate our resistances at an ordinary human level and they affirm our identities as indigenous women and men.
>
> (145)

Although the women depict the atrocities experienced by women, men, and children, they also express relief that Guatemala is no longer at war. Silvestra Ixcoy Coc shares, "When I was working with my embroidery I was sad and afraid that maybe the war would come back. Thank God we are living in peace now" (Gonzales 119). Relief is visually expressed in the embroideries by a balance between the images of weapons, trees, flowers, and a shining sun. Interestingly, many of the figures have smiles stitched on their faces.

The ability to directly depict what the women witnessed, and what their grandmothers and mothers witnessed, is an expression of resistance and power—the very fact that they have agreed to circulate their stories to a wide audience documents their survival. The women stitched images of the trees consistently throughout the embroideries and indicated the ways in which the trees were key to their survival because they offered shelter to the pueblo. Furthermore, the embroideries depict figures standing near trees where the accompanying texts reveal how the pueblo ate roots from those trees and drank water from the moist moss. The embroideries discussed in the previous sections also illustrate survival and performances of power.

Through the rhetorical performance of power, the embroideries document genocide, while also testifying to the survival strategies employed by the CPR-Sierra. Forming the CPR-Sierra and garnering U.N. response are performances of power and survival. This survival is evident in the words of Maria Lux Sica: "Today people are forgetting us, not like before. Now we are free and we have our salt and blankets. Just by telling about it makes me cry. The idea of the book is good for me because after I die I will still have my story in the live light" (93). That the CPR-Sierra experiences are brought to voice in these embroideries is perhaps the most salient performance of power.

A Move toward Decolonization and Self-Determination

The poem that introduces this essay captures the way that the Maya of Guatemala continue to be treated. However, the verses reflect the self-determination evident in the CPR-Sierra embroidery project. These texts are forms of vernacular rhetoric that function to resist an oppressive imperialist system; there is no question that they perform power and resist colonization.

Although Linda Tuhiwai Smith's book is geared toward indigenous researchers, her emphasis on the importance of indigenous self-determination is well illustrated in the embroidery project of the

CPR-Sierra. Smith provides an alternative view of what constitutes "research" as she states that "indigenous communities as part of the self-determination agenda do engage quite deliberatively in naming the world according to an indigenous world view" (125). Whether or not the women of the CPR-Sierra consider themselves to be indigenous researchers, the women realize that they are participating in a project that has historical significance, as many of their responses to the project are reflected in Paula Cuyuch Báten and Petrona Choc Chávez' words, "For me the book is good so that we do not forget our history and guard what we remember" (Gonzales 105), and "I like this project for our expression in relation to our suffering. I want our children to know about the past through our embroideries" (109).

The CPR-Sierra embroidery project has provided an opportunity to (re)vive and (re)visit understandings of testimonio in the new millennium. The embroidery project creates a rhetorical space where more Maya indigenous voices can be included in discussions about human rights violations in Guatemala. Furthermore, the theoretical framework of vernacular rhetoric and the indigenous projects outlined by Smith provide scholars with innovative academic tools to unveil the multiple appeals made in indigenous testimonial texts.

Notes

1. The book is not readily available in the United States, but can be ordered through the Foundations for Education, Inc. website: http://foundations4education.org/index.html. Additionally, donations can be made through this website to help support the embroidery project and other Foundations for Education, Inc. projects.
2. Throughout this essay I do not italicize Spanish or Mayan terms, purposefully. To italicize these terms functions to reify difference. In the context of Guatemala, these terms are part of everyday speech, and therefore, would not be italicized. I only italicize terms when they are already italicized in direct quotations or when drawing attention to a term or phrase for specificity.

Works Cited

Adams, Jacqueline. "Art in Social Movements: Shantytown Women's Protest in Pinochet's Chile." *Sociological Forum* 17.1 (2002): 21–56. Print.

———. "Movement Socialization in Art Workshops: A Case from Pinochet's Chile." *The Sociological Quarterly* 41.4 (2000): 615–38. Print.

———. "When Art Loses Its Sting: The Evolution of Protest Art in Authoritarian Contexts." *Sociological Perspectives* 48.4 (2006): 531–58. Print.

Agosín, Marjorie. *Tapestries of Hope, Threads of Love: The Arpillera Movement in Chile*. 2nd ed. Lanham: Rowman & Littlefield, 2008. Print.

Alvarado, Elvia. *Don't be Afraid Gringo: An Honduran Woman Speaks from the Heart: The Story of Elvia Alvarado*. Trans. and ed. Medea Benjamin. San Francisco: Institute for Food and Development Policy, 1987. Print.

Avant-Mier, Roberto, and Marouf A. Hasian, Jr. "Communicating Truth: Testimonio, Vernacular Voices, and the Rigoberta Menchú Controversy." *Communication Review* 11.4 (2008): 323–45. Print.

Barrios de Chungara, Domitila. *Let Me Speak! Testimony of Domitila, a Woman of the Bolivian Mines*. Ed. Moema Viezzer. Trans. Victoria Ortiz. New York: Monthly Review, 1978. Print.

———. *"Si me permiten hablar ...": Testimonio de Domitila, una mujer de las minas de Bolivia*. Ed. Moema Viezzer. Mexico: Siglo XXI, 1977. Print.

Binford, Leigh. "Empowered Speech: Social Fields, Testimonio, and the Stoll Menchú Debate." *Identities* 8.1 (2001): 105–33. Print.

Calafell, Bernadette and Fernando Delgado. "Reading Latino/a Images: Interrogating Americanos." *Critical Studies in Media Communication* 21.1 (2004): 1–21. Print.

Delgado, Fernando. "Rigoberta Menchú and Testimonial Discourse: Collectivist Rhetoric and Rhetorical Criticism." *World Communication* 28.1 (1999): 17–29. Print.

Gonzales, Ramelle (Romelia), ed. *"Threads Breaking the Silence": Stories of the Women of the CPR Sierra from the Civil War in Guatemala*. *["Hilos rompiendo el silencio": historias sobre las mujeres de la CPR-Sierra de la Guerra Civil en Guatemala]*. La Antigua, Guatemala: Foundations for Education, 2005. Print.

Hauser, Gerard A. *Vernacular Voices: The Rhetoric of Publics and Public Spheres*. Colombia: U of South Carolina P, 1999. Print.

Hauser, Gerard A., and erin daina mcclellan. "Vernacular Rhetoric and Social Movements: Performances of Resistance in the Rhetoric of the Everyday." *Active Voices: Composing a Rhetoric for Social Movements*. Ed. Patricia Malesh and Sharon McKenzie Stevens. State U of New York P, 2009. 23–46. Print.

Huaco-Nuzum, Carmen. "Testimony and Bearing Witness." *Quarterly Review of Film & Video* 18 (2001): 83–91. Print.

Menchú, Rigoberta. *I, Rigoberta Menchú: An Indian Woman in Guatemala*. Ed. Elisabeth Burgos-Debray. Trans. Ann Wright. New York: Verso, 1984. Print.

———. *Me llamo Rigoberta Menchú y así me nació la conciencia*. 16^a ed. México: Siglo Veintiuno Editores, 2000. Print.

Moya-Raggio, E. "Arpilleras: Chilean Culture of Resistance: An Introduction." *Feminist Studies* 10.2 (1984): 277–90. Print.

Ono Kent, A., and John M. Sloop. "The Critique of Vernacular Rhetoric." *Communication Monographs* 62 (1995): 19–46. Print.

———. *Shifting Borders: Rhetoric, Immigration, and California's Proposition 187.* Philadelphia: Temple UP, 2002. Print.

Scholz, T. M. Linda. "Hablando Por (Nos)Otros, Speaking for Ourselves: Exploring the Possibilities of 'Speaking Por' Family and Pueblo in the Bolivian Testimonio *Si Me Permiten Hablar [Let Me Speak!]*." *Latina/o Discourse in Vernacular Spaces: Somos de Una Voz? (Race, Rites, and Rhetoric: Colors, Cultures, and Communication)*. Ed. Michelle Holling and Bernadette Marie Calafell. Lanham: Lexington-Rowman, 2011. 203–22. Print.

Smith, Linda Tuhiwai. *Decolonizing Methodologies: Research and Indigenous Peoples.* 5th impression. 1999. London: Zed; Dunedin: U of Otago P; New York: Palgrave, 2002. Print.

Stoll, David. *Rigoberta Menchú and the Story of All Poor Guatemalans.* Boulder: Westview, 1999. Print.

Tula, María Teresa. *Este es mi testimonio: María Teresa Tula, luchadora pro derechos humanos de El Salvador.* Cambridge: South End, 1994. Print.

———. *Hear My Testimony: María Teresa Tula, Human Rights Activist of El Salvador.* Ed. and Trans. Lynn Stephen. Cambridge: South End, 1994. Print.

Valdivia, Angharad N. *A Latina in the Land of Hollywood.* Tucson: U of Arizona P, 2000. Print.

Xiquín, Calixta Gabriel. *Tejiendo los sucesos en el tiempo [Weaving Events in Time].* Rancho Palos Verdes: Yax Te' Foundation, 2002. Print.

Part IV

Novel Landscapes: Counter-Geographies, Graphics, and Terra-Trauma

Chapter 10

Ciudad Juárez as a Palimpsest: Searching for Ecotestimonios

Alice Driver

Juárez blows like cold wind through the windows of our souls and demands our attention. We embrace its images as if they could fill our own empty spaces, but we cannot hold on.

(Julián Cardona)

The City as a Palimpsest

A palimpsest, traditionally, is a manuscript that, due to disuse, necessity, or desire has been overwritten. It is, in essence, a text with a ghost. The words that have been scraped off and written over, however faintly, give testimony to what came before. For Andreas Huyssen, "The trope of the palimpsest is inherently literary and tied to writing, but it can also be fruitfully used to discuss configurations of urban spaces and their unfolding in time without making architecture and the city simply into text" (7). The spatial dynamic of the city adds a dimension of complexity not seen in a traditional text; symbols on the cityscape can be analyzed as geographical markers inscribing space with meaning. The geography of Ciudad Juárez serves as a witness whose surface is covered with ecotestimonios—graffiti, marches, and posters that create a memoryscape for victims of feminicide giving a more informal, nomadic recounting of events than traditional testimony.[1] In the case of ecotestimonio, geography is the witness, and the voices collected upon its surface are varied. The trope of the palimpsest also allows an analysis of space that is inclusive of memory and history.

At the June 22, 2010, meeting of the Commission on Feminicide in Mexico, parliament member Teresa Guadalupe Reyes Sahagún asserted, "La sentencia del Campo Algodonero no es una sentencia a los asesinos de estas mujeres o de estas niñas: es una sentencia al Estado mexicano." (The ruling on the cotton field is not a ruling against the murderers of these women and girls: it is a ruling against the Mexican state). Reyes Sahagún is referring to the lack of action on the part of Mexican institutions to resolve the murders of eight women whose bodies were dumped in a cotton field in 2001 as damning evidence against the state itself. However, aside from official government actions, a counter-geography also exists, made up of the voices, marches, memorials, and other projects organized by families of the victims and other local and international parties. This rich counter-geography of local memory practices, although less likely to make headlines than sensational photos showing the destroyed bodies of women, is represented in three documentaries: *Performing the Border* (1999) by Ursula Biemann, *Señorita Extraviada (Missing Young Woman)* (2001) by Lourdes Portillo, and *La batalla de las cruces: protesta social y acciones colectivas en torno de la violencia sexual en Ciudad Juárez (The Battle of the Crosses: Social Protest and Collective Actions Against Sexual Violence in Ciudad Juárez)* (2005) by Rafael Bonilla and Patricia Ravelo Blancas.[2] My discussion of these films, informed by interviews conducted with each of the directors, focuses on the formation of a memoryscape as represented in each film and the ethics of representation involved in portraying violated bodies. Each of the directors has also spent a significant amount of time living or working in Ciudad Juárez and/or collaborating with activists and NGOs.

In the article "Memoryscapes" on memory and authoritarian rule in Santiago, Chile, Louis Bickford defines the term memoryscape, focusing on official public monuments and museums. Bickford argues that the power of certain monuments was generated by the meaningfulness of their location during the authoritarian era in Chile (102). In addition, he introduces a metaphor in which he compares memory sites to scars and describes how the open wounds of history heal, leaving behind some mark of their significance (102). According to Bickford:

Public monuments, memorials, and museums shape the physical landscape of collective memory. They are "memoryscapes" that contest official truths of the authoritarian era and give voice to its victims and survivors. From statuary and war memorials, to public art commemorating past events, to roadside historical markers, to plaques highlighting the heroes or villains of history, to museums designed to remember but not repeat the authoritarian past, memoryscapes recapture public spaces and transform them into sites of memory and alternative truth-telling about the authoritarian past.

(96)

His definition includes mostly formal acts of remembering organized or promoted by the state such as museums, monuments, and roadside historical markers. However, such formal acts of remembering have yet to appear in Ciudad Juárez. Bickford discusses how "reconstituted spaces provide sites for graffiti, performances, and public art installations that contest official versions of the past. Rallies often originate or end at these sites" (102). My use of the concept of memoryscape focuses more on informal acts of remembering such as graffiti, marches, posters, and signs or memorials painted/made by individuals in the community.

This essay analyzes filmic representations of feminicide in Ciudad Juárez by looking at the city as a palimpsest or a text upon which citizens and officials have written, erased, and rewritten messages in public space in an effort to control memory discourse. In his discussion of the Holocaust and the politics of memory Huyssen reflects, "The politics of remembering the Holocaust: what to remember, how to remember, when to remember. Cities, after all, are palimpsests of history, incarnations of time in stone, sites of memory extending both in time and space" (101). I argue that a constantly evolving counter-geography of symbolic action, memorials, and symbols in the city reflects the creation of an informal, nomadic, and ephemeral memory space. According to Hermann Herlinghaus, "contemporary cultural conflicts over the borderlands can be understood, to an important degree, as rhetorical conflicts consisting of a struggle over the figurative potentials displayed by speech acts and bodies, and entangled with numerous practices of movement and exchange" (62). Although no official monument currently exists to memorialize the victims of feminicide, the informal work of different groups of citizens, filmmakers, writers, and artists have marked their lives and deaths.

I choose the term palimpsest to discuss the issue of feminicide in Ciudad Juárez because both the geography and the politics of the city work to create what I refer to as spatial amnesia. The city is a space in which the traces of the lives of the victims seem to be slowly erased from public space, discourse, and memory. In terms of geography,

I am referring to tracts of desert like Lote Bravo in which the bodies of victims of feminicide are often dumped.[3] For Monárrez Fragoso, "lo primero que llama la atención, es la manera cómo se abandonan los cuerpos inertes y tiesos en un escenario unidimensional: en los escenarios sexualmente transgresores que son las zonas desérticas, los lotes baldíos, los arroyos, las alcantarillas y en los tiraderos de basura" (The first thing that catches your attention is the way that bodies are abandoned, inert and stiff, in a one-dimensional setting: in sexually transgressive scenes such as deserted zones, empty lots, gutters, sewers, and dumps) (272). The sands of these deserts often swallow up bodies, clothing, shoes, and other evidence, robbing victims of their identity. Steven S. Volk and Marian E. Schlotterbeck discuss the relationship between urban spaces, the desert, and abandoned lots in an analysis of works of cultural production. They describe how,

> The face of urban Juárez is pockmarked by empty lots (*lotes baldíos*) generated by the feverish land speculation that accompanied the first plants. Large parcels of urban space that never reached development stage were simply left vacant. In their movement through the city, poor women on foot traverse these *lotes baldíos*, spaces in which the bodies of murdered women are frequently found. As one journalist observed, "To walk through downtown Juárez is to know and deeply regret that you are a young woman."
> (130)

The political climate of the city, in which governors and other public officials often repeat a discourse that blames women for the crimes perpetrated against them, is one that historically has favored the removal of feminicide memorials erected by citizens. The three films analyzed in this essay demonstrate how ephemeral art such as memorials and crosses constructed by families create a memoryscape in Ciudad Juárez.

Performing the Border

Performing the Border (1999) was the first film to address feminicide in Ciudad Juárez. The video essay focuses on the geographical space of the border and provides an introduction to several issues traditionally related to feminicide (NAFTA, maquiladoras, the sex trade). It is divided into four distinct parts—"The Plant," "The Settlement," "Sex Work," and "The Killings"—which demonstrate how the murders are tied to the specific environment of the border space. In each section Biemann explores how geography, technology, and globalization intersect in the borderlands to promote a culture of disposability.

Ursula Biemann's aesthetic practice was shaped by her lifetime of work as a visual artist. *Performing the Border* was her first film, and she saw it as a chance to experiment with form. In an interview Biemann explained, "For me, *Performing the Border* was like a laboratory to find out what kind of films I would like to make. I didn't have a model" (Skype interview). After filming in Ciudad Juárez and a year of editing, she created a hybrid film which, years later, would be labeled a video essay by Swiss art critic Yvonne Volkart. The film is narrated by the subjective "I" of Biemann, and introduces the viewer to the gendered space of the border. Contemporary art critic Angela Dimitrakaki addresses what she calls the "detached architecture of the image" in *Performing the Border*, and analyzes how Biemann's voice-over is often not connected to any particular image (121). Dimitrakaki explains that "the video essayist's speech (as a voice-over and text) typically does not pose questions: instead, it operates through the statement, which can be either continuous or discontinuous with the image" (121). This juxtaposition of voice and image draws attention to Biemann's interest in artificial constructs created by borders, technology, and the video artist herself.

Performing the Border does not focus specifically on feminicide. Indeed, when Biemann went to the border to film, she had only been aware of the killings of women for three months prior to her trip. In her words, "For me the killing was actually not the reason for me to go there. I had a much more long-term interest in working women on the border and labor issues in the transnational context even ten years before I started this video" (Skype interview). However, once Biemann arrived in Ciudad Juárez she found that women working in *maquiladoras* (factories) and NGOs were talking about the killings, which is how the topic came to be integrated into her project. This is an example of how the voices of local women can form a counter-geography to the official discourse, which tried to cover up the issue of feminicide.

In terms of aesthetic concerns, the filmmaker knew that she did not want to reproduce overused imagery of women. For example, Biemann explained, "I've seen in the news on CNN, for instance, how they deal with the killings. They just drag this mother of a missing girl in front of a camera until she cries and that is that. I don't think that is, politically speaking, taking us anywhere" (Skype interview). Other common imagery in films and news stories on feminicide includes shots of their dead, damaged bodies. Is it necessary to represent horror realistically to give viewers an accurate, if graphic, depiction of the situation?

Biemann's films are tightly constructed and each editing or sound choice has a theoretical underpinning. For example, Biemann strips away all sounds from the natural environment and replaces them with an electronic sound carpet. In a 2008 essay Biemann discussed this choice, stating:

> I am not in search of reality—a notion that has proven to be a fiction in and of itself—but I am interested in generating an artificial construct. Most of my video footage is used without its original sound—no Mexican music, no diesel traffic. The border zone is a synthetic area, and this has been made perceptible through the manipulation and layering of images and an electronic soundscape. Ultimately, these drastic means are used as critical tools with which to sever the image from its signified and to shift the mode from documentary transparency to critical reflection.
> (*Ursula Biemann Mission Report* 15)

By separating the image from the diegetic sound, Biemann forces viewers to consider the border as an artificial construction and creates a surreal environment in which the sounds of daily life have been silenced and replaced by an electronic soundscape.

In contrast to the artificial border space, the women interviewed in the film are preserved as a whole—image and sound remain united. However, within the documentary some women such as performance artist Bertha Jottar discuss how the artificial border and industrial order attempt to turn women into cyborgs, to mechanize their lives and control their time. The industrialized, technological space of the border is poised to engulf the women who inhabit it. Biemann focuses on making connections between the machine culture of *maquiladoras* and surveillance, and she argues that only with the advent of the industrialized age did the serial killer appear.[4] However, Biemann is the only filmmaker who makes a connection between machine culture and serial killers, positing that the murders have, at least in part, been perpetrated by a serial killer.[5] In an article published in 2000, Kathleen Staudt commented "[o]f the total number of women murdered since 1993, approximately one in three of these murders fits the sexualized, perhaps serial-killer profile" ("Globalization and gender" 196).

Biemann made the decision to interview only women in her film. Among those who testify are performance artist Bertha Jottar and activist Esther Chávez. Of course, it was a polemic move on her part to exclude men from the film. However, Biemann explained,

One reason is that you actually end up meeting a lot more women. The [*maquiladora*] workers are women to a great extent, and the NGOs who deal with the women are also women. From what I could see there, guys just hang out being jobless. I don't think they are very important players in the global scenario. It is young girls who are the important actors. Why should I go and interview the bus drivers?

(Skype interview)

The video essay thus comes to represent female voices describing and rewriting the narrative of their city. To date, there has yet to be a film produced that focuses on men as central actors in the anti-feminicide movement.

In the section of the film titled "The Killings," Biemann includes a typed list of case numbers and descriptions of the violence suffered by each of the women who died during her last three months of filming in Ciudad Juárez. The women are anonymous, as Biemann identifies them only by the number of their police file and a description of the violence they suffered. Paired with descriptions of rape, strangulation, and mutilation, these numbers produce a shocking effect. The precise descriptions of violence are juxtaposed with the complete anonymity of the bodies. The director highlights the ethical and moral dilemmas of representing such graphic violence. In a 2004 article, Elena Poniatowska wrote "hoy más que nunca se habla de la frontera por el holocausto de género como llama Sabina Berman el asesinato de más de trescientas setenta mujeres" (today more than ever the border is spoken of for the holocaust of women, as Sabina Berman calls the killing of more than three hundred and seventy women) (88). Not only are acts of unspeakable violence being carried out in the city, but also victims go largely unidentified. Thus, the cityscape is littered with sites of violence, but, as will become evident in the two other documentaries, they are often marked with crosses labeled "*desconocida*" (unknown).

MISSING YOUNG WOMEN

In *Señorita Extraviada (Missing Young Women)* Lourdes Portillo, a self-identified Chicana, narrates her investigation of feminicide in Ciudad Juárez.[6] For Portillo, whose family is from Chihuahua, the documentary is both a personal and a professional investigation. Claudia Sadowski-Smith discusses how Portillo's documentary influenced other Chicano/a artists and became "the catalyst for a surge in representations of the femicide" (77). Her documentary showcases her belief in the capacity of art to transform the conscience of others.

In terms of an aesthetic of representation of victims of feminicide, Portillo describes, "I decided that the most respectful thing to do was to treat them [the victims] like human beings at their best, the way we represent ourselves. I decided to use their names, to use the pictures that the mothers loved, and to never really show the destruction of their bodies. That begets more of the same thing" (Skype interview). According to Elena Poniatowska, Portillo achieved her goals by representing "mujeres casi niñas que tenían una gran alegría de vivir y fueron importantes no sólo para su familia, sino para nosotros, para la sociedad" (young women that had a great joy for life and were important not only to their family but also to us, to society) (94).[7] The filmmaker focuses on bringing to life memories of the victims via the testimony of the mothers and other family members. Unlike Biemann's film, Portillo's seeks to portray the humanity of individual family members and victims of violence. By focusing on the families of the victims as key social actors, Portillo creates a discourse to rival the official one that disseminates photos of dead bodies of victims and questions their morality.

In Portillo's film, several hyper-accelerated frames show cars speeding around the city at dusk so quickly that they turn into a long stream of lights. Conversely, other images are seen in slow motion or are doubled or tripled as if the viewer were watching a mirage in a hot desert and grew unsure of the trustworthiness of her or his own vision. For example, the director shows the tripled image of a young girl wandering in a deserted lot, leaving her looking more like a ghost than an empowered actor in the city. To this end, Portillo as narrator states, "vine a Juárez a perseguir fantasmas y a escuchar el misterio que los rodea" (I came to Juárez to chase ghosts and listen to the mystery that surrounds them). Her use of the blurred image of the young girl suggests that the dividing line between life and death for women in Ciudad Juárez has become so thin as to haunt the living. Sergio de la Mora describes how "A través de *Señorita Extraviada*, Portillo utiliza un diseño visual auto-reflexivo que subraya que los documentales no reproducen la realidad neutralmente" (In *Señorita Extraviada*, Portillo uses a self-reflexive visual design that highlights that documentaries do not reproduce reality naturally) (127). As he makes clear, Portillo employs various techniques to make the viewer question the idea that an image can represent the truth: she films through glass or uses extreme close-ups, distorting images.

The film demonstrates the difficulty of pursuing the perpetrators of both physical and economic violence. Julián Cardona, a photographer for *El Diario* who has lived and worked in Ciudad Juárez since 1993, believes that physical and economic violence have to be analyzed together, and that culprits of both must be more consistently punished by the law. He asserts, "Cuando estás retratando a una sociedad en la que el sistema económico es totalmente inoperante debes considerar no sólo la violencia física que se produce tal sociedad que es totalmente desigualitaria sino también la violencia económica que da vía a la primera" (When you are representing a society in which the economic system is totally ineffective you should consider not only the physical violence that a society of inequality produces but also the economic violence that first causes it) (Personal interview). The links between physical and economic violence can be seen in an analysis of the economic situation of the victims, their geographical home in the city, and the places where their bodies were dumped. In each case, marginalization is the common factor. Victims are so poor that they often cannot afford the price of public transportation, they live in informal housing constructed from materials in landfills, and their bodies are left in abandoned lots, often on the periphery of the city. According to Monárrez Fragoso,

> No es irrelevante, por ejemplo, en el caso de Ciudad Juárez, que cuando un cadáver de mujer es encontrado, tiene 80 por ciento de probabilidades de pertenecer a la zona del poniente de la ciudad, donde se encuentra el mayor déficit de infraestructura urbana en electricidad, agua potable, drenaje y pavimento; donde además se concentra la población inmigrante. (It is not irrelevant, for example, in the case of Ciudad Juárez, that when the corpse of a woman is found, there is an 80% probability that she is from the western zone of the city where one can find the least urban infrastructure in terms of electricity, drinking water, drainage, and pavement; furthermore this is where the immigrant population is concentrated)
>
> (61)

Portillo focuses the camera lens on the zones of the city described by Monárrez Fragoso, linking economic hardship to the low wages provided by international industries and the lack of attention to basic needs permitted by local government.

The director also represents the city as a site of symbolic action: pink crosses painted on a black background on telephone poles, posters of missing girls, and small memorials constructed by families feature prominently in the film. Although the city may be spinning out of control on a globalized level, she makes it evident that citizens work actively to reclaim the geography of the city and install sites of subversive memory to memorialize victims. The official narrative that families of victims of feminicide encounter is one of political will to forget or misrepresent the victims. Portillo shows the efforts of citizens to write their own text onto the city landscape, but she also shows the limited success of those efforts. For example, she interviews a girl on a busy street surrounded by "missing girl" posters and pink crosses, and the young girl states that she is unaware that women had been abducted from the very spot where she is standing.

The role of the mother and her contributions to the symbolic geography of the city are explored by Kathleen Staudt in *Human Rights along the U.S.-Mexico Border* (2009). Her research demonstrates that "Mothers invented public icons and symbols seen everywhere in Ciudad Juárez: pink and black crosses, painted on telephone poles and walls, especially visible on the main thoroughfares of Juárez" (115). Portillo interviews Guillermina González Flores, the sister of one of the feminicide victims, and a founder of the anti-feminicide group Voces Sin Eco (Voices without Echo).[8] González Flores, as founder of the group, initiated the first campaign to paint crosses around the city. The March 20th edition of *El Diario* in 1999 documented the work of the group and described, based on an interview with González Flores, that the intention of the crosses "es mantener vigente todos los días del año un recordatorio sobre el peligro que corren todas las mujeres que viven en Ciudad Juárez" (to maintain every day of the year a valid reminder about the dangers women who live in Ciudad Juárez face) (Carmen Sosa 8C). The pink crosses feature prominently in *Señorita Extraviada,* which shows how they have become incorporated into the cityscape to such an extent that some young girls do not even notice.

Señorita Extraviada highlights how memory of the past is necessary to construct a safe future for women in Ciudad Juárez. Huyssen discusses a shift in sensibility about how societies approach the future that is evident in Portillo's film. He stresses the delicate balance between remembering the past and working for a better future: "If, in the earlier twentieth century, modern societies tried to define their modernity and to secure their cohesiveness by way of imagining the future, it now seems that the major required task of any society today is to take responsibility for its past (some lament this as the present being held hostage by the past)" (101). The tension between memories of past victims of feminicide (maintained by families) and visions of the future spun (by politicians) is central to the documentary. Does collective memory exist in a city with such tensions? When asked about the presence of collective memory, the director replied:

> There is some collective memory when the mothers get together. They are the keepers of memory. They do talk amongst themselves. I know that society is destroyed, the societal fabric. Everybody lives in fear. The children have become very violent. I don't know about collective memory. It's only when they get together—the families or the mothers.
>
> (Skype interview)

Portillo addresses the difficulties of memory cinematically by presenting footage that is blurred as if to triplicate a young girl walking in the desert in one frame. The image, like memory itself, is subject to the ravages of time and interpretation.

After filming *Señorita Extraviada*, Portillo continued to return to Ciudad Juárez and follow the families that appeared in her film. During the process she witnessed the disintegration of the social fabric of Ciudad Juárez as families suffered from overwhelming grief, violence, and harassment by the police. Portillo elaborates, "In following up all the stories, every person's story is the destruction of community and family as we know it. The deaths of these girls have caused that" (Skype interview). This situation represents a real and continuing challenge to the permanence of memory.

The Battle of the Crosses

This question of memory is central to both *Señorita Extraviada* and *La batalla de las cruces (The Battle of the Crosses)*. In a 2005 article on the subject of feminicide, Ravelo stated her belief that "las muertes violentas en esta frontera representan un *sufrimiento colectivo*, un *trauma social*, un *dolor histórico* que permanece en la memoria de la sociedad, en una *memoria lastimada y herida*" (the violent deaths on this border represent *collective suffering, social trauma,* and *historical pain* that remains in the memory of society, a memory that is *hurt and wounded*) ("La costumbre de matar" 150–51). In *La batalla de las cruces* the protectors of collective memory are the mothers of victims, and their testimony is a guiding force throughout the film. The mothers are filmed in the comfort of their kitchens and living rooms, surrounded by sunlight, looking comfortable but sad. Thus the home becomes a site of memory, a place where mothers, families, or community members gather to share stories about victims of feminicide. Domestic space forms a sanctioned memory space and most documentaries produced on feminicide rely heavily on the testimony of women in their homes.

Director Rafael Bonilla collaborated with academic Patricia Ravelo Blancas to produce a documentary that incorporated Ravelo Blancas' years of research on the subject of feminicide into an artifact of historical memory. The film, with a dramatic "voice of God" narration, focuses on how families of victims and other citizens work to preserve the memory of the dead. The reliance on voice-over techniques makes *La batalla de las cruces* the most traditional of the three documentaries in terms of form. This form of indirect address, as Bill Nichols suggests, "invites risks of incomprehensibility (lacking the guiding hand of a narrator)" (183). Rafael Bonilla decided to use the voice-over because "[d]e alguna manera la voz en off sintetiza los textos de Patricia.... Es una voz explicativa que trata de contextualizar el fenómeno" (somehow the voice-over synthesizes Patricia's research.... It is an explanatory voice that tries to contextualize the phenomenon) (Personal interview). However, the melodramatic nature of the voice-over proves problematic because the anonymous, authoritarian voice contrasts sharply with the personal nature of the film. Voice-overs are usually associated with authoritarian, elitist, or paternalistic discourses. Ravelo Blancas and Bonilla do avoid the paternalist critique by using a female voice-over, but the fact still remains that the strong narrative voice overshadows the testimonies of the mothers of victims of feminicide. The voice-over, rather than complementing the interviews, competes for authority with their voices.

Bonilla and Ravelo Blancas, through conversations with the victims' mothers carried out over a number of years, became aware of certain issues of representation that the mothers found unethical. In 2004, when the norteño group *Los Tigres del Norte (The Tigers of the North)* produced the song "Las muertas de Juárez" ("The Dead Women of Juárez"), many of the mothers protested against the song and accompanying video. However, through dialogue with the mothers Bonilla came to realize that

[...] las mamás no estaban enojadas con la canción. Sino estaban enojadas porque en la televisión siempre veían los huesos y los cadáveres de sus hijas. Es decir, eso es lo que les dolía-la parte mórbida de los medios que las lastimaba mucho. Por eso es que desde entonces adaptamos a la actitud de no meter eso en pantalla por respecto y esa es una condición ética (the mothers weren't mad about the song. Rather they were mad because on television they always saw the bones and cadavers of their daughters. That is what hurt them—the morbid part of the media is what hurt them a lot. Because of this we decided to adopt the attitude to not show that in the film, out of respect and because it is an ethical condition).

(Personal interview)

The documentary thus relies on photos and crosses to stand in symbolically for the missing bodies. One technique that the filmmakers use involves showing individual photos of missing women (donated by families or taken from the newspaper) and then typing, letter by letter, their names onto the screen. Thus viewers are introduced to the image before they hear the sound of a typewriter and see the names of victims slowly appear on the screen.

In an interview, Ravelo discussed the central role that the mothers played in making and presenting the film to an audience in Ciudad Juárez: "Las que presentaron el documental fueron tres mamás: Paula Flores, Benita Monárrez y Evangelina Arce. Ellas presentaron porque te digo que nuestra manera de trabajar es diferente. Nosotros somos muy críticos de que las mamás las andan abusando y las andan excediendo y poniéndolos a llorar a todos lados" (Three mothers introduced the documentary: Paula Flores, Benita Monárrez, and Evangelina Arce. They introduced it because our way of working is different. We are very critical of people who abuse the mothers and demand that they cry everywhere) (Personal interview). This comment mirrors what Ursula Biemann said when criticizing how news networks like CNN have used of images of mothers crying for stories on feminicide. The directors were inspired by what they learned of the life of Paula Flores during the process of making *La batalla de las cruces*, and decided to make her the focus of their next documentary, *La Carta (The Letter)*, about the life of Paula Flores.[9] This film, like *La batalla de las cruces*, forms part of a record of historical memory of victims of feminicide and the far-reaching influences of the crimes on families, citizens, and the city. Ravelo discussed the central aims of the film in the following manner:

Principalmente lo que nosotros queríamos era dejar una memoria histórica de esa década en ese documental. La segunda cosa muy importante es que ese material fue un material de esas mujeres y familias para que ellas en todas sus gestiones y actos de protesta pudieran decir "aquí está esta memoria histórica con toda la verdad." (Mainly we wanted to capture the historic memory of that decade in the documentary. The second important thing is that the material was material from the women and families so that they, in all their negotiations and acts of protest, could say "here is true historic memory").

(Personal interview)

The effort to leave an historical memory is especially evident in a shot in which newspaper clippings of murdered girls and women are superimposed over a desert background while the voice-over narrates: "niñas, jóvenes, estudiantes, trabajadoras de la maquila, adolescentes, madres, bailarinas, trabajadoras sexuales" (children, young women, students, factory workers, adolescents, mothers, dancers, sex workers). This section highlights the far-reaching effects of feminicide on girls and women from many different backgrounds. It also focuses on how the physical geography of the desert has, in a sense, "devoured" the bodies of many of the murdered women.

The title, *La batalla de las cruces*, was taken from an article that Ravelo wrote with Héctor Domínguez in 2003.[10] The title, like images from the film, focuses on symbols of the feminicide movement that have become incorporated into the memoryscape of Ciudad Juárez. There are several shots of the eight crosses erected on the cotton fields where the bodies of eight murdered women were found in 1998. A close-up of the pink crosses decorated with purple flowers shows that "*desconocida*" (unknown) is written on several of them. In this instance community members have created a memory space for the unidentified.

The eight crosses in the cotton fields remained, for many years, an important visual marker of feminicide that could be seen when driving by the area. However, recently, as Julián Cardona discussed with me, the city constructed a new hotel on the lot, replacing a memory site with a non-place (Personal interview).[11] In a 2009 newspaper article Judith Torrea described how, due to the construction of the Hotel Conquistador Inn, "Las cruces rosas con los nombres de 8 jóvenes desaparecidas y muertas son sólo un recuerdo en fotos de archivo de periódicos" (The pink crosses with the names of eight young disappeared and dead women are now a memory in newspaper photo archives) (1). Torrea points out that progress in Ciudad Juárez is not detained by terror.

In the case of the cotton-field killings, the interests of urban development trumped those of citizens and families of victims. Jelin and Lagland describe the precariousness of maintaining memory through marking space: "Construir monumentos, marcar espacios, respetar y conservar ruinas son procesos que se desarrollan en el tiempo, que implican luchas sociales, y que producen (o fracasan en producir) esta semantización de los espacios materiales" (To construct monuments, to mark space, to respect and conserve ruins are processes that develop over time, that imply social struggles, and that produce (or fail to produce) the semantization of material space) (3–4). The construction of the hotel can perhaps be considered a lesser form of economic violence—the ability to void an area of symbolic meaning. *La batalla de las cruces* captures the eight crosses on the cotton fields that were, for almost a decade, part of the memoryscape of Ciudad Juárez. In an August 2010 interview academic Tabuenca Córdoba, who has lived and worked in Ciudad Juárez/El Paso her whole life, remembered, just a day earlier, driving by the crosses in Ciudad Juárez. However, she paused just for a moment, shook her head, and said, "I tried to look for the crosses, and I didn't see them. I'm not sure if they're still there" (Personal interview). Although they had been gone for at least a year by that time, the crosses still remained part of the memoryscape of Tabuenca Córdoba.

THE FILMIC MEMORYSCAPE IN CIUDAD JUÁREZ

Performing the Border, *Señorita Extraviada*, and *La batalla de las cruces* focus on physical and human counter-geographies that work against the prevailing discourse in Ciudad Juárez which tries to ignore, erase, or rewrite the stories of victims of feminicide. By emphasizing the importance of symbols on the cityscape, these films highlight how citizens have brought a discussion of feminicide to the forefront and preserve the memory of victims. These films examine the notion of the city as palimpsest and demonstrate the persistence of memory through a conglomeration of signs, voices, and actions that contest the official history.

ACKNOWLEDGMENT

Thank you to the following filmmakers, academics, activists, and photographers for allowing me to interview them: Ursula Biemann, Lourdes Portillo, Patricia Ravelo Blancas, Rafael Bonilla, Julián Cardona, and María Socorro Tabuenca Córdoba. Ravelo Blancas, coordinator of the project of Social Protest and Collective Actions Against Feminicide, also provided me with invaluable materials for my research. Thanks also to Cecelia Carrasco and Molly Molloy, librarians at New Mexico State University who helped make possible my research with the Esther Chávez Cano collection.

NOTES

1. The theoretical term femicide was coined in England in 1801 and popularized by the South African feminist writer and activist Diana E.H. Russell in the books *The Politics of Rape: The Victims of Perspective* (1974) and *Femicide: The Politics of Woman Killing* (1992).

Current use of the word has been made less clear due to the interchangeable use of the terms femicide and feminicide. However, in *Terrorizing Women: Femincide in the Americas* (2010) Rosa-Linda Fregoso and Cynthia Bejarano clarify that, "Building on the generic definition of *femicide* as 'the murder of women and girls *because* they are female' (Russell 2001a, 15), we define *feminicide* as the murders of women and girls founded on a gender power structure" (5). I use the term in this sense.

2. Other films and documentaries on feminicide in Ciudad Juárez include the following: *Ni una más* (2001); *Juárez: Desierto de esperanza* (2002); *Las muertas de Juárez* (2002); *Espejo retrovisor* (2002); *Femicidio, hecho en México* (2003); *16 en la lista: crimenes en Juárez* (2004); *Dual Injustice: Feminicide and Torture in Ciudad Juárez and Chihuahua* (2005); *Juárez Mothers Fight Femicide* (2005); *Juárez: Stages of Fear* (2005); *Juárez, Mexico* (2005); *Preguntas sin respuestas* (2005); *Bajo Juárez: La ciudad devorando a sus hijas* (2006); *Bordertown* (2006); *Border Echos* (2006); *The Virgin of Juárez* (2006); *On the Edge: The Femicide in Ciudad Juárez* (2006); *Juárez: The City Where Women are Disposable* (2007); *El traspatio* (2009); *Silencio en Juárez* (2009); *La Carta* (2010).

3. In a spatial study on violence in Ciudad Juárez published in 2010, Luis Cervera and Monárrez Fragoso clarify that, "En el espacio público es donde se han generado la mayor parte de los asesinos, y hay una menor incidencia en lotes baldíos, parques, tapias y el transporte urbano. Las prácticas sociales que se realizan en la calle, como parte de la esfera pública, representan expresiones de relaciones de poder, y por ende de control, que denotan luchas entre diversos individuos y grupos en la arena social" (Public space is where most of the murders have taken place, and a smaller number have occurred in abandoned lots, parks, walled lots, and on public transport. The social practices that are realized in the street, as part of the public sphere, represent expressions of the relations of power and thus of control. They also show struggles between diverse individuals and groups in the public sphere) (11).

4. The idea that women who work on assembly lines in *maquiladoras* are becoming mechanized can also be seen in Vicky Funari and Sergio de la Torre's documentary *Maquilapolis: City of Factories* (2006). I am thinking specifically of the opening shot of *Maquilapolis* in which several female factory workers are standing in the desert performing the mechanical operations that are required of them on a daily basis in the factories where they work.

5. Biemann based her theory entirely on Mark Seltzer's *Serial Killers: Death and Life in America's Wound Culture* (1998), which came out during the time she was editing *Performing the Border*.

6. Portillo was born in Chihuahua, Mexico but raised in Los Angeles. For Sadowski-Smith, *Señorita Extraviada* "exemplifies an important

milestone in this transnationalization of Chicano/a work, which adds developments outside the United States to an emphasis on the diasporic nature of Chicano/as and Latino/as in the United States" (76).

7. Poniatowska also praises the documentary *Juárez: Desierto de esperanza* by Christina Michaus.
8. Voces Sin Eco, which was founded in 1998, disbanded after three years because González Flores believed that many groups (journalists, NGOs, the media) were trying to profit from the issue of feminicide. However, Guillermina and her mother Paula Flores have continued to be active in the anti-feminicide movement.
9. Ravelo discussed the importance of Paula Flores in the 2004 article "Entre las protestas callejeras y las acciones internacionales: diez años de activismo por la justicia social en Ciudad Juárez." She wrote, "Consideramos que la trayectoria de Paula Flores ha sido importante. Es una mujer natal de Durango que llegó a ciudad Juárez con la ilusión de que su hijo estudiara y de que sus hijas tuvieran una mejor oportunidad de trabajo. Una mujer que, al llegar a Lomas de Poleo en ANAPRA (una ciudad ubicada en la periferia de la ciudad), pensaba como algo ajeno la violencia hacia las mujeres, hasta que inició su peregrinar por la justicia y posteriormente con el encuentro de su hija asesinada" (We think that Paula Flores' trajectory has been important. She is a woman from Durango who arrived to Ciudad Juárez with the dream that her son would study and her daughters would have better job opportunities. A woman who, on arriving to Lomas de Poleo in ANAPRA (a city located on the outskirts of the city) thought of violence against women as something foreign to her, until she began her pilgrimage for justice and after her daughter was killed) ("Entre las protestas callejeras" 24).
10. The article, "La batalla de las cruces: crímenes contra mujeres en la frontera y sus intérpretes" was pubslihed in *Desacatos* in 2003.
11. In *Non-Places: Introduction to an Anthropology of Supermodernity*, Marc Augé defines a non-place as a construction like a mall, airport, or supermarket that is designed to be homogenous regardless of its location to such an extent that it lacks the significance to be regarded as a place.

Works Cited

Augé, Marc. *Non-Places: Introduction to an Anthropology of Supermodernity*. London: Verso, 1995. Print.

Bickford, Louis. "Memoryscapes." *The Art of Truth-telling About Authoritarian Rule*. Ed. Kesenija Bilbija, Joe Ellen Fair, Cynthia Milton, and Leigh Payne. Madison: Wisconsin UP, 2005. Print.

Biemann, Ursula. Skype Interview. July 25, 2010.

Biemann, Ursula, and Jan-Erik Lundström, eds. *Ursula Biemann Mission Report—Artistic Practice in the Field—Video Works 1998–2008.* Umea: Arnolfini, 2008. Print.

Bonilla, Rafael. Personal Interview. June 18, 2010.

Cardona, Julián. Personal Interview. Aug. 20, 2010.

Carmen Sosa, Luz del. "Protestan contra la violencia: Pintan cruces negras." *El Diario* March 20, 1999: 8C. Print.

Cervera Gómez, Luis Ernesto and Julia E. Monárrez Fragoso. "Sistema de información geográfica de la violencia en el municipio de Juárez, Chihuahua: Geo-referenciación y su comportamineto espacial en el contexto urbano y rural (SIGVIDA)." Cuidad Júarez, Chihuahua: CONAVIM, 2010.

Dimitrakaki, Angela. "Materialist Feminism for the Twenty-First Century: The Video Essay of Ursula Biemann." *Ursula Biemann Mission Report—Artistic Practice in the Field—Video Works 1998–2008.* Ed. Ursula Biemann and Jan-Erik Lundström. Umea: Arnolfini, 2008. Print.

Fregoso, Rosa-Linda, and Cynthia Bejarano, eds. *Terrorizing Women: Feminicide in the Américas.* Durham: Duke UP, 2010. Print.

Herlinghaus, Hermann. *Violence without Guilt: Ethical Narratives from the Global South.* New York: Palgrave, 2009. Print.

Huyssen, Andreas. *Urban Palimpsests and the Politics of Memory.* Stanford: Stanford UP, 2003. Print.

Jelin, Elizabeth, and Victoria Langland, eds. *Monumentos, memoriales y marcas territoriales.* Madrid: Siglo XXI, 2003. Print.

Monárrez Fragoso, and Julia Estela. *Trama de una injusticia: feminicidio sexual sistémico en Ciudad Juárez.* El Colegio de la Frontera Norte: Tijuana, 2009.

Mora, Sergio de la. "Terrorismo del género en la frontera de EUA-México: Asesinato, mujeres y justicia en *Señorita extraviada* de Lourdes Portillo." *Cinémas d'Amérique Latine* 12 (2004): 116–32. Print.

Nichols, Bill. *Ideology and Image.* Bloomington: Indiana UP, 1981. Print.

Poniatowska, Elena. "Esa larga cicatriz." *Chicana/Latina Studies: The Journal of Mujeres Activas en Letras y Cambio Social* 4.1 (2004): 88–94. Print.

Portillo, Lourdes. Skype Interview. May 5, 2010.

Radford, Jill, and Diana E.H. Russell., eds. *Femicide: The Politics of Woman Killing.* New York: Twayne, 1992. Print.

Ravelo Blancas, Patricia. "La costumbre de matar: proliferación de la violencia en Ciudad Juárez, Chihuahua, México." *Nueva Antropología* 65 (2005): 149–66. Print.

——. "Entre las protestas callejeras y las acciones internacionales: diez años de activismo por la justicia social en Ciudad Juárez." *Cotidiano: revista de la realidad mexicana actual* 125 (2004): 21–32. Print.

——. Personal Interview. June 18, 2010.

Ravelo Blancas, Patricia, and Héctor Domínguez Ruvalcaba. "La batalla de las cruces: crímenes contra mujeres en la frontera y sus intérpretes." *Desacatos* 13 (2003): 122–33. Print.

Reyes Sahagún, Teresa Guadalupe. "Comisión especial para conocer y dar seguimiento puntual y exhaustivo a las acciones que han emprendido las autoridades competentes en relación a los feminicidios en México." Mexican Legislature, Mexico City. June 22, 2010. Meeting comments.

Russell, Diana. E.H. *The Politics of Rape: The Victim's Perspective*. New York: Stein and Day, 1974. Print.

Sadowski-Smith, Claudia. "Imagining Transnational Chicano/a Activism against Gender-Based Violence at the U.S.-Mexican Border." *Imagined Transnationalism: U.S. Latino/a Literature, Culture, and Identity*. Ed. Kevin Concannon et al. New York: Palgrave Macmillan, 2009. 75–94. Print.

Seltzer, Mark. *Serial Killers: Death and Life in America's Wound Culture*. New York: Routledge, 1998. Print.

Staudt, Kathleen. "Globalization and Gender at Border Sites: Femicide and Domestic Violence in Ciudad Juárez." *Gender and Global Restructuring: Sightings, Sites and Resistances*. Ed. Marianne H. Marchland and Anne Sisson Runyan. New York: Routledge, 2000. 187–200. Print.

———. *Human Rights along the U.S.-Mexico Border: Gendered Violence and Insecurity*. Tucson: Arizona UP, 2009. Print.

Tabuenca Córdoba, María Socorro. Personal Interview. Aug. 19, 2010.

Torrea, Judith. "Amarga justicia para las madres de Ciudad Juárez." *El Mundo*. Unidad Editorial Internet, Nov. 20, 2009. Web. Jan. 2010, http://www.elmundo.es/america/2009/11/20/mexico/1258739292.html.

Volk, Steven S., and Marian E. Schlotterbeck. "Gender, Order, and Femicide: Reading the Popular Culture of Murder in Ciudad Juárez." *Making a Killing: Femicide, Free Trade and La Frontera*. Ed. Alicia Gaspar de Alba and Georgina Guzmán. Austin: Texas UP, 2010. 121–54. Print.

Filmography

Bajo Juárez: La ciudad devorando a sus hijas. Dir. Alejandra Sánchez. FOPROCINE/IMCINE, 2006.

La batalla de las cruces: protesta social y acciones colectivas en torno de la violencia sexual en Ciudad Juárez. Dir. Patricio Ravelo and Rafael Bonilla. Campo Imaginario, 2006.

Border Echoes. Dir. Lorena Mendez-Quiroga. Peace at the Border, 2006.

Bordertown. Dir. Gregory Nava. Perf. Jennifer Lopez, Martin Sheen, and Antonio Banderas. Mobius Entertainment/El Norte Productions, 2006.

La carta. Dir. Rafael Bonilla. FOPROCINE/Huapanguero Volador Films, 2010.

16 en la lista: crímenes en Juárez. Dir. Rodolfo Rodobertti. CPM Films, 1998.
Dual Injustice: Feminicide and Torture in Ciudad Juárez and Chihuahua. Dir. Laura Salas and Tamaryn Nelson. CMDPHD/Witness, 2005.
Espejo retrovisor. Dir. Héctor Molinar. Perf. Manuel Ojeda, Azela Robinson, and Géraldine Bazán. Cine Producciones Molinar, 2002.
Femicidio, hecho en México. Dir. Vanessa Bauche. Perf. Norma Andrade and Sergio González Rodríguez. Justicia con Equidad, 2003.
Juárez: Desierto de esperanza. Dir. Cristina Michaus. Tenzin, 2002.
Juárez, Mexico. Dir. James Cahill. Perf. James Cahill, Roberto Sánchez, and Carmen Perez. Dodging Bullets, 2005.
Juárez Mothers Fight Femicide. Dir. Zulma Aguilar. Nuestras Hijas de Regreso a Casa, 2005.
Juárez: Stages of Fear. Dir. César Alejandro. Perf. Chris Penn, César Alejandro, and María Rebeca. Stages of Fear Joint Venture, 2005.
Juárez: The City Where Women Are Disposable. Dir. Alex Flores. Las Perlas del Mar, 2007.
Maquilapolis: City of Factories. Dir. Vicky Funari and Sergio de la Torre. Independent Television Service, 2006.
Las muertas de Juárez. Dir. Enrique Murillo. Perf. Claudia Bernal, Carlos Cardán, and Eleazar García Jr. Laguna Productions, 2002.
Ni una más. Dir. Alejandra Sánchez. FOPROCINE/IMCINE. 2001.
On the Edge: The Femicide in Ciudad Juárez. Dir. Steev Hise. Detrital Films, 2006.
Performing the Border. Dir. Ursula Biemann. Women Make Movies, 1999.
Preguntas sin respuestas. Dir. Rafael Montero. IMCINE, 2005.
Señorita Extraviada. Dir. Lourdes Portillo. Women Make Movies, 2001.
Silencio en Juárez. Dir. Michela Giorelli. Discovery Channel, 2009.
El traspatio. Dir. Carlos Carrera. Perf. Ana de la Reguera, Jimmy Smits, and Amorita Rasgado. Tardan/Berman, 2009.
The Virgin of Juárez. Dir. Kevin James Dobson. Perf. Minnie Driver, Esai Morales, and Ana Mercedes. Las Mujeres LLC, 2006.

CHAPTER 11

DRAWING THE LINE BETWEEN
MEMORY, HISTORY, AND ARTISTIC
RE/CREATION: MIGUEL GALLARDO
AND CARLOS GIMÉNEZ'S GRAPHIC
TESTIMONIES

Janis Breckenridge

Miguel Gallardo's singular *Un largo silencio* (A Long Silence, 1997) and Carlos Giménez's comic series, *Todo Paracuellos* (The Complete Paracuellos, 2007), graphically depict distinct facets of the Spanish civil war and its aftermath. Gallardo gives voice to his father, transcribing and illustrating his experiences before, during, and immediately after serving with the Republican army. *Todo Paracuellos*, in turn, can be understood as a series of fictionalized, testimonial comics that chronicle the harsh quotidian realities of growing up in the *Hogares del Auxilio Social* (Social Auxiliary Orphanages) during the 1940s and 50s. Paradoxically, these socially committed texts remain firmly rooted in overly familiar *testimonio* paradigms even as they radically experiment with the genre's traditional format, transforming orally transmitted life stories into visual narratives.[1] Although drawing on testimonial discourses and processes, the blurring of factual reportage and fictionalized re/creation, together with the deliberate retelling of seriously significant historical events through a marginalized literary medium once disdained as entertaining and childish, allow these works to break free from testimonio's generic limitations. That is, in openly resisting an oppressive societal silence, these graphic testimonies further defy static narrative paradigms.

Unlike the more distanced or detached professional relationship between the testimonial subject and the trained editor/transcriber typical of the genre, Gallardo and Giménez narrate traumatic events experienced by others that have, at the same time, directly impacted their own personal lives. This essay explores the dynamic between testimonial intent and artistic re-creation at play in their graphic testimonies. Particular attention is paid to aesthetic qualities, especially the connections between graphic format and history, life story, and memory, both personal and collective. Even as these innovative works tenaciously cling to testimonial practices—collecting documentation and data, recording and transcribing the words of testimonial subjects—they increasingly distance themselves from classic testimonial models. *Un largo silencio* and *Todo Paracuellos* literally illustrate novel possibilities for testimonio.

DRAWING TESTIMONY OUT OF THE SHADOWS: *UN LARGO SILENCIO*

Narrated in the first person as reported by the editor/compiler's father, *Un largo silencio* seems at first to strictly adhere to the standards of testimony. The narrative consists of the telling of a life story: a tale of poverty, hunger, hardship, and deprivation. The methodical and chronologically driven narration, replete with precise details including exact prices, actual grades received, meticulous naming of military weaponry, and technical explanations of battle preparation, suggests a deliberately factual and objectively documented account. The book's structure upholds this documentary content and reinforces its testimonial intent. Typical of canonical testimonio texts (à la Rigoberta Menchú, Miguel Barnet, and Domitila Barrios), the title page indicates dual authorship, listing the testimonial subject, Francisco Gallardo Sarmiento, above the transcriber, Miguel Ángel Gallardo. Predictably, the brief prologue asserts the narrative's veracity and describes Gallardo's role as transcriber and mediator for his father. Photographs, letters, and official documents open and close the slender volume.

At first glance then, *Un largo silencio*, whose title refers to the many years that his father refused to talk before he began to repeatedly tell his story, follows conventional testimonial paradigms with respect to both narrative structure and content. The text retains what foundational testimonio critics such as George Yúdice and Marc Zimmerman consider to be the fundamental characteristics of testimonial literature. Transcription of an oral discourse gives voice to a marginalized and silenced individual who stands in for a collective; documentary paratexts confer validity upon an individual life story that personalizes events of historic and social significance. Nevertheless, even at its outset the seemingly traditional format contains unexpected experimental techniques that hint at the more abrupt, radical visual departures that supersede standard testimonio practice and supplant the verbal narration.

The prologue upholds reader expectations regarding orality, truth telling, and the act of giving voice to a silenced protagonist of an overlooked or forgotten history. Yet surprisingly, with the opening words of "Mi padre es un héroe" (My father is a hero) (5)[2] Gallardo overtly defies customary presentation of the testimonial speaker as ordinary and representative of a social group. Rather than claim his father to be a typical Republican soldier as we have come to expect of testimonial subjects who adamantly renounce singularity and exceptionalism, Gallardo blatantly venerates him as a hero for his acts of survival. In a similar vein, the author/compiler explains that this is "Una historia que, a fuerza de oír, se me ha quedado grabada" (a story that, through listening, has remained imprinted upon me) (5). Given the subtle nuances of word choice, the possible translations of *grabada* remain telling: the story has been recorded, engraved, or etched on his mind. In other words, it is implied that the son recalls the testimonial voice by sheer force of repetition rather than actually recording the father's words for the sake of writing the book. Either way, the term *grabada* simultaneously points to both the traditional testimonial process and the visual arts.

It is, however, the cover and the title page that most directly anticipate the text's incorporation of visual material. Even in following the convention of listing both participants as coproducers of the text, these pages prominently display artistic sketches. Shaded drawings of warplanes, a fallen body on the street, and a twisted, open-mouthed horse—reminiscent of Pablo Picasso's emblematic painting of the atrocities of the Spanish civil war, *Guernica*—subtly prepare the reader for the visually inspired text that follows.

Throughout *Un largo silencio*, which could appropriately be described as an illustrated testimonio, penciled drawings substantiate the father's recollections. That is, basic sketches frequently appear in the margins and render, visually, individual people, relevant military equipment, particular modes of transportation, and specific insignia mentioned in the oral testimony. The transcription, increasingly punctuated by such visual material, further undergoes sudden and dramatic shifts in narrative style. In fact, what remains truly unique about this otherwise standard testimony is its rich and eclectic blend of oral, textual, and visual media. The integration of two full-page layouts, pages that literally draw upon historically significant (photo)graphic news (notas gráficas) published in Barcelona's *La Vanguardia*, authenticates the informant's personal memories. These hand-drawn re-creations anticipate and, more importantly, strategically *validate* the author's radical incorporation of comic art or "juxtaposed pictorial and other images in deliberate sequence, intended to convey information and/or to produce aesthetic response" as defined by Scott McCloud (9).

Entire graphic sequences abruptly appear, whether to repeat or supplant the text-based, oral transcription. Inserting graphic layouts radically alters the pace and the emotional effect of the oral testimony. This visualization instills a sense of urgency and, more significantly, fosters an illusion of immediacy. Although critics of testimonio have traditionally rejected the possibility of reader identification,[3] the employment of a visual medium places the viewer in a unique position for seeing and experiencing what the informant recalls. The act of reading becomes secondary as the listener, together with the testimonial subject, engages in the process of bearing witness to (the visual retelling of) traumatic events.

Gallardo's testimonial text undergoes no fewer than five such dramatic transformations or ruptures whereby the predominantly textual transcription suddenly shifts to visual or graphic format. Not coincidentally, these insertions occur with pivotal and intensely emotional, if not altogether traumatic, moments. In each case, the father's otherwise carefully controlled chronological account gives way to an emotionally charged and highly personal story. Breaking the ordered narrative structure, these visually rendered scenes more accurately reflect traumatic memory. As Anne Whitehead elucidates with respect to experimental techniques in narrative fiction, "This method of narration emphasizes the traumatic nature of the memories described, which are not so much remembered as re-experienced or relived" (35). Much in the same way, utilizing visual narration responds to an inherent danger noted by critics of testimonio and trauma: that in their retelling, traumatic events can lose their initial shock, force, or impact.[4] The visual sequences essentially (re)enact traumatic moments. In addition to showing how the testimonial subject remains haunted by these images,[5] events seemingly unfold before the reader's very eyes. No longer merely a passive recipient of testimony, s/he is suddenly thrust into the role of eyewitness.

The first such visualization occurs when describing the rapidly escalating violence taking place in 1936. The testimonial subject's strictly chronological retelling suddenly jumps from preparations for a possible invasion by Franco's forces to the actual event several months later. Then, in graphic format, a series of flashbacks of shocking events—political assassinations, inescapable sounds of gunshots, union membership becoming a requirement to continue employment, and personally enlisting with Republican forces—foreshadow the outbreak of civil war. The stark panels culminate with an illustration of illiteracy among the Republicans. The viewer readily perceives the testimonial subject's unstated but no less profound sense of tragic injustice and impending disaster.

Significantly, the following graphic sequence literally interrupts the oral transcription in mid-sentence. "Mira" (look) (29) commands the father, as he thrusts a photograph corroborating his tale into his interlocutor's (and consequently the reader's) field of vision. The use of direct address underscores the interactive and oral nature of the narrator's account, drawing in the reader. At the same time, the hand-drawn reproduction of a photographic image (one that appears in the text's opening pages) reinforces the factual content underpinning his testimony now rendered, unconventionally, through the medium of comic art.

The illustrated anecdote records the shock of a joyful day shattered by the horrors of war. Gallardo first presents a series of spacious panels depicting leisurely outdoor activities under sunny skies suddenly interrupted by wailing air raid sirens, depicted graphically by means of onomatopoeia, or literally spelling out the vocalized imitation of sound.[6] These initial panels are then powerfully juxtaposed with claustrophobic, dark panels featuring panic-stricken close-ups of those anxiously seeking refuge in an underground bomb shelter. Visual representation creates the illusion of immediacy as the reader, together with the testimonial subject, later emerges from the shelter and witnesses death and destruction. Thick metal shutters protecting storefronts are seen to be mangled and wrenched as if "una mano gigante las hubiera estirado" (a giant hand had yanked them) (30). In contrast, and as though the testimonial subject cannot yet fully grasp the enormity of the atrocity, the corpses of two women with whom he had been happily chatting minutes before appear to be merely sleeping. Only then does he explain his belief that the

Germans were testing "bombas de aire líquido" (liquid air bombs) (30) and thus, like the shutters, their internal organs have been utterly destroyed. By utilizing this dramatic visual format, the author avoids the need to directly report his father's fear, pain, and grief; instead, the text strives to recreate the urgency of the situation and in some measure allow the reader to approximate the traumatic experience.[7]

The final tableau likewise exhibits narrative and visual complexity, particularly with respect to the representation of subjective time and emotional intensity. Aware that nothing good happens to officers in prison camps, Gallardo suffers desperation and despair when assigned to a worker battalion. The visual text conveys his extreme distress by means of a minuscule close-up located at the bottom of a frame dominated by a massive brick wall; the oppressive weight of the very words exposing his thoughts of suicide seem to crush him. At the same time, the layout of the drawings deliberately creates narrative suspense. The final frame on the page states the terrifying fact that his name has been called out. Parallel to the heart-stopping trepidation felt by the vulnerable protagonist, the reader in turn faces an ellipsis and, forced to turn the page (a technique that necessarily slows the pace of the reading), can only anticipate the portentous ramifications.

However, rather than discovering narrative resolution, s/he is instead confronted with an enactment or dramatic repetition of a guard shouting "FRANCISCO GALLARDO SARMIENTO" (52). As with the aforementioned vignette, the use of graphic narrative allows for the visualization of auditory sensations. Much as the ominous sound of air raid sirens permeated the air and consequently filled previous frames, here the scrawled, oversized letters of the testimonial subject's name loom menacingly in the night sky. The terrifying uncertainty of being called out in a concentration camp precipitates paralyzing dread. Time stands still. As if in slow motion, the sound slowly fades away as the disintegrating name, now depicted in shaky letters, morphs into snowflakes and Francisco Gallardo confesses: "Yo oía mi nombre como de lejos pero ya no estaba allí" (I heard my name as if from far away but I was no longer there) (52).

The text then plays out a dramatic flashback in which the testimonial subject recalls witnessing officers, held by the Republicans as prisoners of war, being shot in the back before the eyes of a distraught civilian population. By focusing on their anguished facial expressions rather than on the brutal act, the visual narration emphasizes the traumatic act of bearing witness and further suggests the teller's continued inability or unwillingness to directly confront the atrocity. Again a weighty declaration, "En aquel momento yo pasé el peor mal rato que he pasado en mi vida" (At that moment I went through the worst bad time I have ever gone through in my life) (54), expresses an extreme disillusionment that nearly crushes the diminished protagonist, once again depicted in close-up at the bottom of the frame. The haunting imagery is tellingly employed through flashback and repetitions, key narrative strategies that effectively reproduce the structure of traumatic memory as Whitehead has elaborated. At the same time, the technique of visualization powerfully represents and recreates the continued impact of the horrific past experience, depicting how the subject relives these events, even as the narrative transitions back to the parallel trauma currently being told. Snowy letters crystallize into his shouted name and the testimony quickly advances to a surprisingly abrupt conclusion. Thus singled out, Francisco Gallardo Sarmiento is, unexpectedly, removed from the worker's brigade by a former classmate and subsequently released from the concentration camp.

His testimonio ends with a cursory explanation of how he found a job and met his future wife. Significantly, it is with her photographic image that Gallardo's testimony draws to a close. The brusque ending suggests that this new chapter in his life story provides closure to the traumatic events of the civil war. Nevertheless, the testimonial subject's prolonged inability or unwillingness to directly confront these experiences—directly referred to in the title and subtly reinforced through recurring visual eruptions of his oral testimony—contradict this seemingly happy ending and reveal the haunting nature of traumatic memory.

The graphic sequences scattered throughout *Un largo silencio* depict stories within stories, memories within memories, testimonies within testimonies. Inserting visual narration provides depth by complicating chronological storytelling; recreating or reenacting moments of trauma; drawing the reader in; and ultimately reproducing the processes of witnessing, remembering, and testifying. In short, experimentally employing comic art within an otherwise paradigmatic testimonial text effectively belies the limitations and overly structured nature of classic, edited oral testimonies.

Drawing on Childhood Trauma: Carlos Giménez's *Paracuellos* Series

Similarly envisioning the creative potential of inventive testimonial formats, Carlos Giménez utilizes his preferred medium, comics, to graphically depict growing up in Falangist orphanages. The *Paracuellos* series chronicles the hypocrisies, deprivations, and brutalities suffered within the oppressive confines of these homes. Giménez offers a dramatically new perspective in testimonial literature—portraying the voices, visions, and values of victimized children—while visibly denouncing injustices, maintaining a subtle but acute awareness of the reader, and celebrating the comic medium. Like Gallardo, Giménez concedes to reader and scholarly expectations of testimonio in terms of both content and process even as he experiments with the form of the testimonial genre.

Simultaneously a fictionalized compilation of mediated testimonies and an autobiography, the hybrid text alternates between depicting himself and the other boys in close-ups that draw attention to personal identity and often exaggerate facial expression—particularly with respect to large, expressive eyes—while at other times large groups of children appear from a distance as featureless silhouettes. That is, Giménez's highly stylized drawings, which border on caricature, generally represent the interned children as individualized characters; however, when presenting the boys as an anonymous collective, the cartoon sketches lack personal detail and become intentionally generalized, depicting them en masse without recognizable features. Not only does this illustrative technique effectively show changes in narrative focalization as noted by Danielle Corrado,[8] this oscillation further establishes the simultaneous I/we subject position (the testifier as representative of a group or one among many) that has become fundamental in testimonio.

In the introduction to *Todo Paracuellos* (an edition that collects all six books of the series into one volume), Giménez uncompromisingly defends his choice of alternative representation, the *tebeo* (comics). He first dismisses the notion of comics as trivial or inconsequential: "El hecho de que esto sea un tebeo no debe interpretarse como sinónimo de frívolo o poco serio" (The fact that this is a comic should not be interpreted as synonymous with frivolous or flippant) (18) and then asserts their validity as "Una forma narrativa tan válida como cualquier otra" (A narrative form as valid as any other) (23). Giménez further maintains that nothing has been invented in the drawing of these tales (18). Throughout the introduction he pointedly elaborates upon the extensive testimonial efforts behind his artistic re/creation.

Like Gallardo, Giménez prefaces his fictionalized documentation of the harsh and violent reality of these institutions by claiming the truth-value of his work: each and every episode of the *Paracuellos* series, he insists, is based upon a lived experience. Before serialization, the comics included the actual date and location where the narrated events occurred and in this way, as the author explicitly explains, openly displayed "visos de documento" (documentary overtones) (16). Likewise, in typical testimonial fashion, the author's introduction provides a bullet list of the nine specific homes in which the stories took place. Giménez outlines the weight of archival material behind his creative project, including numerous recorded conversations and a vast collection of documentary evidence such as letters and photographs. He further defends his personal authority to present these stories, having himself experienced five such homes over a period of eight years.

The recollections and contestations presented in *Paracuellos* rely upon numerous testimonial voices. This is both a collective denunciation and autobiographical testimony.[9] If, however, one understands the orphanages themselves to be the work's testimonial subject as much as the children who suffer within them, then it can be argued that Giménez follows the conventions of testimonio by denying the singularity of the auxiliary homes and instead insisting that they are but one example of a perverse brutality common throughout the nation. As he elaborates: "Preguntemos a quienes lo vivieron cómo eran en estos mismos años los cuarteles, las cárceles, los manicomios o cualquier colegio interno y escucharemos las mismas, o muy parecidas, si no peores, historias" (Let's ask those who lived through it what the military barracks, the jails, the mental hospitals or any boarding school was like and we will hear the same, or similar if not worse, stories) (21). To echo critics of Rigoberta Menchú, this is not a "personal" story so much as the story of all such institutions.[10]

Close examination of the introductions to the original editions of *Paracuellos 1, 2,* and *3,* reveals a noteworthy trajectory in the presentation of the comics, a progression of ideas leading up to Carlos Giménez's resolute exposition of the series' testimonial import. These remarks evolve from an interpretation of the comics as a significant contribution to collective memory to an appreciation of their testimonial value to an exhortation of the reader's responsibility in assuming correct posturing so as to fully appreciate the text's emotive impact.

Antonio Martín, renowned historian and critic of Spanish comics, referring to the first volume of *historietas* (cartoons or comics) states: "este ejercicio de memoria es básico frente a los que nos proponen el olvido" (this exercise in memory is essential in the face of those who suggest that we forget). That is, he presents the comics as a defiant act against collective amnesia, as an adamant refusal to engage in the silence following the violence of the Spanish civil war. In so doing, Martín traces the history of the orphanages and includes archival images of Francoist propaganda that both he and the comic vignettes resoundingly debunk. At the same time, his introduction, by strongly advocating Giménez's representation of the "rabia, frustración y tragedia de los niños" (the children's rage, frustration and tragedy) (Martín), hints at the significance of giving voice to a new testimonial subject in this memory work.

In turn, professional Spanish comic artist José María Beá praises the artistic merit of the work. He affirms that with the *Paracuellos* series Giménez, as a "creador testimonial" (creator of testimony), has not only achieved a personal zenith but has also brought about a definitive shift in Spanish comic production. In his estimation, Giménez successfully transforms the genre from reprehensible pandering to "la cultura oficial" (official culture) into a highly artistic contestatory medium offering "una plataforma capaz de plantear contenidos de riguroso valor testimonial" (a medium capable of presenting content of rigorous testimonial value) (Beá).

Jesús Cuadrado, a second-generation critic of Spanish *tebeos*, focuses his introduction to *Paracuellos 3* on textual reception, coaching the reader how to properly approach the comic. Much in keeping with Shoshana Felman and Dori Laub who emphasize the collaborative aspects of testimony and assert that "the listener to trauma comes to be a participant and co-owner of the traumatic event" (57), Cuadrado challenges the reader to surrender to the role of *cómplice* (accomplice).[11] Moreover, Cuadrado opens his introduction, which appropriately utilizes direct address, by confronting the reader with the fact that "si no adopta la personalidad del niño, si no se desliza en su interior, le parecerá todo desmadrado, desmesurado, descompensado. Le parecerá ficticio, falso" (if you do not adopt a child's personality, if you do not go deep down inside, it will all seem diminished, disproportionate, unbalanced to you. It will all seem fictitious, false). In other words, giving voice to an atypical testimonial subject in an atypical testimonial medium requires a willingness on the part of the reader to adopt a unique position.

Anne Whitehead has noted that to feature the narrative viewpoint of a child represents a significant break from classic testimonial practice. In her discussion of Binjamin Wilkomirski's controversial text, *Fragments: Memories of a Childhood, 1939–1948*, she cites a deliberate narrative strategy that could aptly describe *Paracuellos*: "the narrator clearly states that he can only represent his childhood experiences by returning to the child's perspective: 'If I'm going to write about it, I have to give up on the ordering logic of grown-ups; it would only distort what happened' (4)" (Whitehead 38). It is important to bear in mind that in creating the *Paracuellos* series, adult informants, along with Giménez himself, recall childhood experiences and it is precisely this "innocent" or naïve perspective that the comics attempt to represent. At the same time, it should not be overlooked that childhood victimization is mediated through adult consciousness on at least three distinct levels: in the retelling by those who shared their stories with Giménez, in the creative production of the author/transcriber/illustrator, and in the process of textual consumption.

Given this unique narrative positioning together with an explicit awareness of the reader, *Paracuellos* remains remarkable for its unflinching and unrelenting representation of the violence and degradation suffered in the *hogares*. To again cite Corrado, "Los malos tratos no son sugeridos sino expuestos a conciencia en toda su crueldad creando no sólo malestar en el lector sino una aprensión y un miedo que nos aproxima, aunque remotamente, a los sentimientos experimentados por los niños" (Mistreatment is not suggested but rather consciously exposed in all of its cruelty, creating not just discomfort for the reader but also apprehension and fear that brings us closer, though remotely, to the children's feelings) (177). As the text does not shy away from graphic depiction, rather than the overwhelming number of examples that prove the point, I instead find a surprising and notable exception to this rule to be particularly significant.

The sequence "Domingo de visita" ("Sunday Visit") exposes degradations less privileged children voluntarily undertake in order to share the food brought to other boys by their families. A series of frames illustrates various humiliating situations from agreeing to be punched in the face for two figs or to drink ink for a piece of candy, to offering to enslave oneself to another, to consuming undigested bits of food found in the vomit of those who gorge themselves. Yet, jarringly, Giménez inserts an empty frame into this set of panels in which only these words appear: "ahorrémosle al lector escrupuloso el dibujo del niño comiéndose el gargajo" (let's spare the scrupulous reader the drawing of the child eating a loogie) (124). More than 100 pages into a text filled with violence and depravity, this deliberate and ironic visual withholding unexpectedly frustrates the reader's desire to "see" or witness. Excessively formal language, whereby "censorship" is disguised as benevolence, guardedly alludes to the pornography of violence. At the same time, the uncharacteristic display of modesty or shame—one that goes in direct contrast to the unabashed desperation of the hungry children—abruptly reminds the reader of just how deplorable this situation truly is. The empty frame effectively disrupts a chain of mortifying acts and thus lessens the risk of desensitizing readers.[12] In fact, by refusing to visualize the scene, Giménez forces the reader, who must recreate the image internally in order to fill the visual gap, into a more active and participatory role. In the prologue to *Todo Paracuellos*, Juan Marsé, renowned author and journalist, notes that children learn to read images before text and thus declares: "siempre he pensado que un buen narrador visual ha de saber establecer esa complicidad, pidiéndole al lector—sea niño o adulto—un pequeño esfuerzo imaginativo, haciéndole partícipe, por así decirlo, de su creatividad" (I have always thought that a good visual narrator should know how to establish this complicity, asking of the reader—whether a child or an adult—a little imaginative effort, making them a participant, so to speak, in their creativity) (13).

References to active and participatory readership permeate the text, not only with respect to the extra-diegetic reader but also to the young protagonists. Giménez includes a sequence in which puzzled children attempt to decipher the meaning of the forbidding Falangist iconography of the *Auxilio Social*. Ironically, this unwelcoming propagandistic image adorns the gates of the orphanages. Giménez similarly incorporates the logo, which purposefully and forebodingly reinforces the nationalistic ideology driving the institutions, at the opening and closing of every episode. Inserting critical commentary of this omnipresent visual icon within the comic narrative ensures that the image not become invisible due its constant repetition; that is, that the casual reader not overlook its portentous incongruity. Performing a readerly function, the boys offer various explanations of the graphic image—from an eagle to a crocodile to a snake—until one child explains his understanding that "Auxilio Social mata al dragón del hambre" (the Social Auxiliary kills the dragon of hunger) (260). Giménez strategically locates this sardonic prefatory vignette within a visual montage that emphasizes the extreme hunger the boys consistently endure, caustically exposing the harsh reality hidden behind official propaganda. Questioning the symbolic import of the insignia—a visual text—not only disrupts its authority but also serves a self-reflexive narrative function.

In fact, *Todo Paracuellos*, in addition to serving as a testament to the hardships suffered in the orphanages, displays increasingly overt metaliterary tendencies by openly paying homage to the comic medium. Throughout the series, the boys fervently collect and voraciously consume popular comics,[13] act out episodes, invent new scenarios for their favorite superheroes, compete in sponsored writing and drawing contests, and design their own publications within the orphanage. Comics thus provide rare moments of happiness, play, and humor within the austere confines of the institution and are a valued commodity shared among friends or bartered and exchanged for various favors. As one critic has noted, "quien tiene un tebeo tiene, en cierto modo, el poder" (he who has a comic has, so to speak, power) (Marsé 10). For this very reason, comics simultaneously expose their owners to increased vulnerability: loss of a comic produces extreme anguish.

But perhaps the most radical aspect of comics is their potential as a creative outlet for subversive expression. Successfully competing in contests (winning money and getting published) not only validates the children's narrative and artistic talent but, more importantly, this mode of self-expression ultimately signifies a rebellious form of cathartic escape. Not coincidentally, the young Giménez, the child most talented at drawing within the orphanage, is frequently depicted quietly reading *tebeos* or with pencil and paper in hand. Dreaming of becoming a professional comic book illustrator when he grows up, he dedicates himself to drafting his own comic series. "El jinete de la muerte" ("Death's Horseman") is featured as an embedded narrative within *Paracuellos;* several full frames are devoted entirely to displaying his work. The comic is presented to an eager audience of friends and, by extension, to the reader; a subtle reminder that the ideal reader of *Paracuellos* shares their child-like enthusiasm as well as their somewhat immature or "innocent" perspective. "El jinete de la muerte" clearly imitates stock conventions—both thematic and stylistic—of the popular comics the boys read incessantly: masked heroes fight evil villains, throw punches, and seek to avenge wrongs. Even more striking, the child's creative efforts unmistakably mirror the more mature denunciation of injustice and sophisticated artistic style of *Paracuellos*. The young Giménez's cowboy action comic depicts violence without context, notably fistfights that eerily resemble fights among the boys as well as the physical abuse they suffer at the hands of the authorities. Although frequent misspellings typical of a school-age boy suggest a childish naiveté, the illustrations, though not as refined or tightly finished as the "trazo escueto" (concise stroke) (Corrado 180) characterizing the adult author's framing text, remain remarkably well composed.

This metafictive technique of interior duplication reaches a climax in the final book of the *Paracuellos* series with an extended narrative in which a friend of young Giménez, Peribañez, determines to avenge himself for the unpunished theft of his prized pen. Not unlike the "madness" of Don Quixote, the voracious reader (and aspiring writer) begins to enact the noble ideals of his comic heroes. The narrator describes, with dramatic exaggeration, how "En su joven cerebro algo hizo ¡clic!... y todos los tebeos y todas las novelas que había leído hasta entonces, cobraron sentido de golpe" (Something in his young mind went click!... and all the comics and all the novels he had read before then suddenly made sense) (505). Much like "El jinete de la muerte," the subsequent series of action adventures features the heroic young orphan who humorously and poignantly imitates conventions of popular comics. The child, firmly committed to principles of honesty and integrity, performs what he understands to be acts of justice: careful not to steal, he resolutely confiscates and destroys other children's prized possessions. All the while, Peribañez maintains a dual identity: a devious (super)hero in secret, an obedient and pious student in front of authority figures. The ongoing narration of his daring (mis)adventures and narrow escapes culminates with his acquisition of a novel, an object strictly forbidden in the orphanage, that he deems far too precious to destroy. The ensuing ethical dilemma—what to do with the book he covets—precipitates the young Avenger's undoing. Opting to return the book to its rightful owner, he renounces his quest for justice and, much to the other children's relief, no longer performs the role of dutiful and devout pupil. "El vengador" ("The Avenger"), as Marsé astutely notes, "es un espléndido homenaje a los tebeos, a su estructura, a su temática, a su intención y a su función" (is a splendid homage to comics, to their structure, their themes, their intention and their function) (10–11). The final installments of *Paracuellos* then, while still testimonial in intent, become more lighthearted and mischievous, self-consciously engaging in sustained metafictive play with the comic medium.

Not surprisingly, the pleasurable and subversive acts of reading and creating comics, considered to be trashy and a bad influence by those in authority, are regarded as dangerous. As one of the wardens demonically screams: "¡Aquí, en estas porquerías, es donde aprendéis las cosas malas! ¡En esto perdéis el tiempo! ¡De aquí sacáis la violencia!" (Here, in this crap, is where you learn bad things! With this you waste your time! From here you pick up violence!) (179). Thus, comics frequently become an object of unjustifiable censorship and/or a cruel instrument of punishment; they are mercilessly confiscated, ripped up, and even burned. However, for Pablito Giménez, the ultimate offense occurs when Peribañez, himself an avid reader of *tebeos*, heedlessly rips up comics but cannot bring himself to destroy a novel. Incredulous, he demands to know, with biting wit and in frustrated defense of his passion: "¿Qué tendrán los pobres tebeos que todo el mundo los quiere mal?" (What it is about poor comics that everyone has it in for them?) (551). The repercussions of this question, not only in terms of the traditional disdain of comics among scholars and academics but particularly in light of Giménez's deliberate use of the medium within the field of post-Spanish civil war testimony, extends far beyond the intra-diegetic world.

And this brings the reader full circle. Significantly, Giménez concludes his introduction to *Todo Paracuellos* with the following words: "Cuántas veces, de niño, en aquellos hogares pensé, como el Pablito de la serie: 'Yo, de mayor, quiero ser dibujante de tebeos.' No imaginaba que llegaría a serlo precisamente para contar las historias de los Hogares de Auxilio Social" (How many times, as a boy in those homes, did I think, like Pablito in the series: "When I grow up I want to be a comic book illustrator." I had no idea I would become one precisely in order to tell the stories of the Auxiliary Homes) (23). The evolution of the series' paratextual material together with the evolving self-reflexive content of *Paracuellos* openly vindicate the use of comics as a medium for testimony, especially considering that a new testimonial voice and subject position emerge in Giménez's collection—children. It is, in fact, their discussions, reproductions, and embodiments of the visual narratives they enthusiastically consume that best teach us how to approach Giménez's graphic denunciations. *Todo Paracuellos* unmistakably fulfills the testimonial function by depicting collective suffering and injustice while giving voice to the voiceless. At the same time, the text playfully and unapologetically pays homage to the creative potential of comics and, although less directly, the resiliency of youth.

Drawing Conclusions

With their graphic testimonies, Gallardo and Giménez complicate what was already a hybrid form—oral and written discourses—by introducing a further duality between textual and visual representation. Both conform to the classic parameters of testimonio even as they increasingly resist the ordered structure of mediated testimony. Gallardo, whose informant remains haunted by distressing events from his silenced past, replicates traumatic memory by breaking with neatly arranged chronological order and literally illustrating how the subject relives distressing events in their retelling. Gímenez, in keeping with the hypocrisy and malevolence of a deranged institution, eschews the orderly logic of the adult world when re/creating childhood trauma.

In so doing, both authors lay challenging new claims upon the readers of their testimonios. The texts maintain testimonio's underlying project of changing readerly attitudes and promoting social action—a characteristic carefully studied by Kimberly Nance—yet they do so by attempting to forge complicity by means of even greater viewer participation. The reader, perhaps uncomfortably, is placed not merely in the somewhat passive position of witnessing testimony, but instead is thrust into a more active role as the texts attempt to simulate or approximate the initial act of bearing witness. In other words, as Cathy Caruth signals in her discussion of the highly complex and multilayered film, *Hiroshima mon amour,* "a new mode of seeing and of listening—a seeing and a listening from the site of trauma—is opened up to us as spectators" (56). Much as the Spanish civil war has not easily fit into official national narrative or collective memory, Gallardo and Giménez likewise suggest that these memories and life stories cannot be adequately represented or understood using traditional testimonio strategies and frameworks.

Notes

1. Following publication of Art Spiegelman's Pulitzer Prize-winning *Maus,* graphic novels documenting war and social injustice have begun to emerge. These include Emmanuel Guibert's *Alan's War: The Memories of G.I. Alan Cope,* Marjane Sartrapi's autobiographical *Persepolis,* and Joe Sacco's works in comics journalism: *Footnotes in Gaza, Palestine* and *Safe Area Gorazde: The War in Eastern Bosnia 1992–95.* With respect to the Spanish civil war, see Vittorio Giardino's fictional series, *No Pasarán!,* where Max Friedman, detective and retired soldier, returns to the besieged city of Barcelona and the frontlines to seek a missing friend. Giménez's own *Todo 36–39: Malos tiempos (The Complete 36–39: Bad Times),* a four-part comic series, portrays the travails of a typical family in Madrid in order to illustrate the traumatic struggle of the city under siege. Paco Roca and Serguei Dounovetz's *El ángel de la retirada* (the Spanish version of *L'ange de la Retirada*) dramatizes the story of Spanish exiles to France, their experiences within concentration camps, and the conflicts of identity faced by their children; Fidel Martínez and Jorge García detail the plight of female political prisoners under the Francoist dictatorship in *Cuerda de presas*; while Alfonso López, Joan Mundet and Pepe Gálvez alternate textual and visual narrations in order to depict the struggle for democracy before, during, and after the Francoist regime in the graphic biography of Miguel Núñez titled *Mil vidas más.* The Zinn Education Project has made available online Joshua Brown and Peter N. Carroll's graphic booklet titled *Robeson in Spain* (originally published by the Abraham Lincoln Brigade Archive's magazine *The Volunteer* June 2009), aiming to facilitate and promote teaching about

the singer-actor's denunciation of racism and fascism together with his personal involvement in the Spanish civil war.
2. All translations throughout this essay are mine.
3. As Doris Sommer unequivocally declares, "the testimonial 'I' does not invite us to identify with it. We are too different, and there is no pretense here of universal or essential human experience" (108).
4. Anne Whitehead delineates an evolution among trauma theorists who formulate the risk of loss of impact inherent in testimony (from Nicola King to Jean-Francis Lyotard to Cathy Caruth) and in turn offers the following counter argument: "literary fiction offers the flexibility and the freedom to be able to articulate the resistance and impact of trauma. While traditional literary realism may not be suited for rendering traumatic events... more experimental forms emerging out of postmodernist and postcolonial fiction offer the contemporary novelist a promising vehicle for communicating the unreality of trauma, while still remaining faithful to the facts of history" (87).
5. Cathy Caruth, building on observations made by Freud and others, offers the following general definition of trauma: "the response to an unexpected or overwhelming violent event or events that are not fully grasped as they occur, but return later in repeated flashbacks, nightmares, and other repetitive phenomena" (91). She goes on to describe the paradoxes of trauma: "the most direct seeing of a violent event may occur as an absolute inability to know it; that immediacy, paradoxically, may take the form of belatedness" (91–92). Whitehead, in turn, describes how "trauma assumes a haunting quality, continuing to possess the subject with its insistent repetitions and returns" (12). She then studies fictional techniques for representing trauma including the disruption of chronology and linearity, fragmentation, repetition, and dispersion, among other literary devices.
6. Such sound-effect words are common practice in comic literature. For more on the aural component of comics, or creating the illusion of sound through visual techniques, see Catherine Khordoc's insightful study of speech balloons and onomatopoeic labels in *Asterix*.
7. Subsequent graphic sequences likewise depict content of particularly personal and emotional intensity—moments when words fail—that end with unspoken pain and disillusionment. When those he helped during the war fail to acknowledge or return the favor following Franco's victory, Gallardo must come to terms with the fact that "en aquel momento comprendí que la clase a la que yo pertencía era la de los fantasmas y las sombras" (at that moment I understood that the social class to which I belonged consisted of ghosts and shadows) (37). A parallel sense of powerlessness and despair, also depicted visually, overwhelms the protagonist when detained in prisoner of war camps: "mi vida ya no valía nada, sólo era otro nombre en las listas"

(my life was no longer worth anything, I was just another name on the lists) (49).

8. Corrado notes that close-ups communicate the children's point of view; in contrast, depicting them from a distance, whereby the children lose their individual characteristics, conveys the institutional perspective (179). Corrado further points out that low, upward angles convey the boys' perception whereas looking down on the children reinforces the authoritarian power dynamic enjoyed by adults (178).

9. Although Corrado studies *Paracuellos* as an autobiographical text, the comics critic notes techniques that fall outside of the subgenre: namely that Giménez avoids utilizing a first person subject position and instead consistently employs the third person for his own character; the child's name morphs from Carlines to Pablito Giménez, and although the narrator uses a more personal and inclusive *nosotros* (we) in the first volume, later volumes shift to a more distanced and perhaps more objective third-person narrator.

10. Here I refer specifically to the titles of David Stoll's polemical text, *Rigoberta Menchú and the Story of All Poor Guatemalans* and Doris Sommer's article, "Not Just a Personal Story."

11. He further hints at the process of traumatic witnessing by stating that not only did these events happen in Giménez's childhood but in re/creating these memories on paper "lo volvió a vivir en el tablero" (he relived it on the drawing board).

12. In similar fashion, when a horrified delivery man witnesses the savage beating of a boy caught stealing sausage, the change in narrative perspective to someone from outside the *hogar* reminds us that those from within, which now includes the reader, risk normalizing abuse ("El quincenal").

13. Specifically referenced are *Pulgarcito, Coyote, Florita, El Cachorro,* and *El Guerrero del Antifaz.*

Works Cited

Barnet, Miguel. *Biografía de un cimarrón.* La Habana: Instituto de Etnología y Folklore, 1966. Print.

Barrios de Chungara, Domitila. *"Si me permiten hablar...": Testimonio de Domitila, una mujer de las minas de Bolivia.* Ed. Moema Viezzer. Mexico: Siglo XXI, 1977. Print.

Beá, José María. "Paracuellos: La huella infinita." *Carlos Giménez.-.* N.p., n.d. Web. March 2011.

Brown, Joshua and Peter N. Carroll. "Robeson in Spain." Spec. issue of *The Volunteer* Publ. by Abraham Lincoln Brigade Archives (ALBA) 26.2 (June 2009): 1–28. Print.

Caruth, Cathy. *Unclaimed Experience: Trauma, Narrative, and History.* Baltimore: Johns Hopkins UP, 1996. Print.

Corrado, Danielle. "Carlos Giménez y el pacto autobiográfico." *Historietas, cómics y tebeos españoles*. Ed. Viviane Alary. Toulousse: Presses Universitaires de Mirail, 2002. 174–195. Print.
Cuadrado, Jesús. "Paracuellos. El infierno de la memoria." *Carlos Giménez.-*. N.p., n.d. Web. March 2011.
Felman, Shoshana, and Dori Laub. *Testimony: Crises of Witnessing in Literature, Psychoanalysis and History*. New York: Routledge, 1992. Print.
Gallardo, Miguel Ángel. *Un largo silencio*. Alicante: Edicions de Ponent, 1997. Print.
Giardino, Vittorio. *No Pasarán!* 3 Vols. Trans. Stefano Gaudiano, Andrea Gaudiano, Nanette McGuinness. New York: NBM/ComicsLit, 2000–2008. Print.
Giménez, Carlos. "Por si a alguien le interesa." Introducción. *Todo Paracuellos*. By Giménez. Barcelona: Debolsillo, 2007. 15–23. Print.
——. *Todo 36–39: Malos Tiempos*. Barcelona: Debolsillo, 2011. Print.
——. *Todo Paracuellos*. Barcelona: Debolsillo, 2007. Print.
Guibert, Emmanuel. *Alan's War: The Memories of G.I. Alan Cope*. New York: First Second, 2008. Print.
Khordoc, Catherine. "The Comic Book's Soundtrack: Visual Sound Effects in *Asterix*." *The Language of Comics: Word and Image*. Ed. Robin Varnum and Christina T. Gibbons. Jackson: UP of Mississippi, 2001. 156–73. Print.
López, Alfonso and Joan Mundet, ilus. *Miguel Núñez: Mil vidas más*. Written by Pepe Gálvez. Alicante, Spain: Edicions de Ponent, 2010. Print.
Marsé, Juan. "Paracuellos. Aventuras y testimonio." Prólogo. *Todo Paracuellos*. By Carlos Giménez. Barcelona: Debolsillo, 2007. 5–14. Print.
Martín, Antonio. "La obra nacional de Auxilio Social." *Carlos Giménez.-*. N.p., n.d. Web. March 2011.
Martínez, Fidel, illus. *Cuerda de presas*. Written by Jorge García. Bilbao, Spain: Astiberri, 2005. Print.
McCloud, Scott. *Understanding Comics: The Invisible Art*. New York: Harper, 1994. Print.
Menchú, Rigoberta, and Elisabeth Burgos. *Me llamo Rigoberta Menchú y así me nació la conciencia*. Barcelona: Editorial Argos Vergara, 1983. Print.
Nance, Kimberly A. *Can Literature Promote Justice? Trauma Narrative and Social Action in Latin American Testimonio*. Nashville: Vanderbilt UP, 2006. Print.
Roca, Paco, illus. *El ángel de la retirada*. Written by Serguei Dounovetz. Barcelona: Bang Ediciones, 2010. Print.
Sacco, Joe. *Footnotes in Gaza*. New York: Metropolitan, 2009. Print.
——. *Palestine*. Seattle: Fantagraphic, 2001. Print.
——. *Safe Area Gorazde: The War in Eastern Bosnia 1992–95*. Seattle: Fantagraphic, 2000. Print.
Sartrapi, Marjane. *The Complete Persepolis*. New York: Pantheon, 2004. Print.

Sommer, Doris. "Not Just an Personal Story: Women's Testimonies and the Plural Self." *Life/Lines: Theorizing Women's Autobiography.* Ed. Bella Brodzki and Celeste Schenck. Ithaca: Cornell UP, 1988. 107–30. Print.

Spiegelman, Art. *Maus: A Survivor's Tale.* 2 Vols. New York: Pantheon; Random, 1986–1991. Print.

Stoll, David. *Rigoberta Menchú and the Story of All Poor Guatemalans.* Boulder: Westview, 1999. Print.

Whitehead, Anne. *Trauma Fiction.* Edinburgh: Edinburgh UP, 2004. Print.

CHAPTER 12

WITNESSING THE EARTH THROUGH GASPAR PEDRO GONZÁLEZ'S *EL 13 B'AKTUN: LA NUEVA ERA 2012*
(*13 B'AKTUN: MAYAN VISIONS OF 2012 AND BEYOND*)

Louise Detwiler

While a handful of scholarly articles have explored Gaspar Pedro González's 1990s novels as testimonio-like narratives, little has been written to date about his 2006 work, *El 13 B'aktun: la nueva era 2012*.[1] Why? As of this writing, there are tens of millions of electronic results for the Maya and 2012 and yet González's voice is conspicuously absent from these hyperactive conversations. Indeed, noting the online swell in the foreword of his English translation, *13 B'aktun: Mayan Visions of 2012 and Beyond*, Robert K. Sitler writes that "Gaspar González holds a privileged place among better-known authors... who have written about 2012 as the only one who actually *is* Mayan and who has intimate knowledge of the Mayan world" (xiv).[2] While the translated version has only recently become available in 2010, this fact still does not adequately explain why scholars—who in my field of Latin American literature read texts in Spanish as their norm—have so far overlooked this book. Perhaps a better answer is to be found in the fact that the 2012 meme is just not to be taken up by serious academics given the immense controversy surrounding the topic. On the one hand are the unsavory Hollywood associations with movies such as *2012*, and on the other are the related charges of cultural imperialism aimed at a more often than not ill-informed New Age circuit.

While these concerns should not be ignored, the fact remains that the whole point of González's book is to address a first-world reader—including those who have wittingly or unwittingly misrepresented Mayan cultures—regarding an Earth in peril. He does so not necessarily by pointing a finger at New Age-y "Twenty-Twelve-ers," although he does mention that they and related cultural traffickers are an annoyance (49).[3] Rather, he is much more concerned about articulating the effects of five hundred years of oppression that began with the arrival of the *ajq'axepa'*, or the "ones from the other side of the sea" (3). One of the most injurious consequences suffered by the Maya, he explains, was that "ancient knowledge was snatched away from us and replaced with elements imposed from the other culture...but our knowledge did not completely disappear" (3). In reference to this underground knowledge and syncretic identity, he states forthrightly at the outset of his narrative that "on April 18, 2006, we were commanded to reveal things hidden from the eyes of the world" (2). He foregrounds the timing of this disclosure not only by using a specific date, but also by referring to a moment of great importance: "the moment has arrived. It is our job to speak and reveal the secrets so that all humanity, all people of good will, might know them" (3).

The moment González mentions refers to, in part, the upcoming rollover date for the thirteenth B'aktun cycle on December 21, 2012, or a Great Cycle of 5125 years. Although this world age comes to an end, another cycle begins anew given the cyclical nature of time embedded within what many refer to as the Long Count calendar. Victor Montejo, also a Mayan author and scholar, points out that this world age sequence was prophesized to go global: "These prophetic expressions of the indigenous peoples insist *on the protagonist role that new generations must play* at the close of this Oxlanh B'aktun (thirteen B'aktun) and the beginning of the new Maya millennium. The ancestors have always said that 'one day our children will speak to the world'" (emphasis added 120). In each case, these well-versed authors highlight the special quality of this current time period not just for their own communities, but for all of humanity. Further, they do not at all dismiss the 2012 date as a so-called gringo invention, as some scholars have suggested.[4]

The classic testimonio registers that surface within these first few pages of *13 B'aktun* situate the text squarely within this tradition of Latin American literature. While a small library could be filled with the many scholarly books that have attempted to define, defile, or defend testimonio, at its core resides a narrative based on the firsthand account of an eyewitness, or *testigo*.[5] Often motivated by a desire to correct previous official accounts, the eyewitness recalls and reports on traumatic events. A third-party editor may also play a role in writing down this narrative depending upon issues of literacy. Additionally, living a marginalized existence in that region's dominant culture usually characterizes the eyewitness's socioeconomic context. Along these lines, González immediately describes how the Spanish invaders and their descendents continuously oppressed his community over many centuries. Further, he notes early and then often that his account contests the inaccurate ways that his people have been portrayed by others. As a traditional testimonio, González's work has much in common, in fact, with the widely discussed book, *Me llamo Rigoberta Menchú y así me nació la conciencia (I, Rigoberta Menchú: An Indian Woman in Guatemala)*. Both are Maya—Menchú is from the Quiché community and González is Q'anjob'al—and both devote a healthy portion of their narratives to the worldview, customs, and practices of their respective regions in Guatemala. A poetics of urgency is palpable in both narratives as well. It is on this point, however, where the two texts diverge quite dramatically.

While Menchú urgently speaks of the injustices of lives lived and lost during the civil war in Guatemala, González urgently speaks of the injustices of an Earth in peril. And he does so based primarily on his experiences in the spirit world. Given that testimonio follows an aesthetics of referentiality, *13 B'aktun* appears to fall short of this generic mark because the witnessing takes place in a realm that many readers might reject as imaginary or invented. Moreover, the Earth in González's narrative is conceived of as a living entity with its own cosmic subject position. The Earth, in fact, reveals its past and future to González in the spirit world, and he, in turn, speaks on its behalf in his testimonio. What, therefore, is the literary critic to do with the nonhuman, yet biotic, witness who speaks from what seems to be another dimension altogether? Can the Earth co-witness? Can this be testimony?

In this essay, I argue that when viewed ecocritically, the referential act and the eyewitness of testimonio defer to materialist and anthropocentric paradigms.[6] As literary ecocritic Jonathan Tittler notes so cogently, "[w]e are very likely in an early phase in the development of humanism, whose capacity to mount a holistic vision of the universe positions it optimally to surpass anthropocentrism and take us to the next level" (20). González attempts to do just this. Humanity as understood in *13 B'aktun* moves from the anthropocentric to the ecocentric and therefore the traditional figure of the eyewitness is very much demoted, so to speak, in this emptying out process. González's work presents humankind as a much smaller part of the much larger biotic organism, the Earth. This blended biotic entity must rely on the balanced diversity of its many parts for its overall survival rather than upon the monolithic link of human overdetermination. Arriving at an ecocentric notion of humanity means traveling with González to the fuzzy and uncertain space of the spirit world, or what some have described as a fifth dimension of existence.[7] This unfamiliar realm, in fact, is the primary site of referentiality where González witnesses alternative histories of the Earth and speaks on behalf of the Earth.

By reading *13 B'aktun* through the lens of ecology, I ultimately demonstrate that this narrative represents a new subgenre of testimonio, the ecotestimonio, or ecological testimony. To "get at" the ecotestimonio in *13 B'aktun,* first I present and describe a continuum-of-life worldview as often held by paramodern indigenous cultures.[8] Next, I explore the terra-trauma witnessed by González in the immaterial realm of this continuum and how these ecological testimonies serve to decenter humankind's presence on Earth. I then explore this fifth dimension as a legitimate site of referentiality with Gaia theory. In the last two sections, I characterize the nonhuman, yet biotic, witness, whose subjectivity presents a model for the realignment of humanity with the environment. Such a realignment situates heterarchical agency, diversity, and future-orientedness with respect to the Earth as paramount concerns. This "greening" of testimonio reflects the larger recent turn toward ecocriticsm in the field at large. In his epilogue, "Beyond the Telluric Novel" to *The Natural World in Latin American Literatures,* Adrian Taylor Kane points out that "[t]he potential for ecocriticism in Latin American studies is enormous, and given today's pressing environmental concerns, the moment is propitious" (235).

Continuum of Life

A thin volume loosely organized around the dreams and visions of González and his son, *13 B'aktun* weaves in and out of community history and prophesy, as well as poetry, philosophy, science, religion, and calendrics. Among this amalgam of interrelated topics, human beings and the Earth take center stage. He diachronically scrutinizes their relationship while assessing humankind's evolutionary paths. His overall conclusion? In order to save the Earth and therefore themselves, humans must evolve away from the material and instead progress toward the spirit (González 96). To save the material, in other words, humans must become more immaterial in every sense of the word. This evolutionary movement, he notes, can and has been achieved by others, the Maya among them (75).

Yet, how can this be? How does one move both toward and away from the targeted object of the Earth? Is this not an internal contradiction? In a positivist and therefore strictly materialist worldview, perhaps. Indeed, Stan Rowe notes how very unfamiliar this cosmovision of spirit seems to outsiders. In his article, "Ecocentrism and Traditional Ecological Knowledge," he writes that traditional native cultures seem alien to us precisely because of their spiritual sense of connectedness to the Earth. While outsiders may appreciate the daily visible ways of sustainable living found in native communities, Rowe notes that "the essential cultural soul of tribal people—their cosmology and fundamental *beliefs* about themselves in the world they occupy—is relatively inaccessible and strange to us" (par. 5). Further, he convincingly describes the difference between those living in these traditional ways and those looking in through Western eyes. He cites a comprehensive list of scientific disciplines, such as biology and evolution, to make his point regarding this conceptual distance (par. 5). In parallel fashion, Machiorlatti approaches this unfamiliar arena of being with the notion of another dimension altogether. In her article, "Ecocinema, Ecojustice, and Indigenous Worldviews," she explains that "[s]pirit animals, ancestors, guides, and dreaming occupy" a fifth dimension of existence (66). She notes as well that "[t]his expansive worldview does not stop with the planet but extends into the nonmaterial realm ... of spirit and soul" (66). The environment, in this way, is "composed of *all* of the 'worlds' of mother earth, the material and immaterial: land, sky, air, sea, as well as ancestors, spirits, and dreams" (66).

González defines the spirit world in these very same terms and takes pride in how his people have long cultivated the ability to experience it (50). Why, however, does he take his targeted first-world readers to a realm that he knows many have never experienced before nor perhaps will ever accept as existing? Is he not undermining his stated purpose by speaking in such unfamiliar terms to "all humanity" (3)? This question becomes even more puzzling when considering his direct address, for the first time, of the first-world reader in chapter five: "Wise human (sapiens), human of the current era wherever you may be, with all the science that you seek to control at this time, don't laugh at primitive people. You're trapped at a stage that may be worse then theirs. You've gone backwards in comparison" (94). He is quite clear here about the identity of his implied reader. Embedded in his reference to science is a critique of first-world "haves" controlling the world through a concept of science that quite possibly is far behind the knowledge of millennial cultures. I will return to the topic of science in subsequent sections.

The oppositional tone of this direct address also reveals that González is very much aware of the lacunae between his explicitly named reader and his site of enunciation. This awareness means that reaching his reader demands an effective narrative strategy. He witnesses from the spirit world obviously as a sacred cultural practice, yes, but also because in so doing he distances privileged readers from the comfort zones of their daily realities. Like the defamiliarization process of traveling to unknown places, flying through the air with González over this new terrain makes the ecological paradigm shift more vivid and transformative than it might otherwise be. Moreover, he models the wisdom of engaging the material through the immaterial. Lastly, and in line with the Mayan concept of time as cyclical, the disaster scenarios described in the spirit world may have already taken place multiple times in the past rather than merely represent speculative future projections.[9] This notion of time means that prophesy—a prediction about the future based on the cyclical nature of time—becomes testimony throughout González's narrative.[10] Therefore, do his readers experience with him what has already happened, what will happen, or both? These layers of unsettling contexts certainly cannot be read passively. More unsettling still is the fact that he essentially wipes out humanity in order to later resurrect it ecocentrically, as I demonstrate next.

Continuing Life? Material Endings in Immaterial Places

José Ramón Naranjo reads the *Popol Vuh* ecocritically in his article "La ecología profunda y el *Popol Vuh*" (Deep Ecology and the *Popol Vuh*). Using the central premise of the interrelatedness of ecosystems, he finds a highly refined environmental sensibility in these sacred stories of creation. Among them is the idea that humankind's three primary appearances—as mud, wood, and, currently, as corn—were fashioned out of Earth and therefore link human beings directly to the Earth (91). Naranjo notes as well that "cuando el hombre viola las leyes de la Tierra, ... cuando su comportamiento resulta abusivo, predador y negativo para su entorno, cabe la posibilidad extrema del cataclismo corrector" (when man violates the laws of the Earth...when his behavior is abusive, predatory, and negative toward his surroundings, a corrective cataclysm becomes a possibility) (91). While this potential outcome refers to the *Popol Vuh*, as Naranjo briefly notes later in his essay (93) and as I explore below as well in relation to *13 B'aktun*, Gaia theory provides a convincing link between these ancient sensibilities and contemporary science.[11]

González takes his readers to this corrective zone of cataclysmic events by sharing his dreams and visions from the spirit world. Overwhelming scenes of death and destruction comprise nearly the entire first chapter of *13 B'aktun* and reappear in subsequent ones. Their immediate appearance likewise demands immediate attention. However, these scenarios are difficult to read given how thorough and all-encompassing they are. By thorough, I mean that each caustic aspect of nature is described: space, through meteors; air, through tornadoes; fire, through volcanoes; and water, through flooding and hurricanes (6–25). By all-encompassing, I refer to the fact that no being nor living entity on earth is left unscathed: people, birds, plants, animals, and everything in between. His descriptions go beyond illustrating their collective destruction, in fact, to showing their remains smoldering in an apocalyptic aftermath. Even the Earth's topography is destroyed in these visions: "The entire surface was turning into a great gelatinous mass, burning red and smoking, as the planet vomited through volcanoes" (22). I describe these dramatic dreams and visions in some detail below in order to foreground their role in decentering anthropocentric thinking. While the material extremes and excesses of humans obviously do play a major role in harming the Earth, the violent forces of the natural world easily push back against these extremes such that humans do not matter in the final analysis.

In his first dream, an elder with white hair leads González to tour the Earth in ruins (6). The environment on Earth becomes progressively worse with each scene revealed to him. Fire, lack of oxygen, and death characterize his tours (6–7). All of his senses are completely bombarded with the overwhelming sounds of meteors crashing to Earth, with the "burning fumes" that hurt his face, and with the "suffocating atmosphere that made it difficult to breathe" (6–7). Each scenario shows widespread death and devastation: "It was frightening to see the seas boiling, exterminating whatever living beings were there in the depths" (6). Modern cities are no match for this annihilation event, and González witnesses "the remains of machines, vehicles, semi-interred weapons, airplanes, and industries with their tall chimneys still emitting smoke that spread into space" (7). While these disaster scenes are described in detail primarily in the first chapter, they also surface in subsequent ones. In chapter two, for example, his son has terrible visions that include women giving birth to monsters (33).

13 B'aktun provides a number of similar visions such as the one just described when the narrator and his son visit an elderly woman named Katal, who will help them in their mission to share the news of an Earth in grave distress. Much like the hero twins of the *Popol Vuh*, father and son descend into a sacred cave where relics from the classic period still exist on display (18). In a kind of virtual reality environment, they see the history of the cosmos, the planet, and humankind unfold before them on the sides of the cave (20–22). Katal tells them before the event begins that "[n]ow you will see the signs that precede the end of the cycle on the face of the Earth, especially of the b'aktun, of our Lord Ajaw" (20). Like the vision described above, the whirlwind cosmic tour again takes them through nearly indescribable scenes of loss and ruin on planet Earth. Some of their experiences are so horrific that they cannot mention them to the reader (24). Toward the close of their vision journey, the son cries out "[t]his is the end of the world!" and his father nods in agreement (24).

These visions indeed portray humankind's quite pathetic fate, but not as the main focus of what the father and son pair witness together. The core emphasis of these visions remains squarely upon what I can only describe as terra-trauma. The explicit images consistently refer to the destruction of nature through nature, with the fate of humans dangling in parentheses along the way. Not only does González foreground the trauma being inflicted on ecosystems of every kind, but also he shows that humanity is not capable of overcoming the violent forces of the natural world. Humanity, as central to the Earth and its life systems, has been emptied out of meaning as the reader experiences with González complete and utter planetary devastation.

In the Spirit of Gaia: The Fifth Dimension as Referential

The close attention paid to the spirit world begs the following question: What if this world was, well, real? This idea, in fact, is the thesis of Graham Hancock's book, *Supernatural*. A well-known journalist and controversial independent scholar, Hancock writes that "[w]ho are we to say that such entities are just figments of consciousness that have no real existence? What do we really understand about the place that shamans call the 'spirit world' " (95)? While I generally agree with his thesis, for some scholars his work is too nontraditional.[12] For this reason, I pursue a parallel notion below by examining the spirit world of *13 B'aktun* through Gaia theory. Although this scientific theory has yet to receive wide recognition, recent publications and legislation point to an increasingly broader acceptance of its main ideas.

In the dreams and visions just described, the "tool of extermination" often is fire, or *q'aq'* (33). This key natural element provides a crucial link to the contemporary science of Gaia theory, which foregrounds the role of solar warming for life on Earth. Although González laments how science is used to control others, he often refers to modern science in his text—especially quantum physics and a number of famous scientists such as Albert Einstein. Much of chapter two, in fact, describes compelling connections between knowledge found in the *Popol Vuh* and current scientific theories (26–56). The inclusion of time as a fourth dimension under the theory of special relativity, for example, stands out as one of many noteworthy connections. Given Mayan calendrics and their sacred focus on time, this contact point between ancient and modern provides convincing evidence of a highly accurate sense of the complexities of the universe. Following these connections, then, I add another point of contact here in order to illustrate how a seemingly invisible dimension should be taken into consideration as a legitimate referential realm along the continuum of life.

With recent publications such as *Gaia in Turmoil* (2010) and *The Revenge of Gaia* (2006), Gaian science has experienced renewed interest and legitimacy since its introduction in the 1970s by founder James Lovelock.[13] In both Gaia theory and Mayan science as represented by González, the Earth is not a detached, mechanistic planet, nor a highly anthropomorphized entity reflecting human consciousness. Both approaches instead situate the Earth at the intersection of interacting material and immaterial realms. For its part, Gaia theory posits that the Earth has always been a living system that has evolved with its flora, fauna, and later, humankind as an organic whole (Lovelock 162). The Earth functions as a kind of super organism that is so large and intricate that humans cannot perceive it *en masse*. Lovelock explains that Gaia "appears to have the unconscious goal of regulating the climate and the chemistry at a comfortable state for life" (15). Throughout González's text we similarly read of the Earth described as a living being. The elder in his first dream tells him that "the ship on which you now find yourselves is also a living being that was born and that grew by reproducing the diversity of beings it carries" (9). González also consistently makes this same point through his many references to the long-standing beliefs of his community. He frequently states as well that humans cling to just one side, the material, along the continuum of life and therefore cannot perceive the immaterial: "[c]ould our lack of awareness and soul be caused by one of the burdens that weighs most heavily on humanity's back—its warrior's garb from the material world?" (42). Tittler sums up this key idea regarding humankind's inability to perceive itself as part of a larger, living entity by noting that "we cannot get outside the biosphere in order to analyze it dispassionately" (14).

Both Lovelock and González warn that the Earth is quite capable of righting environmental wrongs. In Lovelock's language, this means that a sophisticated feedback loop will eliminate those elements undesirable to the highly refined, yet dynamic, task of sustaining diverse life forms. He cautions that "Gaia now threatens us with the ultimate punishment of extinction" (146). As described in depth earlier, González witnesses multiple extinction events. In addition, he refers a number of times to the grim prophesies found in the *Chilam Balam* and on Monument Six in Tortuguero, Mexico: "At the end of time, those who have harmed the Earth will be exterminated—apparently the entire human race for not having protected her" (González 110).

One of the main underpinnings of Gaia theory comes from the fact that our sun, like most stars, gets hotter over time. In order to accommodate increasingly higher temperatures, the Earth self-regulates to preserve a stasis optimal for life. Lovelock does not agree with the "Goldilocks" theory; that our planet just happens to be in exactly the right place for living systems to thrive (44). He writes that "only for a brief period in the Earth's history was the sun's warmth ideal for life, and that was about two billion years ago" (44). From then until now, the Earth as super organism has managed to organize itself in ways that cope with the effects of this solar warning. Lovelock points out, however, that "by adding greenhouse gases to the air and by replacing natural ecosystems, like forests, with farmland we are hitting the Earth with a 'double whammy'" (45). He believes that we have reached a point of no return because the effects of this one-two punch are no longer reversible (152).

He closes his book on a rather depressing note by suggesting that the best we can do is to "write a guidebook for our survivors to help them rebuild civilization without repeating too many of our mistakes" (156). His final paragraph paints a scene of a group of survivors heading north to the "new Arctic centres of civilization" in order to flee from an overheated world that in most regions has become uninhabitable (159). Lovelock's dramatic final scene echoes the end-of-times visions narrated by González, especially concerning the notion that heat and fire will have essential roles in this termination event. What are signs in *13 B'aktun* are described as data in *The*

Revenge of Gaia. Weather anomalies, climate change, and widespread pollution are three of the more oft-noted items in their respective works. All of these signs and data reveal a living entity in a deplorable state of demise.

The Nonhuman Biotic Witness

According to *13 B'aktun,* the false history of a materialist understanding of the separateness of the Earth and human beings has put the Earth and all life forms in danger. Terra-trauma, however, is bound up with human evolution—or lack thereof—and therefore the two entities and their histories cannot be separated. That the Earth, like humanity, is understood as a biotic corpus, and that the two are as one, serve as the foundation for the act of witnessing found in González's work. Indeed, a new sense of subjectivity surfaces through the nonhuman biotic witness that challenges the traditional testimonio model of the eyewitness who sees and then reports on verifiable events beyond the text.[14] Instead, this blended biotic witness "narrates" past, present, and future events related to its evolution. As mentioned earlier, the Earth's planetary history revealed itself to González and his son on the sides of the cave during his visionary journey with Katal. She tells them: "What you are going to see is *not fiction*; it is nothing new since many of your ancestors maintained communication with the spirit world to build a civilization based on profound knowledge of the intangible" (emphasis added 19). The Earth, therefore, has narrated its history many times before to this community. In addition, planet Earth performed its past and future for González during his first dream with the elder guide. The act of witnessing in *13 B'aktun,* then, refers to a shared and interdependent undertaking. The Earth performs and reveals itself across time to González in the spirit world. González as co-witness then speaks on its behalf.

This atypical witness, sense of subjectivity, and time orientation make even more sense when placed within the cosmic order of Mayan time and space. Each entity has its own set of coordinates—a kind of mathematical subject position, if you will—within the cosmos (29). The Earth, like individuals, possesses its own set of coordinates and therefore also has a unique subject position. "Each component of creation in the universe is there, those that make up the macrosystems and those of the microsystems," González explains (29). This field of coordinates is called the sacred "pop," or straw mat of the universe (29). The pop weaves together space and time such that these coordinates move through the universe together in repeating cycles

(31). González points out that these coordinates of space and time are similar to what "science knows as degrees of latitude and longitude, except in a cosmic and broader sense in the vast universe" (79).

Under this paradigm, then, the Earth indeed has a subject position, as do all of its living systems, within the fabric of space and time. Given the interrelatedness of these systems, the idea of González co-witnessing with a nonhuman entity in a diasynchronic way truly expands the traditionally accepted experiential modality of the eyewitness of testimonio. Add to this the idea of the Earth as a living being described above, and all evidence points to a completely viable option for consideration regarding the act of witnessing. Just as cyborg theory tends to blend technology and humans into a cybernetic organism of cyberspace, so, too, should this melding of human and non-human biotic entities be possible in a fifth dimensional sphere of existence. This scenario represents, in fact, González's aspirational model for an ecocentrically resurrected definition of humanity.

Humanity as Immaterial and Ecocentric

The "greening" of the eyewitness of testimonio serves as a conceptual microcosm for how González redefines humanity in *13 B'aktun*. As Lovelock advises with his "double whammy" idea, less human activity means a healthier Gaia. Both authors agree that human beings must evolve toward a consciousness of the fifth dimension; that is, toward an authentic sense of a continuum between the material and the immaterial. Until this blended state can be incorporated into its notion of subjectivity, humankind will continue to see itself as a separate, and often superior, entity. González counsels his reader that "Everything is related; everything is joined together in the big universe and in the small ones" (99). His emphasis on aspiring to refine the spiritual over the material stands out, in fact, as an alternative truth code pervading the entire text.

González is so intent on adequately conveying this alternative code of the spirit that he devotes many pages to analyzing humankind's evolutionary history through the *Popol Vuh*. Much more than an aside about Mayan cultures, this section scrutinizes each of the three creation events and concomitant evolutionary paths (26–56). González wonders if our descent into materialism, in addition to harming the Earth, has not cut us off from being able to perceive these other dimensions and their entities (42). In order to right these wrong turns in the trajectory of the combined evolution of humankind and the Earth, the narrator notes that the war to be waged is not against one another or nature, but rather against the demons within: "It is easier to tame the beasts of nature... than our own beasts" (100–01). By turning humanity inward to struggle with itself spiritually rather than dominate nature, González places humans on a new path that doubly articulates both engaging and disengaging the Earth simultaneously. While this "immaterial approach" informs González's overall project of witnessing from the fifth dimension and moving humanity from the anthropocentric to the ecocentric, going inward also necessitates a rebirth whereby humanity then reengages the Earth in ecocentric and future-oriented ways.

The idea of looking ahead rather than into the past sounds simple enough, but actually this sense of orientation often fails as critical theories tend to tackle issues in the past and the present. This paralysis of critique comprises one of the main points of Patrick D. Murphy's "Ecofeminism and Postmodernism: Agency, Transformation, and Future Possibilities." Murphy asserts that ecofeminism provides a set of principles that serve as forward-looking transformational concepts with which to improve the Earth for all in the future. Among these principles are agency and diversity. He points out that ecofeminism assigns agency "to everyone who is human but also to the various nonhuman 'actors' who share the world with us" (51). Additionally, ecofeminism insists upon "healthy biological diversity and life as an interconnected web, as a heterarchy rather than a hierarchy" (51). Agency and diversity understood in these ways serve to diffuse anthropocentrism. In other words, human agency is not constructed as dominant, but rather cedes power to many diverse, and equal, actors.

These transformational concepts surface in the closing chapter of *13 B'aktun*. After having plunged humanity's anthropocentrism quite literally into hell on Earth, González ends his narrative with a call to action for the future. He does so in the following passage, worth quoting in its entirety:

> Dear reader, wherever you may be, let me make clear to you that this isn't a novel like others you've read. The others we read while feeling distant from them, like passive receptors of information, like spectators at a movie we watch from our own perspective. But in this one, you are an actor, a participant. You can't remain indifferent to what you've read because you're already within the drama of life in this world.
>
> (127)

He also informs the reader that his text will have no conclusion because, he writes, "I ask that you finish the last chapter" (128). González again directly reaches out to his readers to call attention to both their agency and their embeddedness within "the drama of life." In so doing, he emphasizes heterarchical connections by reminding his readers that there is no vertical distance, in fact, between what they have just read and their lives. Text, narrator, reader, and world are all as one. The future beckons all to act in these interconnected ways rather than close the book and move on to something else that feels more important. To González, there is nothing more important than the future of the planet. He appeals to this notion, in fact, by continuously reminding his readers that the world as we know it is not nearly as secure or stable as one might believe it to be. Toward the end of his book, he asks: "What would you do if you knew with certainty that the end of the world would occur in the year 2012?" (128).

THE ECOTESTIMONIO ENDING

With an unwavering sense of future, convincing efforts to address ecological harm, and persistent drive to unsettle the supposedly secure and ironclad material boundaries of its readers, *13 B'aktun* falls under what Kimberly Nance has defined as "deliberative" testimonio.[15] She writes that "the future orientation of deliberative testimonio requires a hybrid and much more sophisticated rhetorical strategy, one that will persuade readers to think critically about the world at the same time that it confronts them with a personal obligation to combat injustice" (38). González definitely asks his readers to think critically about the world, and, I would add, about themselves and their just or unjust relationship to it. The world in his text, however, is not the strictly social world of traditional testimonio texts; rather, it is the Earth as living organism and a fifth-dimensional realm.

The ecotestimonio model to emerge from the pages of *13 B'aktun* challenges, therefore, many long-standing tenets of the classic testimonio narrative. Terra-trauma, rather than human trauma, takes center stage. The nonhuman biotic *testigo* of Earth and González co-witness from an immaterial world of spirit. Time orientation often refers to a future based on the cyclical nature of past events, or prophecy. In all of these ways, the lens of ecology brings the materialist and anthropocentric paradigms of the very referential testimonio text into sharp focus for further scrutiny and critique.

NOTES

1. These novels are: *La otra cara (A Mayan Life)* and *El retorno de los mayas (Return of the Maya)*, first published in Spanish in 1992 and 1998, respectively. The only scholars who have addressed *El 13 B'aktun* to date are Robert K. Sitler, R. McKenna Brown, and

Martin Pflug. See their respective scholarship entries in the works cited section.
2. Sitler and other scholars are quick to point out that the term "Maya" does not adequately convey the linguistic, cultural, and geographic diversity of the many groups so often defined by this umbrella term. Moreover, scholars note too that the Maya have not disappeared and are many millons strong across multiple countries and regions. I use the term in this essay in part due to a lack of viable alternatives. I do so, however, with these caveats in mind.
3. All quotations in this essay refer to Stiler's English translation, *13 B'aktun: Mayan Visions of 2012 and Beyond*.
4. Lisa K. Miller's *Newseek* article, "Y2K for a New Age," is representative of this line of thought. She offers the following quote from one of her interviewees: "In Mexico... the real Maya think of 2012 as 'a gringo invention.' " In general, most academicians reject the topic of 2012 outright.
5. Noteworthy testimonio scholars in the U.S. include John Beverley, Georg Gugelberger, Elzbieta Sklodowska, Doris Sommer, Marc Zimmerman, and George Yúdice. For a comprehensive bibliography on other scholars and testimonial studies in general, see Maier and Dulfano (9–17) and the works cited section in Nance (193–206).
6. Just as a feminist approach often interprets a narrative by highlighting the textual treatment of women and issues of gender, or a Marxist approach studies class differences, an ecocritical hermeneutics at its most basic refers to a critical examination of ecosystems and environmental concerns.
7. The first three dimensions are space (length, width, and depth) and the fourth dimension is time. My use of the term fifth dimension is based on Jennifer A. Machiorlatti's article "Ecocinema, Ecojustice, and Indigenous Worldviews" (66). This realm is also referred to as the Otherworld (Sitler 69) or, most commonly, the spirit world.
8. I borrow this term from Patrick D. Murphy, who defines paramodernism as "an ideological formation in which beliefs and cultural practices run alongside of modernity or postmodernity in the contemporary world" (note 1, 58).
9. A female prayer-maker named Katal tells González and his son during their visions with her in a sacred cave that what they are about to see "is not fiction" (19). However, later she tells them that what they see are signs of events to come. Therefore, the text ultimately remains open-ended on the time orientation of these events.
10. The notion of time as cyclical represents an additional item regarding the ways in which the traditional testimonio text relies on contemporary Western paradigms. A testimonio that predicts a future based on past events conjures up multiple and simultaneous senses of time. In the model described by Kimberly Nance in *Can Literature Promote Justice?*, testimonios fall into three main categories as defined by time

orientation and narrative stance: those that gaze accusingly into the past (forensic) (23), those that denounce or praise in the present (epideictic) (25), and those that persuade or dissuade with respect to the future (deliberative) (21). Note that these models are much more complex than I have summarized them here. Although *13 B'aktun* often tends to narrate in the past, present, and future all at once, the future-oriented nature of both its title and most of its content makes a strong case, as I state in the conclusion, for categorizing it as a deliberative text.

11. Naranjo makes two main points regarding Gaia theory. He first notes that Gaia theory accounts for the Earth's atmosphere as a biological construction given how it has suppressed gases harmful to life (93). He also points out that the Gaia hypothesis is the first scientific manifestation of the ancient principle of a living Earth (93).

12. Although Hancock's books, as he himself has acknowledged many times, do not receive wide acceptance by the academy, their originality, depth, and breadth should invite dialogue and consideration by scholars of all disciplinary backgrounds and mindsets.

13. Lovelock devised the term Gaia with the help of novelist William Golding in 1969 (22). One convincing example of the slow but steady circulation of a living planet idea is the case of Bolivia. As of this writing, Bolivia not only has laws in place in its own country to treat the Earth as a living entity, but also it is drafting a United Nations treaty to propose that this concept be accepted internationally.

14. This process has been contested in many ways. Most scholars note the performative aspect of giving testimony, in addition to issues of veracity and editorial inscription. Here, however, my critique refers not to this process but rather to the very concept of the human eyewitness itself.

15. The closing ambiguity of *13 B'aktun* is much more present in the Spanish than in the English, which omits the final six lines of González's narrative. The Spanish text ends with two violent *sacudidas* (shakings), and father and son screaming for one another. The last line of the Spanish consists of a series of exclamation points, leaving the reader to wonder whether the world is, in fact, ending. The English version ends on a decidedly positive note by associating the brightness of the ceremonial fires with the "light of the New Era" (129). This editorial change was approved by the author. Regardless of the ending, however, the prevailing notion of an unstable planet remains consistent throughout the entire narrative.

Works Cited

Brown, R. McKenna. "Who Owns the Mayan Apocalypse? Identity Claims in *El 13 B'aktun* by Gaspar Pedro Gonzalez." 107th Annual Meeting of the American Anthropological Association, San Francisco. Nov. 23, 2008. Presentation. Web. April 28, 2011.

———. "Gaspar Pedro González' *El 13 B'aktun*: An Internal Vision of the Mayan Apocalypses." Carolina Conference of Romance Languages, U of North Carolina, Chapel Hill. March 29, 2008. Presentation. Web. April 28, 2011.

Crist, Eileen, and H. Bruce Rinker, eds. *Gaia in Turmoil: Climate Change Biodepletion, and Earth Ethics in an Age of Crisis*. Cambridge: MIT, 2010. Print.

González, Gaspar Pedro. *El trece b'ak'tun: la nueva era 2012*. Guatemala: Cholsamaj, 2006. Print.

———. *13 B'aktun: Mayan Visions of 2012 and Beyond*. Trans. Robert Sitler. Berkeley: North Atlantic, 2010. Print.

Hancock, Graham. *Supernatural: Meetings with the Ancient Teachers of Mankind*. New York: Disinformation, 2007. Print.

Kane, Adrian Taylor, ed. "Epilogue: 'Beyond the Telluric Novel.' " *The Natural World in Latin American Literatures*. Ed. Adrian Taylor Kane. Jefferson: McFarland, 2010. 233–36. Print.

Lovelock, James. *The Revenge of Gaia: Earth's Climate Crisis & the Fate of Humanity*. New York: Basic, 2006. Print.

Machiorlatti, Jennifer A. "Ecocinema, Ecojustice, and Indigenous Worldviews: Native and First Nations Media as Cultural Recovery." *Framing the World: Explorations in Ecocriticism and Film*. Ed. Paula Willoquet-Maricondi. Charlottesville: U Virginia P, 2010. 62–80. Print.

Maier, Linda S., and Isabel Dulfano, eds. *Woman as Witness: Essays on Testimonial Literature by Latin American Women*. New York: Peter Lang, 2004. Print.

Menchú, Rigoberta, and Elisabeth Burgos. *Me llamo Rigoberta Menchú y así me nació la conciencia*. Barcelona: Editorial Argos Vergara, 1983. Print.

———. *I, Rigoberta Menchú: An Indian Woman in Guatemala*. Introd. and ed. Elisabeth Burgos-Debray. Trans. Ann Wright. 1984. New York: Verso, 1993. Print.

Montejo, Victor. *Maya Intellectual Renaissance: Identity, Representation, and Leadership*. Austin: U of Texas P, 2005. Print.

Miller, Lisa. "Y2K for the New Age." *Newsweek*. May 2, 2009. Web. June 5, 2009.

Murphy, Patrick D. "Ecofeminism and Postmodernism: Agency, Transformation, and Future Possibilities." *Women, Ecology, and the Environment* 9.3 (1997): 41–59. Print.

Nance, Kimberly. *Can Literature Promote Justice?* Nashville: Vanderbilt UP, 2006. Print.

Naranjo, José Ramón. "La ecología profunda y el *Popol Vuh*." *Anales de literatura hispanoamericana* 33 (2004): 85–100. Print.

Pflug, Martín. "*El 13 B'aktun*: La transculturación y la destransculturación de una cosmovisión milenaria." *Proceedings of the Joint 2009 Conference of the National Association of African American Studies & Affiliates*, February 9–14, 2009: *Culture Session*. Baton Rouge: NAAAS & Affiliates, 2009. 129–43. Web. April 28, 2011.

Popol Vuh: The Mayan Book of the Dawn of Life. Trans. Dennis Tedlock. 1985. New York: Touchstone-Simon & Schuster, 1996. Print.

Rowe, Stan. "Ecocentrism and Traditional Ecological Knowledge." *Ecospherics Ethics*. N.d. N. pag. Web. Jan. 25, 2011.

Sitler, Robert K. "Gaspar Pedro González: The First Maya Novelist." *SECOLAS Annals* 28 (1997): 67–72. Print.

——. Foreward. *13 B'aktun: Mayan Visions of 2012 and Beyond*. By Gaspar Pedro González. Trans. Robert Sitler. Berkeley: North Atlantic, 2010. Print.

Tittler, Jonathan. "Ecological Criticism and Spanish American Fiction: An Overview." *The Natural World in Latin American Literatures*. Ed. Adrian Taylor Kane. Jefferson: MacFarland, 2010. 11–36. Print.

2012. Dir. Roland Emmerich. Columbia Pictures, 2009. Film.

Conclusion

"Something That Might Resemble a Call": Testimonial Theory and Practice in the Twenty-First Century

Kimberly A. Nance

In theory as well as in practice, testimonio's centrifugal force is undeniable. That outward trajectory is not only geographic; testimonio's generic variety has grown apace. As a Latin Americanist and literary scholar brought up on the old new narrative and the magical variety of realism, I cannot help but experience a flash of déjà vu at this veritable boom. It is not just that once again a genre has emerged from Latin America to go global. There is also something familiar about the sequence of scholarship. First come claims that a movement is not only grounded in the region but is somehow generically defined by one particular moment and milieu. Then, in the midst of the celebration of its authentically Latin American character, a movement slips that early critical yoke, spreading beyond the region even as it continues to develop within. Critics are faced with a choice: either declare that whatever overruns those early geographic and generic bounds cannot be the real thing or else revise their definitions in light of new developments. Like the scholars who elected to study the magical realism of Toni Morrison and Salman Rushdie alongside that of Gabriel García Márquez and Isabel Allende, essayists in this collection have opted to follow testimonio from its canonical beginnings in Latin America through new forms and into new places. Many of these essayists focus on new testimonios and those that are still in progress; others—for instance, Julia Medina in her essay on guerrilla narratives—loop back to reconsider older texts in a new light. And they are not alone: testimonial theory has now been used to study texts ranging from Caribbean novels to Indonesian working class autobiographies, from transcripts drawn from truth commissions in Rwanda to Inuit stories of the Canadian Arctic.

But acknowledging the centrifugal movement of testimonio and testimonial criticism is only half the story. The very observation that testimonio is evolving beyond its former boundaries entails an implicit claim that the new productions are somehow still testimonio. While bearing in mind Louise Detwiler and Janis Breckenridge's well-founded caution against "endlessly picking apart" the genre (see their introduction), certain questions are still worth asking. What counts as testimonio, and why does it matter? At the same time that critics were beginning to police the boundaries of testimonio, the publishing industry was rapidly broadening the use of the term, having caught on to testimonio's marketing value. Paralleling the burgeoning application of the term "magical realism" to an ever-broader range of works, productions that in earlier times might have been promoted as memoir, biography, or autobiography began to be tagged as testimonios. Although the circuit of mutual comparison and endorsement never quite reached the level of "if you liked Rigoberta Menchú, you'll love this new testimonio," at least by the 1980s the back covers of some new testimonios bore laudatory blurbs from established testimonialistas, and by the end of the twentieth century that label was regularly applied to far less politically charged texts.

When virtually any sort of life writing is promoted as testimonio, the genre's social and political dimension—and its potential effectiveness—can be diminished. Overly exclusive definitions of testimonio pose barriers to productive solidarity, a risk to which Patricia Connolly devotes extended attention, and Breckenridge makes a compelling case that testimonio is not bound by canonical structures of mediated testimony (see their earlier essays). At the same time, definitions that are overly inclusive also carry risks. That risk is especially high when the category of testimonio is stretched to cover memoirs of relative privilege, where hypertrophic expansion can lead to what physician and activist Paul Farmer has termed "fictional solidarity." "Not all forms of suffering are equivalent," he insists, and "the risk of stretching the concept of rights to cover every possible case is that obscene inequalities of risk will be drowned in a rising tide of petty complaint" (231).

So what are the centripetal forces that continue to draw testimonios together in the twenty-first century? What unites the new cultural productions studied here with earlier testimonios, and what is the relationship between these essays and earlier testimonial criticism? Turning first to the testimonios described here, many of them lack one or more of the characteristics often put forth by critics as defining the genre: not only Latin American provenance, but also collaboration between subaltern and professional, homogenous political stripe, first-person perspective, and nonfictional narrative (even, in the case of the CPR-Sierra textiles, the narrative itself.) What remain as constants are efforts to translate an experience of injustice into a cultural production that will promote change by engaging others to act, a working definition that still bears a family resemblance to the qualifications set forth when Casa de las Américas publishing house first created a category for testimonio in its annual prize competition.

Accounts of the origins of that prize—including transcripts of foundational conversations that took place in 1969 among Ángel Rama, Isadora Aguirre, Hans Magnus Enzensberger, Manuel Galich, Noé Jitrik, and Haydee Santamaría—all attest to the strong connection between testimonio and social action that was present from the outset (Rama). Ambrosio Fornet characterizes the creation of the testimonial prize category as a response to "la oleada factográfica que, como resultado de las expectativas revolucionarias, empezaba a azotar el continente" (the documentary tidal wave that, as a result of revolutionary expectations, was beginning to sweep the continent) (138), when what was at stake was nothing less than the place of writers in revolutionary movements. "The incorporation of this award category," Pablo Calvi suggests, "provided a Latin American answer to the controversial question about the role of intellectuals in politically loaded times, a question that had festered ever since it was raised in *Les Temps Modernes* by Jean Paul Sartre and Albert Camus almost twenty years before" (66). While the judges were interested specifically in Latin America and the Caribbean and in written text—not surprisingly, since the prize was to be awarded by a Cuban publisher—it is notable that there were no further specifications as to the shape that a testimony should take, much less any expectation that testimonio should constitute some sort of anti-artistic expression. On the contrary, as parameters for the prize were developed, the form was expressly left open, and artistic quality counted.

Testimonies must document some aspect of Latin American or Caribbean reality from a direct source. A direct source is understood as knowledge of the facts by the author or his or her compilation of narratives or evidence obtained from the individuals involved or qualified witnesses. In both cases reliable documentation, written or graphic, is indispensable. The form is at the author's discretion, but literary quality is also indispensable.

(qtd. and trans. in Beverley 155n.)

Also present from the outset was a sense of testimonio as overrunning established boundaries. Carmen Ochando Aymerich asserts that one impetus for the new prize category was precisely a growing body of submissions "cuyas características textuales salían fuera de los cauces de las modalidades tradicionales" (whose textual characteristics spilled over the banks of traditional modes), and that after the category was established it would continue to broaden, owing both to "la trayectoria de los textos" (the trajectory of the texts) and "las apreciaciones de los miembros de los jurados" (the critical responses of jury members) (32).

In reading the critical essays as well, I was struck first by what is missing in contrast with earlier work on testimonio. These writers display no surprise that speakers would shape their discourse to suit particular political purposes and audiences, or that others, including members of the speakers' community, might try to reshape that discourse to serve a different agenda. Both rhetorical intention and contestation are taken as givens. Also largely absent is the misprizing of desire as equivalent to effect; the essays here look to potential outcomes without presuming success. They allow for the possibility that a given testimonio might prove less than effective, as evident when Nancy Gates-Madsen examines in her essay the constraining force of the socially sayable in *My Name Is Light*. Missing as well are expectations that successful testimonios will necessarily have immediate and local effects. The projects described here are long term and wide ranging. Conspicuously present in these pages are the critics themselves. Rather than writing themselves out of the picture in an attempt at self-effacement or romantically fusing with their subjects, many of the scholars represented here have chosen to cast a critical eye on the potential social consequences of their own actions, as when Leigh Binford reflects on his work with Fabio Argueta, or T. M. Linda Scholz stands before CPR-Sierra embroideries in a Guatemalan marketplace.

For all of their theoretical diversity, the essays in this volume are also united by an approach that might be termed "ecological." Detwiler and Alice Driver focus their essays explicitly on ecotestimonios, but all of the essays effectively situate testimonio as a living organism in interrelationship with a particular environment. Rather than attempting to dissect and anatomize, these writers have chosen to observe in vivo, at junctures ranging from early development to production, editing, and reception. Judging from their observations, testimonio as a project to increase social justice is alive and well. Of course, the news that the genre continues to thrive in the twenty-first century is not entirely positive; maps of testimonial production also serve as indexes of actual injustice, and the production of testimonios is no guarantee of amelioration.

Literature in general has been described as a "prosthesis of the mind" (Holquist 83). That term is particularly apt to testimonio, which points at once to loss and to recovery, to what is missing and what is possible—a quality that David Foster terms an "interplay between lament and resistant promise, between oppressed individuals and the awakening collective" (see Foster's earlier essay). Where established mechanisms of justice have been ineffective, absent, or complicit, testimonios seek to supplement or substitute. That work may take the form of post hoc formal hearings, as in the case of the truth commissions studied by Lynn Stephen in her essay, or far less formal media such as the rumors in Corinne Pubill's essay. Testimonios serve not only to describe and diagnose, inscribing a local injustice in the social system that made it possible; they also seek to persuade audiences to intervene. As readers might recognize, the title of this essay comes from Jean-François Lyotard's formulation of the "pact" that he regarded as necessary for testimony to lead to action. "Something that resembles a call" must be met by someone who not only recognizes that call for help, but also recognizes him or herself as one who can—and should—assist (Lyotard 121).

In illuminating the connections between otherwise abstract social, economic, and governmental policies and the lives of individuals, testimonios may be uniquely suited to help bridge gaps between resolution and reality. Efforts to address human rights abuse that end with endorsement of abstract propositions, David Reiff concludes, are doomed to fail because "the solutions that they propose are not real solutions, the history they touch on is not the actual history, and the world they describe is not the real world" (9). He cites a report from the United States Institute of Peace, noting that 60 years after the United Nations Convention on Genocide, "the world agrees that genocide is unacceptable and yet genocide and mass killings continue"; the challenge now, the report continues, is to "stop allowing the unacceptable" (Reiff 2). In religious, forensic, and ethical contexts, testimony rests on expectations of personal accountability for one's actions, not only for the witness who testifies, but also for those who witness the testimony. In live contexts, the result may be a sort of mutual production that Melissa Guzman examines in her essay on radio testimonios. In any medium, the most effective testimonios present justice not as an accomplishment but rather as an unfinished project. They seek to persuade audiences to bend that arc further.

In this regard, testimonios' frequent focus on ordinariness—both of the victims of injustice and of those who work (or might work) to combat it—anticipates some very recent work in the area of applied ethics. Claims of ordinariness are a powerful means of persuasion on both sides of the moral spectrum, as Madeleine Hron observes in her article "Ordinary Killers," applying testimonial theory to Jean Hatzfield's 2003 collection of accounts from Rwanda. In 2011, Philip Zimbardo, famous for the 1971 Stanford prison experiment in which students assigned to play the roles of guards were induced to behave in sadistic ways toward their fellow-student prisoners, is embarking on a project to promote the opposite outcome—actions of moral bravery (Choi). The first step, Zimbardo explains, is to make people aware of mechanisms that promote or permit injustice: "bystander inaction, diffusion of responsibility, the power of the group, obedience to authority and the like." Next, he hopes to demonstrate how ordinary people come to do heroic things. Zimbardo stresses the need to "democratize heroism," "to change the mentality of people away from the belief that they're not the kind who do heroic deeds to one where they think everyone has the potential to be heroic." "It's amazing," he observes, "that there has been research on evil for years, but almost no research on heroism" (qtd. in Choi).

Zimbardo is undoubtedly correct when it comes to academic research, but in fact such research has been going on empirically all over the world, and for stakes far higher than publication and citation. With few resources and under difficult conditions, not only have ordinary individuals resolved to perform acts of moral bravery, community organizers have become expert at convincing other ordinary people to undertake such acts. Chronicles of such ordinary heroism are a defining element of many testimonios, which often feature detailed accounts of how individuals make their own decisions to act and then persuade others to join them. Frequently they also present the counterexamples of people who fall prey to the mechanisms that Zimbardo warns against. Recent research in neurology, psychology, and communication theory also offers new explanations for the effectiveness of some testimonios and the practical failure of others. Investigations of the operation of the justice motive in human life (Furnham), the neurological underpinnings of empathy (Eisenberg), and the ways in which both fictional and nonfictional narratives can affect audiences' attitudes and actions (Appel, Brock, Green, Leung, Richter, Strange) are enriching the sociocultural field of testimonial studies. In significant ways, academic researchers are beginning to discover what many producers of testimonio have already learned.

Perhaps the most encouraging development in twenty-first-century testimonial scholarship is the growing recognition of that empirical expertise in promoting social action. Among the recent programs in which testimonios have been studied in the context of actual social justice projects is the Transitional Justice Data Base Project established in 2005 at the University of Wisconsin-Madison, whose funders include the National Science Foundation as well as the United States Institute of Peace. The project's activities include both theoretical and applied work on response to atrocities, including qualitative and quantitative evaluation of international and domestic legal mechanisms, truth commissions, amnesty, reparations, and lustration. The Literature and Justice Project begun in 2007 at the University of Southern California also brings together faculty and students to read testimonios and other literary accounts of injustice alongside models of justice from political philosophy and social theory. In 2008, Donna Bickford reported on a similar program in "Using Testimonial Novels to Think about Social Justice." Projects such as these demonstrate clearly that testimonial scholarship has moved beyond a focus on what testimonialists might lack (for instance, literacy), to an appreciation of what so many of them possess: field-proven analytical and rhetorical skills. No longer only objects of literary or cultural scrutiny in the academy, testimonios are also finding a place as guides for academic research on social justice and plans for concrete interventions. Taking its cues from testimonio itself, productive testimonial criticism requires approaches that are similarly provisional, improvisational, and empirically informed—proceeding with a mixture of faith and skepticism, but nevertheless proceeding.

Works Cited

Appel, Markus. "Fictional Narratives Cultivate Just World Beliefs." *Journal of Communication* 58.1 (2008): 62–83. Print.

Appel, Markus, and Tobias Richter. "Persuasive Effects of Fictional Narratives Increase over Time." *Media Psychology* 10 (2007): 113–14. Print.

Beverley, John. *Against Literature*. Minneapolis: U of Minnesota P, 1993. Print.
Bickford, Donna M. "Using Testimonial Novels to Think About Social Justice." *Education, Citizenship and Social Justice* 3.2 (2008): 131–46. Web. June 21, 2011.
Calvi, Pablo. "Latin America's Own 'New Journalism.' " *Literary Journalism Studies* 2.2 (2010): 63–83. Web. June 22, 2011.
Caminero-Santangelo, Marta. "At the Intersection of Trauma and Testimonio: Edwidge Danticat's *The Farming of Bones*." *Antípodas: Journal of Hispanic and Galician Studies* 20 (2009): 5–26. Web. June 21, 2011.
Choi, Charles Q. "Too Hard for Science? Philip Zimbardo—Creating Millions of Heroes." April 22, 2011. *Scientific American*. Web. June 21, 2011.
Eisenberg, Nancy. "Empathy-Related Emotional Responses, Altruism, and their Socialization." *Visions of Compassion: Western Scientists and Tibetan Buddhists Examine Human Nature*. Ed. Richard Davidson and Anne Harrington. New York: Oxford UP, 2002. 131–64. Print.
Farenga, Vincent. "Report: The Literature & Justice Project 2007–2008." Department of Comparative Literature, University of Southern California. 2008. Web. June 21, 2011.
Farmer, Paul. *Pathologies of Power: Health, Human Rights, and the New War on the Poor*. Berkeley: U of California P, 2003. Print.
Fornet, Ambrosio. *La coartada perpetua*. México: Siglo XXI, 2002. Print.
Furnham, Adrian. "Belief in a Just World: Research Progress over the Past Decade." *Personality and Individual Differences* 34 (2003): 795–817. Print.
Green, Melanie, and Timothy Brock. "In The Mind's Eye: Transportation-Imagery Model of Narrative Persuasion." *Narrative Impact: Social and Cognitive Foundations*. Ed. Melanie Green, Jeffrey Strange, and Timothy Brock. Mahwah: Erlbaum, 2002. 315–42. Print.
——. "The Role of Transportation in the Persuasiveness of Public Narratives." *Journal of Personality and Social Psychology* 79 (2000): 701–21. Print.
Holquist, Michael. *Dialogism: Bakhtin and His World*. London: Routledge, 1990. Print.
Hron, Madelaine. "Gukora and Itsembatsemba: The 'Ordinary Killers' in Jean Hatzfeld's *Machete Season*." *Research in African Literatures* 42.2 (2011): 125–46. Web. April 22, 2011.
Lyotard, Jean-François. *The Differend: Phrases in Dispute*. Trans. Georges Van den Abbeele. Minneapolis: U of Minneapolis P, 1984. Print.
Moquin, Heather. "Breathing Out 'The Songs that Want to be Sung': A Dialogue on Research, Colonization and Pedagogy Focused on the Canadian Arctic." PhD thesis. University of Glasgow, 2010. Web. June 21, 2011.
Ochando Aymerich, Carmen. *La memoria en el espejo: Aproximación a la escritura testimonial*. Barcelona: Anthropos, 1998. Web. June 21, 2011.

Payne, Leigh A., Tricia D. Olsen, and Andrew G. Reiter. *Transitional Justice Data Base*. University of Wisconsin-Madison. 2005. Web. June 21, 2011.

Rama, Ángel et al. "Conversación en torno al testimonio" (Transcripción del diálogo desarrollado entre los jurados y organizadores del Premio Casa de las Américas en febrero de 1969: Ángel Rama, Isadora Aguirre, Hans Magnus Enzensberger, Manuel Galich, Noé Jitrik, Haydee Santamaría). *Casa de las Américas* 36.200 (1995): 122–25. Print.

Reiff, David. "The Persistence of Genocide." *Hoover Institution Policy Review* 165 (2011). Web. June 21, 2011.

Strange, Jeffrey. "How Fictional Tales Wag Real-World Beliefs." *Narrative Impact: Social and Cognitive Foundations*. Ed. Melanie Green, Jeffrey Strange, and Timothy Brock. Mahwah: Erlbaum, 2002. 263–86. Print.

Strange, Jeffrey, and Cynthia Leung. "How Anecdotal Accounts in News and in Fiction Can Influence Judgments of a Social Problem's Urgency, Causes, and Cures." *Personality and Social Psychology Bulletin* 25 (1999): 436–49. Print.

Suryomenggolo, Jafar. "Defining Indonesia from the Margins: Working Class Autobiography as Part of the Nation's Collective Memory." *Indonesia and the Malay World* 39.114 (2011): 221–43. Web. June 21, 2011.

Notes on Contributors

Leigh Binford (Professor of Anthropology and Chair of the Department of Anthropology, Sociology, and Social Work at the College of Staten Island) is the author of four books, including *Landscapes of Struggle: Politics, Community, and the Nation-State in Twentieth Century El Salvador*. His fieldwork in Mexico and El Salvador focuses on rural social economies, peasantries, international migration, human rights, civil war, and postwar reconstruction. His current research addresses the consequences of post - civil war neoliberal policies for former Farabundo Martí Front for National Liberation rebels and their supporters.

Janis Breckenridge (Assistant Professor of Spanish at Whitman College) specializes in twentieth-century Latin American literature. A recipient of the Feministas Unidas Essay Prize for her essay on testimonial film, Janis has published numerous articles that address such diverse subjects as Latin American cinema and fiction, literary and visual testimony, children's literature, lesbian sexuality, and the parodic treatment of travel literature. Her current research focuses on human rights and collective memory in literature, film, and public space in Argentina.

Patricia Connolly (MA in English Literature from the University of Vermont) is currently a doctoral candidate in Feminist Studies at the University of Minnesota. Her research focuses on the ways in which testimonio has been taken up by contemporary feminist activist groups and literary writers, the political and imaginative possibilities enabled by hybrid writing forms, and questions of representation and reception in relation to these texts.

Louise Detwiler (Associate Professor of Spanish and Department Chair at Salisbury University) has published numerous articles on twentieth-century Latin American and Latina writers. A former recipient of the M/MLA Women's Caucus Distinguished Paper Award for her work on testimonio, her current research focuses on the representation of ecological and environmental voices within life writing.

Alice Driver (Ph.D. in Hispanic Studies from the University of Kentucky) has published articles and interviews and is currently the Managing Editor of *Nomenclatura: aproximaciones a los estudios hispánicos*. Her article "Of the

Flesh: Graphic Images of Feminicide in Ciudad Juárez" will be published in the fall of 2012 in *Restructuring Violence in the Spanish-Speaking World*.

David William Foster (Regents' Professor of Spanish and Women and Gender Studies at Arizona State University) directs the Brazilian studies program at ASU. His research focuses on urban culture, with emphasis on gender and Jewish diaspora issues in Buenos Aires and São Paulo.

Nancy J. Gates-Madsen (Assistant Professor of Spanish at Luther College) is the co-translator of *Violet Island and Other Poems*, a bilingual anthology of the work of Cuban poet Reina María Rodríguez. She has published various articles about the legacies of authoritarianism in the Southern Cone, and her current scholarship explores the literary and cultural silences left in the wake of dictatorship.

Melissa Guzman (Graduate student of Sociology at the University of California, Santa Barbara) studies the interactive and collective aspects of religious communities. She is currently exploring how Latina/o immigrant Pentecostals affirm a sense of civic engagement and formulate a type of "spiritual citizenship" in their daily lives.

Julia M. Medina (Assistant Professor of Spanish at the University of San Diego) specializes in nineteenth- and twentieth-century Latin American literature and critical theory. She has published articles that deal with political manifestoes, photographic images, cartoons, prologues, *crónicas*, and autobiographical narratives. Her current research focuses on the intersection between visual culture, nonfiction, resistance, and intellectual representations in Central America.

Kimberly A. Nance (Professor of Spanish at Illinois State University) has published three books together with 25 articles and book chapters on Latin American literature, coauthored a Spanish composition text, and served on the Modern Language Association's Executive Committee on the Teaching of Literature. Her 2006 book, *Can Literature Promote Justice?* (Vanderbilt University Press), was named a CHOICE Outstanding Academic Book.

Corinne Pubill (Assistant Professor of Spanish and French at Salisbury University) focuses her research on women writers of the Southern Cone. Her publications, including an interview with writer María Teresa Andruetto, explore the use of memory, politics, and insile in the production of narrative.

T. M. Linda Scholz (Assistant Professor at Eastern Illinois University) studies the connections between rhetorical theory and criticism, postcolonial feminist theory, subaltern studies, and Latina/o and Latin American Studies. Her most recent publication, "Hablando Por (Nos)Otros Speaking for Ourselves: Exploring Possibilities of 'Speaking Por' Family and Pueblo in the Bolivian Testimonio Si Me Permiten Hablar [Let Me Speak!]," appears in *Latina/o Discourse in Vernacular Spaces: Somos de Una Voz?*

Lynn Stephen (Distinguished Professor of Anthropology at the University of Oregon and Director of the Center for Latino/a and Latin American Studies) studies migration, the intersection of culture and politics, and how political identities articulate with ethnicity, gender, class, and nationalism in relation to local, regional, and national histories, as well as systems of governance in Latin America. She has conducted fieldwork in Mexico, El Salvador, Chile, Brazil, and the United States. Her newest book is titled *Transborder Lives: Indigenous Oaxacans in Mexico, California, and Oregon.*

INDEX

Note: letter 'n' followed by locators denotes note numbers.

Abu-Lughod, Lila, 20, 22
Acevedo, Luz, 45
Acta de independencia de Chile (1818), 66
Acta general de Chile (documentary film, Littin), 59–66
　conditions of production of, 60–1
　first section of, 62–5
　significance of acta term to, 65–6
Actas de Marusia (film, Littin), 67n6
Acteal massacre, 114–15
activism, *see* social action and social movements
Adams, Jacqueline, 166
agency, 2
　guerilla warfare and, 71, 78
　heterarchical, 224
　lack of, 132
　nonhuman, 233
　political, 168
　process of testimonio and, 48, 50, 110
　see also subjectivity
Agosín, Marjorie, 166, 168, 172
Aguirre, Isadora, 241
alienation, *see* insile
Allende, Isabel, 239
Allende, Salvador (Chilean president), 66
Alsino y el cóndor (film, Littin), 68n10
Alvarado, Elvia, 173
Amnesty International, 123, 125, 168

Andruetto, María Teresa, 141, 143nn2–3
　see also *La mujer en cuestión*
anthropocentrism *vs.* ecocentrism, 223–4, 226–8, 233–4
anthropology, *see* ethnography
anti-testimonio, 4, 131
　function of, 141–2
　rumors and, 133, 136, 138–9, 140–1
Antofagasta, Chile, 66n6
APPO (Popular Assembly of the Peoples of Oaxaca), 118, 119–20, 122, 123
Aragón, Ramiro, 120–1, 123, 124
Arce, Evangelina, 193
archiving/archive concept, 110
　oral testimony as, 109, 111, 126
　repertoire concept and, 116–17, 124
Argentina
　CONADEP, 66, 143n1, 144
　H.I.J.O.S., 90–1, 102n4
　junta trial/courtroom testimony, 113
　memory boom, 102n3
　military regime description, 142–3n1, 143n4
　oppression in, 133
　Ribera, Campo de la, 137, 139, 144n8
　truth commission, 110, 111, 112, 114, 243, 245

Argentina—*continued*
see also children of the disappeared; *La mujer en cuestión*; *My Name is Light*
Argento, Analía, 99–100, 103n19, 104n25
Argueta, Fabio, 11–12, 13–15, 29–30, 242
Arias, Arturo, 1, 76
Arpillera Movement (Chile), 166, 168, 172
Atencio, Rebeca, 148
Augé, Marc, 197n11
authenticity
camera's eye and, 58
documentation and, 204
incomplete, 160n2
mediated testimonio relationship and, 16, 159–60n2
multiple, 141
testimonio definition and, 147, 239
autobiography, 5
vs. fiction, 88
hybrid texts and, 208, 218n9
as testimonio, 82n6, 240
see also *Todo Paracuellos*
Avant-Mier, Roberto, 169
A veinte años, Luz (Osorio), see *My Name is Light*

Balibar, Etienne, 21
Barnet, Miguel, 1, 82n5, 202
Barrios de Chungara, Domitila, 173
Bartow, Joanna R., 2–3
Batalla de Chile (documentary, Guzmán), 59
La batalla de las cruces: protesta social y acciones colectivas en torno de la violencia sexual en Ciudad Juárez (documentary, Bonilla and Ravelo Blancas), 182, 191–5
Báten, Inocenta Cuyuch, 174
Báten, Paula Cuyuch, 176

Beá, José María, 210
Behar, Ruth, 20, 21, 23–5
Bejarano, Cynthia, 196n1
Bell, Beverly, 38, 53n7
Bellinghausen, Herman, 121–2, 124
Bello, Andrés, 82n9
Benjamin, Walter, 74
Beverley, John
  as foundational critic, 3, 235n5
  metonymy, 140
  orality, 159n2
  passé status of testimonio, 4, 19, 38, 41, 81–2n2
  subalternity, 17, 141
  testimonio definition, 12, 73, 82n6, 88, 133
  testimonio's effect on readers, 18–19
  truth of Other, 142
Beyond Terror: Gender, Narrative, Human Rights (Goldberg), 90
Bickford, Donna, 245
Bickford, Louis, 182–3
Biemann, Ursula, 182, 184–7, 193, 196n5
Binford, Leigh, 4, 242, 249
Biografía de un cimarrón (Barnet), 1
biological determinism, 97–8, 100
body, the, 92
  evidence of crime, 104n24, 122–3
  feminism and, 39–40
  knowledge source, 97–8
  repertoire and, 117
  social structures and, 44–5
Bolivia, 110, 111, 115–16, 236n13
Bonilla, Rafael, 182, 191–5
border crossing, 24–5
border/peripheral spaces, 76, 183, 184–7
botín de guerra (spoils of war), *see* children of the disappeared
Bourdieu, Pierre, 13
Bourgois, Philippe, 32n8
Bravo, Estela, 103n20
Breckenridge, Janis, 4, 240, 249

Brown, Joshua, 216n1
Brown, R. McKenna, 234–5n1
Burgos-Debray, Elisabeth, 17, 83n13

Cabandié, Juan, 103n18, 104n25
Cabezas, Omar, 75, 82n9
  see also *La montaña es algo más que una inmensa estepa verde*
Calafell, Bernadette, 169
Calveiro, Pilar, 142
Calvi, Pablo, 241
Cambiando Vidas (religious radio program), 148–62
  as institutional domain of interaction, 150–1
  organization of testimonio on, 152–4
  requests for help on, 155–8
  transcripts, 148
Campo Algodonero, 182
Camus, Albert, 241
Can Literature Promote Justice? Trauma Narrative and Social Action in Latin American Testimonio (Nance), 3, 50, 89, 235–6n10
capitalism
  academic critique of, 27, 28, 29, 33n15
  displacement of revolutionary politics, 19
  poverty and, 24
  vs. testimonio, 41
Cardona, Julián, 189, 194
Carey-Webb, Alan, 18
Carlotto, Estela, 104n24
Carroll, Peter N., 216n1
La Carta (documentary, Ravelo Blancas and Bonilla), 193
Caruth, Cathy, 89, 216, 217n5
Castillo, Debra, 5
censorship, 65, 214
Cervera, Luis, 196n3

El chacal de Nahueltoro (film, Littín), 67–8n10
Chávez, Esther, 186
Chávez, Petrona Choc, 176
Chilam Balam (Mayan texts), 230
childhood, *see Todo Paracuellos*
children of the disappeared, 90–100, 143n2, 144n8
  complex family relationships, 94–100, 103–4nn21–5, 103n16
  exposure of abduction, 91–4, 103n19
  identity politics, 90, 97–100, 104n23
  real life cases, 103–4n21, 103n18, 104nn23–4
Chile, 33n17, 62, 63, 68n11
  Acta de independencia de Chile (1818), 66
  Arpillera Movement, 166, 168, 172
  Chilean Church, 64
  truth commission, 111
  see also *Acta general de Chile*
Christian Base Community movement (El Salvador), 11, 13–14
Christian Democratic Party (Chile), 33n17
Ciudad Juárez, Mexico, 4, 181–97
  community destruction in, 191
  memoryscapes in, 194–5
  poverty/violence connection in, 189
  spatial amnesia in, 183–4
  spatial study of violence in, 196n3
  symbolic action in, 189–90
class politics, 13–14, 66–7n6
  anthropology and, 23, 25
  class fantasies, 30
  continued importance of, 19
  decline of, 12–13, 15, 19, 23
  rural proletarianization, 27–8, 31n3

clichés, 132
CNTE (Coordinadora Nacional de Trabajadores de la Educación), 119
cocalero unions (Bolivia), 19
collaboration, *see* mediated testimonio relationship; polyvocalism/polyvocal testimonies
collective testimonios, *see* polyvocalism/polyvocal testimonies
comic art
  artistic merit, 210
  aural component, 217n6
  subversive potential of, 212–15
  as valid narrative form, 208
  see also *Un largo silencio*; *Todo Paracuellos*; visual narration
communication studies, 169
Communist Party (Chile), 66–7n6
complicity
  fear and, 143n1, 172
  reader, 212, 216
  with repressive forces, 93, 95, 134, 135, 136
Comunidades de la Población en Resistencia-Sierra, *see* CPR-Sierra embroidery project
CONADEP (Comisión Nacional sobre la Desaparición de Personas), 66, 143n1, 144
Connolly, Patricia, 4, 240, 249
context, interactional, 151, 153–4, 155–9
continuum of life, *see* material-immaterial relationship
conversation analysis (CA), 148, 149–51, 159
Córdoba, Tabuenca, 195
Corrado, Danielle, 208, 211, 218n8
COR-TV (Corporation of Public Radio and Television, Mexico), 119

counter-geographies, 182, 183, 185, 195
  see also Ciudad Juárez, Mexico
CPR-Sierra embroidery project (Guatemala), 4, 165–76
  as atypical testimonio, 241
  as cultural resistance, 168–9, 170–1, 175
  described, 167–8, 171–2, 173–4
  importance of, 166–7
  as remembering, 173–4, 176
  researcher relationship with, 165–6, 242
  as vernacular rhetoric, 170, 172
Cuadrado, Jesús, 210
Cuba, 74–5, 81
Cuban Women Now (Randall), 44
Cué, Gabino, 125
cyborgs/cyborg theory, 5, 186, 232

Delgado, Fernando, 169
Delgado Aburto, Leonel, 73, 74, 76, 82nn7–8
deliberative testimonio, 50, 91, 234, 236n10
Demeure: Fiction and Testimony (Derrida), 88, 89
democracy, 169
denunciation
  complicity with, 136
  ineffectual, 31n7
  of injustice, 209, 213, 215, 216n1
  see also insile
Derrida, Jacques, 88, 89
Detwiler, Louise, 4, 240, 242, 249
developmentalism, 28, 78, 79, 80
De vuelta a casa: historias de hijos y nietos restituidos (Argento), 99–100, 103n19, 104n25
El Diario (newspaper), 190
Díaz del Castillo, Bernal, 73
Dimitrakaki, Angela, 185

Dirty War (Argentina), *see* Argentina
  the disappeared, 102n3, 144n8
  in documentary film, 63–4
  leveling concept and, 135–6
Disappearing Acts: Spectacles of Gender and Nationalism in Argentina's "Dirty War" (Taylor), 93
Discipline and Punish (Foucault), 18
documentary film
  eyewitness figure/role, 65
  La batalla de las cruces, 182, 191–5
  Performing the Border, 182, 184–7, 196n5
  privacy and, 58, 60
  Señorita Extraviada, 182, 187–91, 196–7n6
  theory of, 57–8
  truth in, 114, 188
  voice-over technique, 62, 185, 192, 194
  see also *Acta general de Chile*
domestic space, 191–2
Domínguez, Héctor, 194
Driver, Alice, 4, 242, 249–50
Duchesne-Winter, Juan R., 83n12
Dulfano, Isabel, 2

Eagleton, Terry, 31n6
"Ecocentrism and Traditional Ecological Knowledge" (Rowe), 225
ecocentrism *vs.* anthropocentrism, 223–4, 226–8, 233–4
"Ecocinema, Ecojustice, and Indigenous Worldviews" (Machiorlatti), 225, 235n7
ecocriticism, 223–4, 235n6
"Ecofeminism and Postmodernism: Agency, Transformation, and Future Possibilities" (Murphy), 233

ecotestimonio, 4, 181, 224, 234, 242–3
Ecuador, 111, 115–16
editorial inscription, *see* mediated testimonio relationship
El Mozote massacre (El Salvador), 13
El Quiché (Guatemala), 18, 166, 173, 174
El Salvador, 29
  Christian Base Community movement, 11, 13–14
  civil war, 11, 12, 14–15
  FMLN, 11, 15, 31n4, 74, 83n10
  peace treaty (1992), 71
  poverty in, 23–4
  truth commission, 111
Eltit, Diamela, 2–3
embodiment, 117, 122–3, 140
  see also body, the; oral testimonio
embroidery project, *see* CPR-Sierra embroidery project (Guatemala)
empathy, 244–5
Enzensberger, Hans Magnus, 241
epideictic testimonio, 91, 92, 93–4, 236n10
essentialism, 20, 22, 30, 45–6
ethics, applied, 244
ethics of representation, 58–9
  for children of the disappeared, 96–7
  feminicide victims, 182, 185–6, 187, 188, 192–3
  individual privacy and, 60
  of trauma/terror, 90
ethnography, 20–9
  testimonial function, 20–3, 32n8–9
  Translated Woman, 23–5
  Worker in the Cane, 23, 26–9
evasion of detection, 172, 174
exile, 59, 61, 143n1
  see also insile

Farabundo Martí National
    Liberation Front (FMLN, El
    Salvador), 11, 15, 31n4, 74,
    83n10
Farmer, Paul, 240–1
Faudree, Paja, 115–16
fear
    collective memory and, 191
    collective paranoia and, 131
    complicity with oppression and,
        143n1, 172
    guerilla warfare and, 77–8
    insile and, 134–5, 139, 141
    leveling concept and, 136
Feld, Claudia, 102n3
Felman, Shoshana, 88–9, 110, 210
feminicide, 4, 181
    anti-feminicide movement, 190,
        197n8
    border spaces and, 184–5, 187
    ethics of representation, 182,
        185–6, 187, 188, 192–3
    vs. femicide, 195–6n1
    graphic representation of, 185–6
    impact on families, 194
    memorials to victims, 189–90
    public spaces and, 196n3
feminism/feminist term, 39–40, 41,
    235n6
    see also *Playing With Fire*; *Telling
        to Live*
Fernández Benítez, Hans M., 3
fiction
    vs. history, 160n2
    as testimonio, 88–9, 201–2
    truth-value and, 208–9
fifth dimension, 235n7
    see also spirit world/spirituality
*Fire from the Mountain: The Making
    of a Sandinista* (Cabezas), see
    *La montaña es algo más que una
    inmensa estepa verde*
flashback, 207
Flores, Paula, 193, 197n8–9

Ford-Smith, Honor, *see Lionheart
    Gal: Life Stories of Jamaican
    Women*
forensic testimonio, 91, 92, 93–4,
    236n10
Fornet, Ambrosio, 241
Foster, David William, 243, 250
Foucault, Michel, 18
Foundations for Education,
    Inc., 167
Fox, Vicente, 123
*Fragments: Memories of a Childhood,
    1939–1948* (Wilkomirski), 210
Fragoso, Monárrez, 184, 189,
    196n3
Fregoso, Rosa-Linda, 196n1
Frente Patriótico Manolo
    Rodríguez, 67n8
Funari, Vicky, 196n4
Funes, Mauricio, 83n10

Gabriel Ríos, Juan, 120–1
Gaia in Turmoil (Crist, Rinker, and
    McKibben, eds.), 229
Gaia theory, 236n11, 236n13
    ancient Mayan belief and, 227,
        229–30
    spirit world and, 224, 228–31
Galich, Manuel, 241
Gallardo, Miguel, *see Un largo
    silencio*
Gallardo Sarmiento, Francisco,
    202
    see also *Un largo silencio*
García Márquez, Gabriel, 60
Gates-Madsen, Nancy J., 4,
    242, 250
General Workers Confederation
    (CGT, Puerto Rico), 28
genocide, 172, 175, 243
Giardino, Vittorio, 216n1
Giménez, Carlos, 213, 214
    see also *Todo Paracuellos*
Goffman, Erving, 150

INDEX

Goldberg, Elizabeth Swanson, 90, 97
Golding, William, 236n13
Gonzales, Ramelle (Romelia), 167
González, Gaspar Pedro, see *El 13 B'aktun: la nueva era 2012*
González Flores, Guillermina, 190, 197n8
Gramsci, Antonio, 14
Grandin, Greg, 110, 111
Grandmothers of the Plaza de Mayo, 87, 90–1
  rhetoric of, 97–100
  see also children of the disappeared
graphic testimony, see comic art; *Un largo silencio*; *Todo Paracuellos*; visual narration
Greenfield, Conetta Carestia, 68n10
Guatemala, 115–16
  civil war, 172, 173, 223
  human rights violations, 166
  peace treaty, 71
  truth commission, 111
  US influence, 173
  see also CPR-Sierra of Guatemala; Mayan indigenous communities
guerilla warfare, 71, 77–8, 166, 173–4
Guevara, Ché, 74, 78, 80
Gugelberger, Georg, 235n5
Guttman, Matthew, 32n8
Guzman, Melissa, 4, 244, 250
Guzmán, Ruth, 121, 123
Guzmán Patricio, 59

Haiti, see *Walking on Fire: Haitian Women's Stories of Survival and Resistance*
Hancock, Graham, 228, 236n12
Harding, Timothy, 19, 31n7

Harvey, David, 33n15
Hasian, Marouf A., Jr., 169
Hatzfield, Jean, 244
Hauser, Gerard A., 167, 169–70, 172
hegemony, 17, 28, 29, 71
  see also neoliberal economic model
Herlinghaus, Hermann, 183
heroism, 244
Herrera de Noble, Ernestina, 104n24
H.I.J.O.S. (Sons and Daughters for Identity and Justice against Forgetting and Silence, Argentina), 90–1, 102n4
'Hilos rompiendo el silencio': *Historias sobre las mujeres de la CPR-Sierra de la Guerra Civil en Guatemala* (CPR-Sierra), 166
history
  vs. fiction, 160n2
  historical processes, 73–4
  memory and, 176, 191–2, 193–4
  oral archiving of, 115–16
  oral testimony and, 113–15, 124–5
  testimonio's contribution to memory, 75–6, 81, 141
  truth commissions and, 110–11
Hood, Edward Waters, 75
Hron, Madeleine, 244
Huaco-Nuzum, Carmen, 169
humanism, 223–4
Human Rights along the U.S.-Mexico Border (Staudt), 190
human rights organizations, 64, 65, 123, 125, 168
Huyssen, Andreas, 181, 183, 190
hybrid texts, 208

I, Rigoberta Menchú (Menchú)
  controversy, 114, 126n2
  effect on first world readers, 18–19
  intimate relationships, 173
  metonymy, 140, 209
  paradigmatic testimonio, 1, 41, 83n13
  popularity, 12, 17
  truth value of, 126n2
identity politics
  anthropology and, 23, 25
  children of disappeared, 90, 97–100, 104n23
  Grandmothers of the Plaza de Mayo and, 87
  International Convention of the Rights of the Child (1990), 103n15
  oral testimony and, 109
  oversimplification/romaticization of, 90, 97–8, 98–100, 102
  rise of, 12–13, 19
illustrated testimonio, *see* visual narration
immigrants, 24–5, 152, 189
India, *see* Sangtin Writers
indigenous communities
  claims of injustice, 171–2
  continuum-of-life worldview, 224, 225–6
  history of language use, 110, 115–16, 125–6
  Mexican populations, 118
  oppression of, 165
  paramodernism, 224, 235n8
  scholarly attention to, 166–7
  self-determination, 167, 175–6
  stories of remembering by, 172–4
informant role, 2, 23
  see also mediated testimonio relationship

insile, 137–42, 143n1
  of Andruetto, 141
  defined, 139–40, 143n3
  fear and, 134–5, 139, 141
  as individual/alienating, 131, 137, 139, 140–1, 142
  institutionality, 150–1, 158–9
  interactional context, 151, 153–4, 155–9
International Convention of the Rights of the Child (1990), 103n15
intrusive camera, 57–8, 61

Jackson, Michael, 20
Jamaica, *see Lionheart Gal: Life Stories of Jamaican Women*
Jara, René, 88
Jelin, Elizabeth, 113, 194
Jitrik, Noé, 241
La Jornada (newspaper, Mexico), 123
Jottar, Bertha, 186
justice motive, 244–5

Kane, Adrian Taylor, 224
Kapferer, Jean-Noël, 144n10
Kaufman, Susana G., 113
Khordoc, Catherine, 217n6
King, Linda, 115
Kinzer, Steven, 83n17
Klubock, Thomas Miller, 110, 111
knowledge production, 53n7
  orality and, 52n4, 115–16
  polyvocalism and, 45, 47, 49, 50
  repertoire and, 123–4
  writing as, 117
Krippendorf's Tribe (film), 22
Kunz, Marco, 96–7

Lagland, Victoria, 194
Landless Workers Movement (MST, Brazil), 19

INDEX 261

Langer, Lawrence, 87
language/language use
   conversation analysis (CA), 148, 149–51, 159
   cultural specificity and, 46
   vs. discourse, 29
   ethnography and, 32n9
   everyday/vernacular, 83n12, 148
   indigenous history, 110, 115–16, 125–6
   ironic, 211
   politics of, 39, 52n4, 83n12
   in translations, 102n6
   in trauma narratives, 89
   see also rhetorical strategies
Un largo silencio (Gallardo), 201–2, 202–7, 215–16, 217n7
Latina Feminist Group, *see Telling to Live: Latina Feminist Testimonios*
latinidades, 39
Latour, Bruno, 114–15
Laub, Dori, 88–9, 110, 116, 210
Law in a Lawless Land (Taussig), 32n9
Let Me Speak! Testimony of Domitila, a Woman of the Bolivian Mines (Barrios de Chungara), 41
leveling concept, 135–6
life writing, 5, 6
   see also autobiography; testimonio identification/definition; testimonio metamorphosis
LIMEDDH (Liga Mexicana por la Defensa de los Derechos Humanos), 123
Lionheart Gal: Life Stories of Jamaican Women (Sistren Theatre Collective), 38–9
   creative process, 48, 51
   language use, 52n4
   name use, 52n6
   place-based framing, 48–9
   polyvocal structure, 39, 44, 46, 50

Lispector, Clarice, 2–3
literacy, 159n2, 223
literature, 16–17, 17–18, 142
Literature and Justice Project, 245
Littin, Miguel, 67n7, 67n10
   see also *Acta general de Chile*
Long Count calendar (Mayan), 222
Lote Bravo, Mexico, 184
Lovelock, James, 229–31, 232, 236n13
Lúkacs, Georg, 132–3
Lyotard, Jean-François, 243

MacArthur Genius Fellowship, 24–5
McCarthyism, 26–7
mcclellan, erin daina, 167, 169–70, 172
McCloud, Scott, 204
Machiorlatti, Jennifer A., 225, 235n7
magical realism, 239–40
Maier, Linda S., 2, 4, 41
Mallon, Florencia, 23, 26, 28, 33n17
Mantero, José María, 74
maquiladoras, 186, 196n4
Maquilapolis: City of Factories (documentary, Funari and Torre), 196n4
"The Margin at the Center: On Testimonio" (Beverley), 82n6
Márquez, Gabriel García, 239
Marsé, Juan, 212, 214
Martín, Antonio, 209–10
masculinity/hypermasculinity, 75
massacre at Acteal, Chiapas (Mexico), 114–15
massacre at El Mozote (El Salvador), 13
material-immaterial relationship, 225, 229–31, 232–3
Maus (Spiegelman), 216n1

Mayan indigenous communities
   2012 meme, 221–2, 235n4
   Chilam Balam, 230
   cyclical notion of time, 222, 226, 234, 235–6n10
   "Maya" term, 235n2
   Popol Vuh, 226–7, 229
   see also CPR-Sierra of Guatemala; *El 13 B'aktun: la nueva era 2012*
mediated testimonio relationship, 2
   authenticity and, 16, 159–60n2
   child/adult mediation, 211
   effect on testimonio's impact, 33n17
   vs. personal life story, 202
   in religious testimony, 149, 151, 153–4, 155–9
   testimonio definition and, 88, 148
Medina, Julia M., 4, 240, 250
Me llamo Rigoberta Menchú y así me nació la conciencia (Menchú), see *I, Rigoberta Menchú*
memory, 5
   collective, 134, 190–1, 191–2, 209–10, 216
   in documentary film, 188, 193–4
   effect on testimonio authenticity, 160n2
   monuments/memorials, 182–3, 189–90, 194–5
   oral testimony and, 109–10, 113
   as resistance, 168
   rumor and, 131, 140, 144n10
   storytelling and, 172–4
   testimonio's contribution to, 75–6, 81
   traumatic, 207
   writing and, 117
The Memory Box of Pinochet's Chile (Stern), 112–13
memoryscapes, 182–3, 194–5
Menchú, Rigoberta, 166
   see also *I, Rigoberta Menchú*

metonymy
   vs. alienation, 142
   atypical, 140
   as fundamental testimonio characteristic, 40, 43–4, 203, 208, 209
   vs. polyvocal structures, 40, 43–4, 46, 170
Mexico
   Commission of Feminicide, 182
   indigenous language use, 115–16
   massacre at Acteal, Chiapas, 114–15
   Oaxaca social movement (2006), 110, 118–25
   Zapatista Army of National Liberation, 19, 81n1
   see also Ciudad Juárez, Mexico
Miara, Samuel and Beatriz, 104n22
military/militarization, 67n6, 83n16
   see also guerilla warfare; war/warfare
Miller, Lisa K., 235n4
mining, 67n6
Mintz, Sidney, 23, 26–9, 32n14, 33n16
modernism, 33n15
Monárrez, Benita, 193
La montaña es algo más que una inmensa estepa verde (Cabezas), 71–2
   as conqueror-warrior narrative, 73
   construction of guerillero self, 77, 81
   fighting/warfare, 77–8
   hypermasculinity, 75
   revolutionary rhetoric, 78–9
   romantic foundational-nationalism, 74
   title's significance, 76
Montejo, Victor, 222
Monument Six (Tortuguero, Mexico), 230
Mora, Sergio de la, 188
Moreiras, Alberto, 72

Morrison, Toni, 239
Mouesca, Jacqueline, 67n10
Moviemiento Renovador (El
 Salvador), 15, 31n4
Moya-Raggio, E., 166
La mujer en cuestión (Andruetto),
 131–42
 as alternative history, 141–2
 as anti-testimonio, 133
 fear, 134–5, 139–40
 leveling concept, 135–6
 novel definition and, 132–3
 power of rumor in, 137–9
Murphy, Patrick D., 233,
 235n8
My Name is Light (Osorio), 87–102
 plot summary, 91
 reader engagement, 92–3
 representation of complexity,
  94–7, 98–100
 revealing past injustice, 90–4, 101
 sentimentality/romanticism,
  96–7, 101–2
 as testimonio, 89

Nance, Kimberly A., 3, 250
 deliberative testimonio, 50, 91,
  234, 236n10
 epideictic testimonio, 91, 92,
  93–4, 236n10
 forensic testimonio, 91, 92, 93–4,
  236n10
 reader action, 215–16
 testimonial rhetoric, 91, 92, 93,
  102n5, 235–6n10
 testimonio definition, 89
 testimonio goals, 123
 trauma narratives, 101
Naranjo, José Ramón, 226–7,
 236n11
narrative strategies/structures, 39,
 44, 207
 see also orality;
  polyvocalism/polyvocal
  testimonies; visual narration

narrative voice, 62, 65
nationalism, 74
 independence, 115–16
 language use/vernacular and,
  83n12
 truth commissions and, 110–11
National Republican Alliance
 (ARENA) Party (El
 Salvador), 15
National Science Foundation, 245
*The Natural World in Latin
 American Literatures*
 (Kane), 224
neoliberal economic model, 12
 displacement of class politics, 19
 guerrilla nostalgia and, 71
 healing from dictatorships
  and, 111
 hegemony of, 28
 Sandinistas and, 74
 testimonio's relevance under,
  29–30
New Social Movements (NSMs), 19
Nicaragua, 83n16
 *see also La montaña es algo más
  que una inmensa estepa verde*;
  *Perra vida: memorias de un
  recluta del servicio militar*
Nichols, Bill, 192
Noble-Herrera, Marcela and Felipe,
 104n24
non-governmental organizations
 (NGOs), 38, 45,
 52n2
non-places, 197n11
No Pasarán! (Giardino), 216n1
Nordstrum, Carolyn, 32n9
novels, definition of, 132–3,
 141

Oaxaca, social movement of 2006
 (Mexico), 118–25
Ochando Aymerich, Carmen,
 242
O'Connell, Joana, 15

orality, 16–17
   as hallmark of testimonio, 148, 159n2, 203, 215
   knowledge production and, 52n4, 115–16
   power of, 138–9
oral testimonio, 4
   as archive, 109, 111, 126
   defined, 110
   importance of context, 112, 115, 125, 159
   motivation to act, 123
   performance and, 116–17
   in social movements, 116, 121–5
   in truth commissions, 110–15
   see also rumor
ordinariness
   testimonio definition/function and, 51, 89, 203, 244
   vernacular rhetoric and, 174
orphanages, *see Todo Paracuellos*
Ortega, Daniel, 75
Osorio, Elsa, *see* My Name is Light
ostracism, *see* insile
other, the, 142
   anthropology and, 21–2
   blaming, 135–6, 143n1
   distancing from, 20–1
   rumors and, 138–9
   testimonio scholarship and, 16–17, 18
   see also insile

PACs (Civilian Defense Patrols, Guatemala), 171, 173
Palazón Saez, Gema, 97–8
palimpsest trope, 181, 183–4, 195
Paracuellos series (Giménez), *see Todo Paracuellos*
paramodernism, 224, 235n8
Payeras, Mario, 78
Peoples Revolutionary Army (ERP, El Salvador), 11, 14

performance studies, 116–17, 126
performativity, 111, 236n14
Performing the Border (documentary, Biemann), 182, 184–7, 196n5
Perra vida: memorias de un recluta del servicio militar (Sobalvarro), 72
   distance/disillusionment in, 79–80, 81
   fighting/warfare in, 77–8
   lack of subaltern subject, 73
   production of, 75–6
   title's significance, 77
Peru, 115–16
Peruvian Truth Commission, 111, 112, 114
Petras, James, 19, 31n7
Pflug, Martin, 234–5n1
Pinochet, Augusto, 59, 61
place-based framing, 48–9
Playing With Fire: Feminist Thought and Activism through Seven Lives in India (Sangtin Writers), 37–8
   language use, 52n4
   name use in, 52–3n6
   place-based framing, 48–9
   polyvocal structure, 39, 44–5, 52n3
   process in, 47–8, 49–50
polyvocalism/polyvocal testimonies, 39, 52n3
   effect on reader/text relationship, 40, 44, 48–9
   history of, 44
   process-based approach, 47–51
   tensions within, 37–8
   truth function of, 44–7
   vernacular rhetoric and, 170–1
   see also rumor
Poniatowska, Elena, 187, 188
Popol Vuh (Mayan text), 226–7, 229
Popular Party (Puerto Rico), 26

Portillo, Lourdes, 182, 187–91, 196n6
postmodernism, 33n15
  vs. class politics, 15
  decline of testimonio and, 12–13, 19
  self/other divide and, 21–2
  trauma expression and, 217n4
poststructuralism, 19, 20, 31nn5–6, 32n8
poverty
  in Chile, 63
  as dictatorial policy, 64
  in El Salvador, 23–4
  essentialism and, 30
  as justification for subversiveness, 137
  in Mexico, 118
  progressive church and, 13–14, 32n14
  violence and, 189
power
  collaborative projects and, 47
  in mediated testimonio relationship, 16, 148
  poststructuralism and, 31n5
  in reader/text relationship, 49
  rumor and, 138–9, 141–2
  vs. subversive potential of testimonio, 17–18
  vernacular rhetoric and, 174–5
press/media, 123, 143n1
privacy, documentary film and, 58, 60
process-based approach to testimonio, 40, 47–51
progressive church, 13–14, 32n14
Pubill, Corinne, 4, 243, 250
public spaces, 182–4, 194–5, 196n3
Puerto Rico, 26–9

Rabasa, José, 114–15
Radway, Janice, 18
radio, *see Cambiando Vidas*
Radio Cacerola (Mexico), 123
Rama, Ángel, 241
Randall, Margaret, 41, 44, 47
Ravelo Blancas, Patricia, 182, 191–5, 197n9
readers, 170
  contradictory narrative effects, 134, 140
  defamiliarization, 226
  effects on testimonio, 16, 18–19
  first world targets, 18–19, 72–3, 222, 225–6
  hegemony's effect on, 29
  local targets, 171
  motivation/discouragement of, 3, 92, 102, 243
  participatory reading, 147–8, 210–12, 224–6, 233–4
  polyvocal narrative structure and, 40, 44, 48–9
  power relationship with text, 40, 49
  strategies to engage, 50, 92–3, 244–5
  visual narration effects, 204–6, 207, 211–12, 215–16
  as witnesses, 124, 210, 211
Reading Autobiography: A Guide for Interpreting Life Narratives (Smith and Watson), 5, 6
Reading the Romance (Radway), 18
Reati, Fernando, 137, 139
Recabarren, Luis Emilio, 66–7n6
Rege, Sharmila, 43
Reggiardo Tolosa, Matías, 104n22
Reiff, David, 243
religion/religious testimony, 13–14, 26, 32n14
  see also *Cambiando Vidas*; spirit world/spirituality
repertoire, 110, 116–17, 123–4
repetition, 207, 217n5
report, *see* rumor

resistance, 19
  cultural resistance, 51, 168–9,
    170–2, 175
  rumor and, 142
  silence and, 140
  as survival, 46
  see also CPR-Sierra embroidery
    project (Guatemala); guerilla
    warfare; social action and
    social movements
Reuque, Isolde, 33n17
The Revenge of Gaia (Lovelock),
  229–31
Revolutionary Armed Forces of
  Colombia (FARC), 19
Reyes Sahagún, Teresa
  Guadalupe, 182
rhetorical strategies, 242, 245
  accumulation, 64
  deliberative, 50, 91, 234, 236n10
  epideictic, 92, 93–4, 236n10
  forensic, 91, 92, 93–4, 236n10
  infiltration, 60
  in public space, 183
  question use, 50, 62
  in state oppression, 135–6, 137,
    143n1
  three types of, 3, 91, 236n10
  vernacular rhetoric, 169–76
  see also identity politics
Ribera, Campo de la (Argentinian
  detention center), 137, 139,
  144n8
Ricoeur, Paul, 134
*Rigoberta Menchú and the Story of
  All Poor Guatemalans* (Stoll),
  114, 126n2, 173
The Rigoberta Menchú Controversy
  (Arias), 1
Rivero, Eliana, 148
Robeson in Spain (Brown and
  Carroll), 216n1
Rodríguez, Ileana, 76
Rosaldo, Renato, 21
Roseberry, William, 13, 31n3

Ross, Fiona, 112
Rostow, Walt, 26–7
Rowe, Stan, 225
rumor, 4, 131–44, 243
  as anti-testimonio, 133, 136,
    138–9, 140–1
  functions of, 134
  leveling concept and, 135–6
  memory and, 131, 140, 144n10
  as narrative device, 132–3
  power of, 137–9, 141–2
Rushdie, Salman, 239
Russell, Diana E.H., 195n1
Rutila Artés, Carla, 103n18

Sadowski-Smith, Claudia, 187,
  196–7n6
Said, Edward, 42–3
Saldaña Portillo, María Josefina, 76,
  78–9
Sánchez Maya, Yessica, 121
Sandinista Revolution (Nicaragua),
  74, 83n16
  *see also Perra vida: memorias de
    un recluta del servicio militar*
*Sandino's Daughters: Testimonies of
  Nicaraguan Women in Struggle*
  (Randall), 44
Sangtin Writers, 4, 37–8, 44–5,
  47–50, 52nn1–3
Santamaría, Haydee, 241
Santiago, Chile, 62
Santiago Sánchez, Elionai, 118–25
  detention and torture of, 118–21
  press conference/oral testimonio
    by, 121–5
Sarkar, Bhaskar, 116
Sarlo, Beatriz, 114
Sarmiento, Domingo Faustino, 82n9
Sartre, Jean Paul, 241
scenario framework, 126
  oral testimony and, 110, 121,
    122–5
  summary, 117–18
Schlotterbeck, Marian E., 184

Index

Scholz, T.M. Linda, 4, 169, 242, 250
science, 225, 226, 227, 229
Scilingo, Adolfo, 102n3
second person narrative, 92–3
Seider, Rachel, 112
Seltzer, Mark, 196n5
Señorita Extraviada (documentary, Portillo), 182, 187–91, 196–7n6
Serial Killers: Death and Life in America's Wound Culture (Seltzer), 196n5
sexual violence, 112, 114
    see also feminicide
Sica, Maria Lux, 175
silence/silencing, 6, 143n1
    anti-testimonio and, 132, 140–1
    insile, 139–40
    repression of social action, 121
    romanticization of trauma, 101–2
    subalternity and, 30
    truth commission's countering, 111
    see also insile; subalternity
Sistren Theatre Collective, 38–9
    see also *Lionheart Gal: Life Stories of Jamaican Women*
Sitler, Robert K., 221, 234–5nn1–2
Sklodowska, Elzbieta, 160n2
    as foundational critic, 235n5
    reader/text relationship, 73
    testimonio definition, 72, 88
Smith, Linda Tuhiwai, 170
    colonialism, 171
    indigenous self-determination, 167, 175–6
    indigenous storytelling, 172–3
    indigenous survival, 174
Smith, Sidonie, 5, 6
SNTE (Sindicato Nacional de Trabajadores de la Educación), 119
Sobalvarro, Juan, 75

Sobalvarro, Juan, *see Perra vida: memorias de un recluta del servicio militar*
social action and social movements, 1
    anti-feminicide movement, 190, 197n8
    Arpillera Movement (Chile), 166, 168, 172
    Christian Base Community movement (El Salvador), 11, 13–14
    motivation as function of testimonio, 18–19, 240, 241, 244–5
    Oaxaca social movement of 2006 (Mexico), 110, 118–25
    oral testimony function, 116, 121–5
    vernacular rhetoric and, 169–70
    see also resistance
sociology, 148, 149–51, 159
solidarity, poetics of, 72
Sommer, Doris, 216n3, 235n5
South Africa, 111
South African Truth and Reconciliation Commission, 112
Southern California, University of, 245
Spanish civil war (1936–9), 201, 205–7, 209–10, 212, 216
spatial amnesia, 183–4, 194–5
Spiegelman, Art, 216n1
spirit world/spirituality, 223
    continuum of life, 225–6
    as fifth dimension, 235n7
    Gaia theory and, 224, 228–31
    human evolution and, 232–3
    visions of terra-trauma, 227–8
Spivak, Gayatri, 30, 138
Staudt, Kathleen, 186, 190
Stephen, Lynn, 4, 243, 251
Stern, Steve, 112–13
Stoll, David, 114, 126n2, 166, 173

strategic humanism, 22
subalternity, 12–13, 141
  authenticity of voice, 73
  decline of class politics and, 15
  first world reflections and, 18
  as hallmark of testimonio, 223
  literary exclusion, 17
  paternalism and, 78–9
  rumor and, 138–9
  silence and, 30
  use of testimonio, 41
  see also voice, giving of
subjectivity, 5
  anthropologists and, 20, 22, 23
  first world co-optation of, 72–3
  guerilla, 75, 76
  nonhuman, 224, 231–2
  vs. political action, 31n6
  see also agency
Subject to Change: The Lessons of Latin American Women's Testimonio for Truth, Fiction, and Theory (Bartow), 2–3
Supernatural (Hancock), 228
surveillance, 186

Taso, don, 23, 26–9
Taussig, Michael, 32n9
Taylor, Diana
  archive *vs.* repertoire, 116–17
  complicity with repressive forces, 93
  "once-againness", 124, 125
  scenario framework, 110, 117–18, 121, 122–5
Taylor, Julie, 112
Teatro x la identidad (Theatre for Identity), 103n16, 143n2
television, 119, 123

Telling to Live: Latina Feminist Testimonios (Latina Feminist Group), 38
  effect of collaboration on members, 50
  language use, 52n4
  name use, 53n6
  place-base framing, 48
  polyvocal structure, 39, 44, 45, 47–8
  theorizing *latinidades*, 39
Les Temps Modernes (Sartre and Camus), 241
Terrorizing Women: Feminicide in the Americas (Fregoso and Bejarano, eds.), 196n1
testigo, *see* witnessing
testimonial function, anthropological, 20–3, 32nn8–9
testimonio identification/definition, 82n6
  vs. anti-testimonio, 133
  armed struggle and, 72
  categories/types, 3, 91, 235–6n10
  deliberative testimonio, 50, 91, 234, 236n10
  epideictic testimonio, 91, 92, 93–4, 236n10
  first-person account, 133
  forensic testimonio, 91, 92, 93–4, 236n10
  indigenous contexts, 170–1
  intuitive approach, 4–5
  metonymy, 40, 43–4, 203, 208, 209
  as motivation for action, 89, 110, 215–16, 243–5
  origins, 239
  social/political dimension, 28–9, 51, 73, 240
  summary, 147–8, 202–3, 222–3
  vs. testimonial function, 20

truth, 88, 89, 203, 241–2
urgency and, 4, 12, 51, 88, 147, 223
testimonio metamorphosis, 1–4, 5, 239–41
    broadened definition of, 89, 102n5
    changing Latin American political terrain and, 15
    ecotestimonio, 224, 242–3
    nonhuman witnessing, 231–2
    vs. passé status, 4, 19, 38, 41, 81–2n2
    scholarly reception, 12–13, 16–19
    traveling theory and, 42–3
    see also oral testimonio; polyvocalism/polyvocal testimonies; visual narration
Testimony: Crises of Witnessing in Literature, Psychoanalysis and History (Felman and Laub), 88–9
Theatre for Identity *(Teatro x la identidad)*, 103n16, 143n2
Theidon, Kimberly, 111–12, 113, 114, 115
theology, 149–50
Theory of the Novel (Lúkacs), 132–3
third-person testimony, 112, 114
El 13 B'aktun: la nueva era 2012 (González), 221–34
    as ecotestimonio, 224
    Gaia theory and, 228–31
    material/immaterial relationship, 224–5, 229–30
    nonhuman witnessing, 224, 231–2, 234
    reader engagement, 224–6, 233–4
    science and Mayan knowledge, 229
    terra-trauma, 226–8, 230–1, 236n15
    as testimonio, 223–4
    translation of, 221, 235n3

Los Tigres del Norte (music group), 192–3
time, 206
    constraint on testimonio's legitimacy, 73
    as fourth dimension, 229, 235n7
    future orientation, 233–4
    Mayan/cyclical, 222, 226, 234, 235–6n10
    passage of, 79
Tittler, Jonathan, 223, 230
Todo Paracuellos (Giménez), 201–2, 207–15
    metafictive technique, 212–15
    participatory reading, 210–12
    as testimonio, 207–9
Todo 36–39: Malos tiempos (Giménez), 216n1
Torre, Sergio de la, 196n4
Torrea, Judith, 194
torture, 118, 120–1, 122
transitional justice, 110–11, 126n1, 245
Translated Woman: Crossing the Border with Esperanza's Story (Behar), 23–5
trauma/trauma narratives
    difficulty articulating, 88–9, 101, 217n4
    ethics of representation, 90
    as hallmark of testimonio, 223
    meaning-making, 113
    narrative strategies, 207
    as reliving experiences, 218n11
    romanticization, 101–2
    terra-trauma, 224, 226–8, 230–1, 234, 236n15
    visual narration and, 204–6, 217n7
traveling theory, 42–3
Trouillot, Michel-Rolph, 21–2
truth commissions, 65–6, 109–15, 125, 243

truth/truth value, 142
  construction of, 109–10
  controversy, 126n2
  courtroom and, 113–14
  difficulty of portraying traumatic facts, 217n4
  documentary films and, 114, 188
  fictional accounts and, 208–9
  as hallmark of testimonio, 88, 89, 203, 241–2
  multiple/complicated, 115, 173
  vs. performativity, 236n14
  "political", 125
  polyvocalism and, 44–7
  rumor and, 132
  vs. truth effect, 16
  visual narration and, 205
Tula, María Teresa, 173

unions, 28–9, 119
United Nations, 236n13
United States
  evolutionist triumphalism and, 26–7
  Guatemalan civil war, 172, 173
  impact of underdeveloped nations on, 18–19
  Latino/as in, 149, 152
  Sandinistas and, 74
United States Institute of Peace, 243, 245
urban spaces as palimpsests, 181, 183–4, 195
urgency
  narrative structure and, 141
  passing of, 12, 15, 41, 71, 82n2
  testimonio definition and, 4, 12, 51, 88, 147, 223
  visual narration and, 204–6
Urtecho, Coronel, 73, 82n8
Uruguay's truth commission, 111
Uttar Pradesh, India, *see* Sangtin Writers

Valdivia, Angharad N., 169
Valparaíso, Chile, 63, 68n11
Vásquez, Evelin Karina, 103–4n21, 104n23
Verbitsky, Horacio, 102n3
vernacular rhetoric, 169–76
Villa, Pancho, 24
violence
  graphic depiction, 211–12, 218n12
  nationalism and, 111
  physical/economic ties, 189
  sexual violence, 112, 114
  society's complicity, 136
  spatial aspects, 196n3
  see also feminicide
visual narration, 203–6
  effect on readers, 204–6, 207, 211–12, 215–16
  metonymy, 208
  trauma and, 204–6, 217n7
Voces Sin Eco (Mexico), 190, 197n8
voice, giving of, 4
  anthropology and, 22–3
  children and, 208, 210, 215
  CPR-Sierra embroidery project and, 168, 175, 176
  as goal of testimonio, 12, 87, 141–2, 147–8, 159n2, 170, 201, 203
  limits to, 16, 18, 73
  memoryscapes and, 182–3
  right to speak/truth commissions, 112–13
  vernacular rhetoric and, 170–1
  see also mediated testimonio relationship; polyvocalism/polyvocal testimonies; rumor
voice-over technique, 62, 185, 192, 194

Volk, Steven S., 184
Volkart, Yvonne, 185

Walker, Janet, 116
Walking on Fire: Haitian Women's Stories of Survival and Resistance (Bell), 38
  approach to readers, 48, 50
  knowledge production in, 53n7
  language use, 52n4
  name use in, 53n6
  polyvocal structure, 39, 44, 45–6, 48
  process/methodology focus, 47
war/warfare, 76
  children as "spoils of war", 98, 99
  criticism of, 80–1
  guerilla warfare, 71, 77–8, 166, 173–4
  Spanish civil war (1936–9), 201, 205–7, 209–10, 212, 216
  testimonio identification and, 72
Watson, Julia, 5, 6
Whitehead, Anne, 204, 207, 210, 217n4–5
Wilkomirski, Benjamin, 210
Williams, Gareth, 18
Williams, Raymond, 19
Wisconsin-Madison, University of, 245

witnessing, 2
  anomalous, 5
  blurring with testifier role, 49–50
  in documentary film, 65
  eyewitness as active social agent, 111
  nonhuman, 224, 231–2, 234
  oral testimony and, 109, 124
  readers as witnesses, 124, 210, 211
  reliving trauma through, 218n11
  testimonio definition and, 88, 223
  visual narration and, 204–6, 207, 216
  see also truth commissions
Woman as Witness: Essays on Testimonial Literature by Latin American Women (Maier and Dulfano, eds.), 2, 41
Worker in the Cane: A Puerto Rican Life History (Mintz), 23, 26–9
Writing Caste/Writing Gender: Narrating Dalit Women's Testimonios (Rege), 43

Yúdice, George, 3, 77, 147, 203, 235n5

Zapatista Army of National Liberation (EZLN, Mexico), 19, 81n1
Zimbardo, Philip, 244
Zimmerman, Marc, 3, 88, 203, 235n5